Mao Zedong

for Lynn and Matthew,
with love

Mao Zedong

A Political and
Intellectual Portrait

MAURICE MEISNER

polity

First published in 2007 by Polity Press

Polity Press
65 Bridge Street
Cambridge CB2 1UR, UK

Polity Press
350 Main Street
Malden, MA 02148, USA

ISBN-10: 0-7456-3106-1
ISBN-13: 978-07456-3106-6
ISBN-10: 0-7456-3107-X (pb)
ISBN-13: 978-07456-3107-3 (pb)

A catalogue record for this book is available from the British Library.

Typeset in 11.25 on 13 pt Dante
by SNP Best-set Typesetter Ltd, Hong Kong
Printed and bound in Great Britain by ••

For further information on Polity, visit our website: www.polity.co.uk

Contents

Preface

Mao Zedong conceived and led the most popular revolution in world history. The numbers of people actively involved in the great revolutionary movement that swept over the vast Chinese countryside in the late 1930s and 1940s are historically unprecedented. And the numbers whose lives were profoundly transformed by the upheaval must be counted in the hundreds of millions. In scope and scale, and in its thoroughgoing character, the Chinese Communist Revolution was probably the greatest of all modern revolutions, overshadowing the French and Russian revolutions with which it is often compared.

While Mao Zedong was a great revolutionary, he became increasingly despotic as a ruler, a not uncommon development in the history of revolutions. He organized the peasants of China to destroy ancient forms of oppression and authority only to replace them with the alien authority of his own deified image. He liberated the Chinese nation from the shackles of foreign imperialism – and "built a country," as his successor Deng Xiaoping put it – only to shackle the people of the country to the onerous demands of the doctrine of "continuous revolution." The two sides of Mao – the revolutionary and the tyrant, the social liberator and the political dictator – cannot easily be reconciled. But both must be taken into account in any serious consideration of his long revolutionary career.

Both Mao Zedong's successes and failures, his achievements and his crimes, enfolded on a grand scale, defining several crucial historical eras. Mao was the political leader of the long Chinese Communist Revolution for nearly two decades as well as its principal theoretician and military strategist. And he reigned over the People's Republic of China for more than a quarter of a century. The duration of Mao's political dominance is unprecedented in the history of modern revolutions, providing an unusual political and ideological continuity between the revolutionary and post-revolutionary periods. This study seeks to take advantage of that continuity to explore questions relating to the social nature and limits of the

Chinese Communist Revolution as revealed in Mao Zedong's long political and intellectual life.

As an account of Mao Zedong's revolutionary career, this book is no more than a sketch, primarily addressed to readers who seek a short biographical introduction to the public life of an unfamiliar subject. It cannot be substituted for Philip Short's superb and comprehensive biography *Mao: A Life* (New York: Henry Holt, 2000) or Stuart Schram's pioneering study *Mao Tse-tung* (New York: Simon and Schuster, 1967), a volume which retains its vitality and historical insightfulness four decades after its publication.

In tracing Mao's political history, this volume emphasizes his encounters with (and reinterpretation of) the inherited body of Marxist-Leninist theory, and the relationship between his "sinified" version of Marxism and his political practice, both as a revolutionary and a ruler. This emphasis does not derive from any belief that Mao enriched the Marxist tradition. His intellectual and theoretical contributions to Marxism were meager, at best. Rather it was his departures from the basic premises of Marxism that are important for understanding both the positive and negative aspects of his political career, as will be suggested in the pages that follow.

Acknowledgments

The intellectual and political portrait of Mao Zedong that is sketched on the following pages owes much to the work of many scholars who have written on the history of Chinese Communism over the past 60 years. I am especially indebted to Stuart R. Schram and the late Benjamin Schwartz, pioneers in the critical study of Mao Zedong and the Chinese Revolution. My warmest thanks are due to Louise Knight, Editorial Director of Polity Press, who encouraged me to undertake this project several years ago, and to members of the Polity editorial staff in Cambridge and Oxford, especially Ellen McKinlay, Emma Hutchison, and Caroline Richmond, who generously helped along the way. I am enormously grateful to an anonymous outside reader for Polity who provided a lengthy and stimulating commentary on the original manuscript while gently pointing out glaring omissions and errors. I am above all grateful to my wife and partner, Lynn Lubkeman, who read and corrected two drafts of the entire manuscript as well as many bits and pieces along the way. She has contributed to the writing of virtually every sentence. It is to Lynn, and our son Matthew, that this volume is affectionately dedicated.

China

- — International Boundary
- — — Provincial Boundary
- Hunan Province Name

A Note on Chinese Names

Chinese personal and place names in this volume are rendered in the now generally accepted Pinyin system of romanization. There are exceptions, however. The Wade–Giles system has been retained for Chinese names which are most familiar to Western readers in their older form – such as Sun Yat-sen and Chiang Kai-shek. It has also been retained for the names of Chinese authors and book titles which were published in Wade–Giles transliteration, usually before 1979. Thus, Mao Zedong appears as "Mao Tse-tung" in citations of the earlier Western-language translations of his writings.

1

Youth, 1893–1921

Family background and education

Mao Zedong was the leader of the greatest peasant uprising in world history, the architect of a unique revolutionary strategy by which the rebellious countryside conquered the cities. The revolution that grew over two decades in the vast rural hinterlands of China in the 1930s and 1940s was not a traditional peasant jacquerie. Rather, the Chinese Communist Revolution, paradoxically, was carried out under a Marxist banner, a doctrine that largely excluded peasants from any progressive role in the making of modern history.

Yet however great the incongruity between ideology and social reality, the Maoist revolution was one of the few peasant movements in history to achieve a lasting political success, propelling Mao Zedong to supreme power in the world's most populous land – and propelling China toward that long elusive nationalist goal of "wealth and power" in the modern world.

Mao Zedong could not have claimed to have sprung from the impoverished and hungry peasant masses he was to organize under a Communist banner. The young Mao grew to maturity in relatively comfortable circumstances. Among the 300 or so families who lived in the village of Shaoshan in the southern province of Hunan, the Mao family was one of the most prosperous. His father had fled the chronic conditions of poverty and famine under which most peasants labored by joining the imperial army at the age of 16. By virtue of thrift – and no small measure of luck – he returned to his village after six years with sufficient money to purchase a few acres of land and to marry. By the time Mao Zedong, the first of the family's three sons to survive infancy, was born on December 26, 1893, his enterprising father had transformed himself into a "rich" peasant. He expanded his landholdings, hired two farm laborers, and also became a petty landlord, a moneylender, and a mortgage-holder. He further augmented his income by trading grain. As Mao later recalled, his father "simply purchased grain from the poor farmers and then transported it to the city merchants, where he got a higher price."[1]

Thus the Mao family was rising at a time when most rural families were falling ever deeper into debt and poverty in the waning years of the Qing dynasty, the last in the long line of China's imperial regimes. It was a time when hunger chronically stalked the land, with famines ravaging large parts of Hunan province in the 1890s and during the first decade of the new century. But amidst the deepening rural crisis, the Mao family prospered. Mao Zedong grew up in a spacious compound situated in a lovely valley surrounded by hills, ponds, and terraced rice fields. The young Mao had his own bedroom, a rare luxury in rural China.

The father's financial success permitted his eldest son to acquire a traditional and later a modern Western-type education. Mao Zedong began to work on the family farm at the age of six, but two years later he was enrolled in the local village school where he was taught classical Confucian texts. Mao disliked the Classics, he later recalled, but he learned them well, quoting the ancient texts to his advantage in his often bitter arguments with his father as well as in later political writings and speeches. And the young Mao did acquire a love of reading, a pleasure he pursued with considerable passion throughout his life. What he most enjoyed were the romantic novels telling the tales of peasant rebellions, heroic rebels, and political intrigues. Popular novels such as *Romance of the Three Kingdoms*, many dating from the Ming dynasty, were beyond the pale of Confucian orthodoxy. Mao recalled: "I used to read [these outlawed books] in school, covering them up with a Classic when the teacher walked past. . . . I believe that perhaps I was much influenced by such books, read at an impressionable age."[2]

Mao attended the village school for five years, working part-time on the family farm. He graduated in 1907, at the age of 13, and went to work full-time for his father, combining manual farm labor with the task of keeping the financial records for the various family businesses. In his spare hours, he read traditional novels and histories – and also books that advocated modernization to save China from foreign colonization.

Mao Zedong's iron will, which came to characterize his political career, was evident at an early age. In 1909 the 15-year-old Mao was determined to attend a middle school (the Dongshan Higher Primary School) where the Western "new learning" was part of the curriculum. There ensued a prolonged struggle with his father who had arranged to apprentice his son to a rice shop in a nearby commercial town. But in the end, as was usually the case, the younger Mao had his way, and his father grudgingly agreed to pay his tuition and living expenses. He was to continue to do so for another decade.

At the Higher Primary School, located in a nearby county, Mao Zedong entered the world of China's traditional gentry elite. Less than 1 percent of boys, and virtually no girls, were afforded a middle-school education in early twentieth-century China. As Mao recalled his first impression of the Higher Primary School, the first time he had been away from home: "I had never before seen so many children together. Most of them were sons of landlords, wearing expensive clothes. . . . Many of the richer students despised me because usually I was wearing my ragged coat and trousers."[3]

Nonetheless, Mao's studies went well over the next two years, especially in ancient Chinese history and classical literature. And he was introduced to politics for the first time:

> I made good progress at this school. The teachers liked me, especially those who taught the Classics, because I wrote good essays in the Classical manner. But my mind was not on the Classics. I was reading two books sent to me by my cousin, telling of the [1898] Reform movement of K'ang Yu-wei [Kang Youwei]. One was called Journal of the New People and was edited by Liang Ch'i-ch'ao [Liang Qichao]. I read and reread these until I knew them by heart. I worshipped K'ang Yu-wei and Liang Ch'i-ch'ao.[4]

There was nothing particularly radical about Mao's intellectual and political proclivities when he arrived in the provincial capital of Changsha in the spring of 1911 to attend a secondary school. While he had some sympathy for poor peasants at an early age, he opposed the use of illegal or violent means to remedy their plight. Mao later recalled his ambivalent attitude about hungry peasants who forcibly seized rice supplies during a severe food shortage: "My father was a rice merchant and was exporting much grain to the city from our district, despite the shortage. One of his consignments was seized by the poor villagers and his wrath was boundless. I did not sympathize with him. *At the same time I thought the villagers' method was wrong also.*"[5]

During his youth Mao's political inclinations were no more radical than his social attitudes. His boyhood hero was the mid-19th-century Hunanese statesman Zeng Guofan, a conservative Confucian who had rescued the Qing dynasty and the gentry-landlord class by bloodily suppressing the Taiping peasant rebels. He continued to view Zeng as a hero well into his adulthood. On the eve of the republican Revolution of 1911, the young Mao was still a monarchist: "I considered the Emperor as well as most officials to be honest, good and clever men. They only needed the help of

Kang Youwei reforms."[6] Among students and young intellectuals in the waning days of the monarchy, Mao's political views were rather moderate, indeed quite conventional.

Mao Zedong's political radicalization began with the Revolution of 1911. Those events excited political imaginations, even though the actual battles were far less weighty than they appeared to be at the time – and the end results bitterly disappointing. Mao Zedong, approaching his 18th birthday, withdrew from the secondary school in the provincial capital and enlisted in the army of a Qing dynasty commander who had defected to the revolutionaries. He spent six months as a soldier, largely on uneventful garrison duty in Changsha. When the last Qing emperor abdicated in February 1912, Mao assumed that the revolution had come to a successful conclusion. He resigned from the army and decided to "return to my books."[7]

Following his demobilization, Mao was uncharacteristically less than fully certain about what he wanted to do. He aimlessly pursued a number of alluring advertisements for the many new "modern" schools that had opened in Changsha, among them a police school, a law school and a soap-making school. He briefly attended a business school, but withdrew on discovering that most of the courses were taught in English. He then embarked on what he called a "period of self-education," spending most of his time reading Western books (in Chinese translation) in the recently established Hunan Provincial Library. He read the authors who had molded the thought of China's new Westernized intelligentsia – Adam Smith, Darwin, Mill, Spencer, Rousseau, and Montesquieu. The young Mao was particularly influenced by the Social Darwinism of Spencer, with its enormous emphasis on the inevitability of struggle. In the hands of its influential Chinese translator and annotator, Yen Fu, the notion of "the survival of the fittest" took on a profoundly nationalist meaning – and an implicitly anti-traditionalist one. What Social Darwinist texts conveyed to Mao was the message that the "wealth and power" of the nation was the main value to which all other values must be subordinated, not excluding traditional cultural values, if need be.[8]

Although Mao was to remain emotionally attached to many aspects of the Chinese cultural heritage, traditional values were now subordinated to the higher goal of the preservation and regeneration of China as a nation-state in a world of competing nation-states. He also derived from Social Darwinism a belief in the necessity and value of struggle *per se*, which, along with powerful nationalist impulses, were to remain enduring features of his thought.

Pressed by his father to pursue a career, and threatened with the loss of financial support if he did not do so, Mao eventually decided to become a teacher. He enrolled in the Hunan Provincial Fourth Normal School in Changsha, a teacher training college, in the spring of 1913. He remained a student for five years, graduating in 1918 with the equivalent of a college degree. During this period, he later recalled, "my political ideas began to take shape" and "I acquired my first experiences in social action."[9]

Yet there are few hints of Mao's future radicalism in the political ideas he expressed during these years, at least as they appear in his surviving school essays and classroom notes. His great hero remained the conservative Confucian Zeng Guofan. Quotations from Zeng's writings appear frequently in Mao's early essays, as do passages from the texts of Confucius and Mencius. Among the great sages of world history, he listed Confucius together with Jesus and Socrates.[10] And among contemporary political figures, he sometimes favored those who enforced "order," including the brutal governor of Hunan province (1913–16), Tang Xiangming, who slaughtered the followers of Sun Yat-sen.

The New Culture movement

The crucial era in the radicalization of Mao Zedong, as for many young students and intellectuals, was the period of intellectual Westernization and cultural iconoclasm known as the "New Culture movement," 1915–19. The first phase in the broader May Fourth movement, the New Culture movement followed in the wake of the Revolution of 1911 – or, more precisely, it followed from its failure to achieve what Mao would later call its "bourgeois-democratic" tasks. Power in the new Republic was usurped by the militarist Yuan Shikai, who drove Sun Yat-sen into exile and established a military dictatorship. The abortive democratic promise of the Revolution was accompanied by failures on all other fronts. The new state was repressive but weak; incapable of bringing about genuine national unification, it prepared the way for the chaotic age of warlordism, and provided no impetus for modern economic development. Nor did the 1911 Revolution do anything to alleviate the foreign economic and political impingements that had turned China into a semi-colony and "the sick man of Asia."

While China's emerging "Westernized" intelligentsia were disappointed with the failure of the Revolution of 1911, they were outraged when contemporary politicians cynically manipulated old Confucian traditions for reactionary political ends. Most prominent among such scoundrels was the militarist "President" of the Republic himself, Yuan Shikai, who resurrected ancient imperial traditions and rituals to legitimate his dictatorial rule, proclaimed Confucianism the state religion, and eventually staged an ill-fated effort to reestablish the monarchy with himself as the first emperor of the Xin (or "New") dynasty. Yuan's imperial ambitions verged on parody. But it was this contemporary association of tradition with political reaction that contributed to giving the New Culture movement its virulently iconoclastic thrust.

The New Culture movement began when China's most influential Westernizing intellectual (and later the first leader of the Chinese Communist Party), Chen Duxiu, returned from exile in Japan. In the autumn of 1915 Chen founded the periodical *New Youth* which attracted to its editorial board China's leading Western-oriented intellectuals and molded the consciousness of an entire generation of Chinese students.

The message the *New Youth* conveyed to Mao's generation of students was that traditional Confucian values were not only ill-suited to China's survival in the modern world, but morally inferior to Western values as well. The persistence of old Chinese traditions was not only responsible for the plight of China, but inimical to the freedom and happiness of the individual. Thus the urgent task confronting the Chinese intelligentsia was first to uproot the oppressive old Chinese culture and then replace it with the dynamic and liberating values of Western science and democracy. "Destruction before Construction" was the motto of the New Youth group long before it became a Maoist injunction.

To regenerate China, the New Youth intellectuals advocated a "cultural revolution," for they believed that transforming the consciousness of the people was the essential precondition for meaningful social and political change. The effort was to be directed mainly to the youth of China, for young people were relatively uncorrupted by the traditions of the past and thus more amenable than their elders to undergoing a fundamental change of consciousness. Young people were seen as the bearers of a new culture and a new society – and thus Chen Duxiu iconoclastically entitled his journal *New Youth* in a land where age was traditionally venerated.

The intelligentsia's overwhelming concern with deficiencies in Chinese culture and morality led them, at first, to seemingly ignore the threat of foreign imperialism. They believed that the fundamental problems of China resided within, in grave defects in Chinese culture and society. Until there was an internal "cultural revolution," there was little hope of effectively responding to the foreign threat. For much the same reason, the *New Youth* intellectuals initially rejected active political participation.

For if the crisis of China was deeply rooted in basic defects in the culture and psychology of the Chinese people, then political activity in so diseased a society offered little hope of getting to the root of the malady. What China required was a "cultural revolution," and this was the first and essential precondition for meaningful political action.

Neither the rather strained effort to appear unconcerned with the immediate threat of imperialism nor the distrust of politics could long survive. The dramatic events surrounding the incident of May 4, 1919, recast the New Youth intellectuals as the forerunners of the nationalism and political activism of the much celebrated May Fourth movement. But many of the other beliefs prominent in the writings of the New Youth group – especially the iconoclastic assault on tradition, the emphasis on consciousness as the decisive factor in history, the concept of cultural revolution, and the faith in youth – survived to mold the intellectual and political history of the modern Chinese intelligentsia.

Few were more profoundly influenced by these beliefs than the young Mao Zedong. Commenting on the various activist student groups that began to emerge around 1917, Mao recalled:

> Most of these societies were organized more or less under the influence of *New Youth*, the famous magazine of the Literary Renaissance, edited by Chen Duxiu. I began to read this magazine while I was a student in the normal college and admired the articles of Hu Shi and Chen Duxiu very much. They became for a while my models, replacing Liang Qichao and Kang Youwei, whom I had already discarded."[11]

Many of the "culturally revolutionary" ideas Mao derived from the *New Youth* magazine were to influence his reception and reinterpretation of Marxism in the 1920s.

Mao Zedong's first published article – an essay on the virtues of physical exercise – appeared in the April 1917 issue of *New Youth*.[12] There is little in his unpublished writings before 1917 – school essays, classroom notes, and personal letters – to suggest that he would be attracted to the radical cultural iconoclasm of Chen Duxiu and the New Youth group. In these early writings he frequently quoted Confucius, Mencius, and other traditional sages. He continued to express admiration for the conservative Confucian statesman Zeng Guofan, as well as for Confucian reformers such as Kang Youwei.[13] The contrast with Chen Duxiu and other New Youth intellectuals – who believed Confucianism was the source of China's social evils and national weakness – is striking.

Mao's esteem for the Confucian tradition was accompanied by an authoritarian preference for "law and order." In a school essay written in

1912, the earliest of his surviving writings, he contrasted the ignorance of the common people with the "good laws" of Shang Yang, or Lord Shang, a Legalist statesman of the 4th century BC whose anti-feudal reforms are credited with providing autocratic efficiency to the state of Qin. "Laws and regulations are instruments for procuring happiness," the young Mao wrote, but "at the beginning of anything out of the ordinary, the mass of the people [*limin*] always dislike it."[14] This hardly foreshadows Mao's celebrated populist "faith in the people."

Mao's early authoritarian preferences were not confined to ancient history. He had a surprisingly favorable opinion of the Military Governor of Hunan province, Tang Xiangming (1886–1975), who was known as "Tang the Butcher," and even for the dictator Yuan Shikai (who had appointed Tang Military Governor), on the grounds that they had maintained a degree of order in a chaotic age.

Mao's rather benign views of autocratic rulers – from Shang Yang to Yuan Shikai – hardly accorded with the new intelligentsia's celebration of "Mr Democracy." And his propensity to easily draw on the Confucian tradition was incongruous with the iconoclastic condemnations of Confucianism that filled the pages of the *New Youth* magazine. But on one crucial issue, the belief that the fundamental problem of China's plight in the modern world resided within, in deficiencies in the psychology and thought of the Chinese people, the young Mao seemed predisposed to the New Culture movement diagnosis. Like the New Youth intellectuals, Mao had a profoundly nationalist concern with the foreign impingement on China. But he also believed that the cultural and moral renovation of the Chinese people was the first and essential task.

This view found expression in his essay on physical education, where Mao deplored the weakness of China but attributed that condition not to foreign imperialism but rather to the deterioration of "the physical condition of our people."[15] He repeated a theme common in nationalist ideologies by suggesting that the strengthening of the bodies of individual citizens would eventually yield national strength. As models to emulate, he looked to the two most successful cases of late "conservative modernization" – Germany and Japan. "Among the civilized nations of today," he wrote during World War I, "it is in Germany that [physical education] most flourishes. Fencing has spread to all corners of the country. Japan, for its part, has *bushido*."[16]

Mao was unwilling to rely solely on foreign examples of national self-strengthening. He suggested that there was much to learn about physical education from "the writings of the ancients," and he thus quoted liberally from Confucius and praised the practices of his childhood hero, Zeng Guofan, to support his prescriptions for building strong bodies that "contain knowledge and house virtue."

A striking feature of Mao's essay is his emphasis on the efficacy of the human will. As if announcing one of the central features of the doctrine that was to be known as "Maoism," he wrote: "Physical education not only harmonizes the emotions, it also strengthens the will. . . . the principal aim of physical education is military heroism. Such objects of military heroism as courage, dauntlessness, audacity, and perseverance are all matters of will."[17]

Yet there was little that was radical about Mao's first published essay. "A Study of Physical Education" is a rather conservative nationalist message on "the effectiveness of exercise in strengthening a country."[18] There is only one faintly iconoclastic note. In an implicit criticism of the Confucian literati's traditional disdain for physical activity – symbolized by the scholar's gown and long fingernails – he wrote:

> Our country has always stressed literary accomplishment. People blush to wear short clothes. Hence there is the common saying: 'A good man does not become a soldier.' . . . Students feel that exercise is shameful. . . . Flowing garments, a slow gait, a grave calm gaze – these constitute a fine deportment, respected by society. Why should one suddenly extend an arm or expose a leg, stretch and bend down?"[19]

The text of Mao's essay provides few clues to its author's intellectual and political future. But it must have been enormously exciting for the 23-year-old Mao – still a student at a provincial normal college who had yet to travel beyond his native province of Hunan – to have an article published in so prestigious a journal as *New Youth*. Now based in Beijing, the *New Youth* magazine had become the principal organ of China's radical and iconoclastic intellectuals. Its editors and contributors were the most prominent members of China's Westernizing intelligentsia, many of them now on the faculty of Beijing University.

It was under the influence of the iconoclastic writings published in *New Youth* that Mao Zedong was gradually radicalized. While Mao's essay on physical education was cast in mostly traditionalist terms, by the summer of 1917 he was becoming increasingly critical of "our country's ancient learning," which was the reason, he concluded, "why we have not made any progress, even in several millennia." Very much in the New Youth spirit, he compared Chinese learning with Western methods and recommended the latter: "Today anyone who is resolved to pursue learning, and yet does not follow [Western] principles, will not be able to attain excellence."[20] And in a letter to a former teacher, written in August 1917, Mao complained that "my countrymen have accumulated many undesirable customs, their mentality is too antiquated, and their morality is extremely bad."[21]

Although Mao was increasingly influenced by the iconoclastic New Youth group, he felt a need to balance his rejection of traditional Chinese values with a critical stance toward the West. This led him to fall back on one of the most banal themes in modern Chinese (and Western) intellectual history – the notion of combining the best of both "the East" and "the West." Thus, the 23-year-old Mao wrote in late 1917: "I have long thought about setting up a private school, which would combine the strengths of classical education and modern schools."[22] And in reporting on the progress of an evening school he and other students at the Changsha Normal School had established to provide educational opportunities for workers who could not afford an education (and where Mao taught history), he approvingly noted that "all the students lined up and bowed three times to the national flag and the portrait of Confucius."[23]

Mao's continuing attachment to aspects of the Chinese tradition, and his efforts to combine what he deemed of value in the Chinese cultural heritage with "Western learning," stands in striking contrast to the views of the more iconoclastic New Youth intellectuals. Hu Shi, for example, found little of value in the Chinese tradition and thus advocated "all-out Westernization." Even more striking is the contrast between Mao and Chen Duxiu, soon to be the first leader of the Chinese Communist Party. In 1915 Chen addressed an issue that had preoccupied Chinese intellectuals for more than a decade – the desirability of blending the "spiritualism" of the East with the "materialism" of the West. It was an appealing – and easy – formula for intellectuals attracted to the values associated with Western economic and military power but unwilling to surrender their own cultural heritage. Chen, however, found nothing to recommend the notion. He contrasted the inertia and decadence of "the East" with the dynamism and youthful spirit of "the West" – and he found the two incompatible. Not only were Western values imperative for China's survival in the modern world, they were morally superior to old Chinese values as well. And it was fruitless to attempt to merge two such starkly opposite cultures. While the West was young and vibrant, China was old and decaying – and its moribund culture had nothing to contribute to modern civilization. The only solution, he emphasized time and again, was to completely destroy the diseased old culture and replace it with the democratic and scientific values of the West.[24]

While Chen's condemnation of the Chinese cultural tradition may seem extreme, his iconoclastic views were shared by most members of the New Youth group. Mao Zedong, by contrast, held a far less uncompromising view of the relevance of the Chinese tradition to modern times. While he was hardly a traditionalist – indeed, his basic intellectual values were to be increasingly drawn from the West – he had a relatively sympathetic attitude toward the traditional cultural heritage. And he wished to preserve as much of tradition as seemed salvageable for modern nationalist ends.

The contrast between Chen's and Mao's attitudes toward traditional culture foreshadows the differences in their reception of Marxism at the close of the decade. Chen, the uncompromising anti-traditionalist and Westernizer, was to receive Marxism as the most advanced expression of modern scientific thought – and he was to embrace it as a universally valid doctrine whose dictates applied to China as they did elsewhere. But Mao Zedong's inclination to salvage what he could of the traditional cultural heritage suggested a greater sensitivity to the particular conditions of China. And that foreshadowed a greater willingness to revise the inherited body of Marxist theory to suit those conditions.

The influence of Western ideas

During his final year at the Normal School in Changsha (1917–18), Mao Zedong was more intensively exposed to the Western intellectual tradition than ever before. Although he never mastered a foreign language, by 1917 Chinese translations of Western writings were readily available and Mao read widely in Western philosophy and social theory – Plato, Aristotle, Kant, Hobbes, Spinoza, Nietzsche, and Spencer, among others.

Mao's intensive study of Western writings during the 1917–18 academic year was guided by his influential ethics teacher Yang Changji, who had spent a decade studying Western philosophy in Japan, England, and Germany. A disciple of Kant, Yang hoped to combine Western philosophy with a revitalized Chinese culture rather than replace the tradition with Western ideas in wholesale fashion, a stance that Mao found congenial. Although his aim was to reform Chinese culture, not discard it, Yang, nonetheless, was an ardent supporter of the iconoclastic *New Youth* magazine. It was Yang who had introduced Mao to that most influential of periodicals – and later to leading members of the New Youth group. Yang's ideas had inspired Mao's essay on "physical education" – and Yang had arranged for its publication in *New Youth*. And it was Yang who encouraged Mao to read Friedrich Paulsen's *System of Ethics*, a rather banal and philosophically idealist neo-Kantian work which was to become best known for the extensive marginal notes that Mao wrote in the copy he read during the winter of 1917–18.[25]

These notes on Paulsen reveal something of Mao's thought on the eve of the May Fourth movement of 1919 and his conversion to Marxism in 1920. And the notes provide insights, less into the reasons he was attracted to Marxism than into some of the intellectual predispositions that he was to bring to his interpretation of the doctrine. Most striking is the full-blown appearance of a powerful voluntarist strain. In the winter of 1918 it mainly took the form of emphasizing the heroic powers of individual human consciousness. Next to a passage in the text where Paulsen asserts that "human beings are capable of changing their basic natures by using their wills," Mao approvingly wrote "the power of the will" and "the power of the mind."[26] And elsewhere Mao wrote:

> The great actions of the hero are his own, [they] are the expression of his motive power, lofty and cleansing, relying on no precedent. His force is like that of a powerful wind arising from a deep gorge, like the irresistible sexual drive for one's lover, a force that will not stop, that cannot be stopped. All obstacles dissolve before him.[27]

The annotations in the Paulsen volume also foreshadow Mao's enormous emphasis on the value of struggle, which satisfied an essential demand of human nature:

> a long period of peace . . . would be unbearable to human life. . . . Could human life stand the Great Harmony? . . . waves of competition and friction would inevitably break forth that would disrupt the reign of Great Harmony . . . chaos too has value in real life. When we read history, we always praise the era of the Warring States. . . . It is the times when things are constantly changing and numerous men of talent are emerging, that people like to read about. When they come to periods of peace, they are bored . . . human nature is delighted by sudden change.[28]

The young Mao's belief that struggle, constant change, and even chaos were not only the sources of creativity but necessary to satisfy elemental human needs – his striking (if perhaps dubious) belief that "human nature is delighted by sudden change" – foreshadowed the emphasis on the value of ceaseless struggle that was to so profoundly mold his interpretation of Marxism. It was a belief that also foreshadowed the dystopian strain that was to appear in his later vision of the socialist utopia, the embryo of an idiosyncratic view of the communist utopia as a time of endless contradictions and struggles.

The value Mao placed on struggle and ceaseless change did not rest easily with his continuing attachment to tradition. Traditionalists favor conservative continuity with the past; they are not "delighted by sudden change." The Chinese tradition especially prized harmony with the social and natural worlds, not struggle to change them. Thus it is not surprising that Mao was becoming increasingly critical of tradition in 1918. What is surprising, in retrospect, is that Mao's growing anti-traditionalism was expressed in a celebration of the virtues of Western-style individualism.

The primacy of the individual is one of the dominant themes in Mao's commentaries on Paulsen. "There is no higher value than that of the individual," Mao wrote, and "there is no greater crime than to suppress the individual." Therefore, he demanded that "our country's three bonds must go." The "three bonds" are the essence of Confucian morality – the obedience of the minister to the prince, the son to the father, and the wife to the husband.[29] And he further dismissed China's "two thousand years of scholarship" as little more than "unthinking learning."[30]

Not only was the individual personality to be released from the constraints of tradition, Mao insisted that the value of the individual took precedence over the group and even the nation. At a time when Chinese nationalism was growing, and would soon burst forth in the May Fourth movement, Mao wrote:

> I do not agree with the idea that the life of the individual derives from the life of the nation in the same way that the four limbs derive from the body. The life of a nation, including its politics and language, all began well after the human race had evolved. . . . The individual came before the nation; the individual did not come from the nation. . . . Paulsen's view [that the nation is great and the individual is small] reflects the fact that he lived in Germany, which is highly nationalistic.[31]

Mao Zedong's exaltation of the primacy of the individual marked a radical break with the Chinese tradition, which rigidly subordinated the individual to the group – family, community, or state. It was an anti-traditionalism that found its most extreme expression in his celebration of what he called "true egoism," by which he meant that "the self is the center of all things and all thought, self-interest is primary for all persons."[32] He further declared: "Some say that we must believe that moral law comes from the command of God. . . . This is a slavish mentality. Why should you obey God rather than obey yourself? You are God. Is there any God other than yourself?"[33]

This extreme individualism, combined with the exaltation of struggle, marked the zenith of the young Mao's anti-traditionalism and the height of the influence of Western ideas – at least before his conversion to Marxism. The Western intellectual influences were a curious and ill-digested combination of the liberal concept of the autonomy of the individual and Nietzsche's notion of the "superman" who rejects the "slave morality" of tradition in favor of his own will or "self." Mao had read portions of Nietzsche and Schopenhauer, from whom he no doubt derived his image of the hero as "the truly great person" whose actions are "his own," relying on "no precedent."

Mao attempted to soothe this radical rupture with tradition by suggesting that "self-interest" and "egoism" were compatible with "our Confucian theory of ethics." But it was a feeble attempt, and although Mao was to retain an emotional attachment to aspects of the Chinese tradition, the intellectual sources that he now drew upon were mostly borrowed from the West.

Anarchist influences

After his graduation from the Normal School in Changsha in April 1918, the 24-year-old Mao Zedong became a leader of the New People's Study Society, one of the many radical student groups that were springing up in various Chinese cities in the early May Fourth era. The society largely devoted itself to the anarchist-inspired "work-study" program, which aimed to send Chinese students to France. The program championed the ideal of combining work with study; but it also had the eminently practical purpose of enabling Chinese students to finance their education by working in French factories, which were suffering from labor shortages after the slaughters of World War I. Not only were there special economic opportunities in France, it was erroneously believed, but a romantic image of France as the cosmopolitan homeland of modern democracy and revolution was widespread among young Chinese intellectuals, an image disseminated in the pages of *New Youth* by Chen Duxiu and others since 1915.

Mao Zedong was one of the principal organizers of the work-study movement in Hunan. Lacking firm plans following his graduation, he went to Beijing in September 1918 along with a group of 20 Hunanese students to prepare for the journey to France. But Mao did not accompany his fellow students to Europe. He later claimed that he remained in Beijing because "I felt that I did not know enough about my own country, and that

my time could be more profitably spent in China."[34] Contributing to that
feeling, perhaps, was a lack of funds and a reluctance to study the French
language. Mao was not to set foot on foreign soil until three decades later
when, in 1950, as leader of the newly established People's Republic, he was
to journey to Moscow.

Meanwhile, since Mao was no longer a student, he was no longer finan-
cially supported by his father. In searching for work, he enlisted the assistance of his former ethics teacher, Yang Changji, who recently had accepted
a professorship at Beijing University. Yang wrote a letter of introduction to
Li Dazhao, the head of the University Library and a leading member of the
New Youth group, who provided Mao with a minor job as a library assistant. It was not an entirely satisfactory situation:

> My office was so low that people avoided me. One of my tasks was to reg-
> ister the names of people who came to read newspapers, but to most of
> them I didn't exist as a human being. . . . I tried to begin conversations
> with [several noted intellectuals] on political and cultural subjects, but
> they were very busy men. They had no time to listen to an assistant
> librarian, speaking southern dialect.[35]

There were compensations for the intellectual slights, the menial
work, and the material hardships. Although Mao remained very much
on the margins of the vibrant student intellectual and political life of
Beijing University, he did informally attend lectures, and was a member
of several student societies. He also was a frequent guest at the home
of Professor Yang Changji (whose daughter, Yang Kaihui, he married
in 1921).

While Mao was employed at the Beijing University Library, Li Dazhao
became the first prominent Chinese intellectual to embrace the message of the Russian October Revolution. For Li, writing in late 1918, the
Bolshevik victory heralded a universal wave of revolution that would
shape the history of the 20th century no less profoundly than the French
Revolution had influenced the course of the 19th century. Li greeted the
October Revolution in chiliastic – if not yet Marxist – fashion, hailing
Bolshevism as an irresistible revolutionary force about to sweep over the
world. "Such mighty rolling tides," he declared, are

> beyond the powers of the present capitalist governments to prevent or
> stop, for the mass movement of the twentieth century combines the
> whole of mankind into one great mass. . . . all those dregs of his-
> tory . . . such as emperors, nobles, warlords, bureaucrats, militarists, and
> capitalists. . . . will be destroyed as though struck by a thunderbolt. . . .
> The dawn of freedom has arrived![36]

Mao was greatly influenced by Li's passionate response to the Russian Revolution and his image of universal revolutionary tides sweeping the world. Similar images of irresistible revolutionary waves were to appear in his own writings in 1919. But there is little evidence to support Mao's later claim that, "Under Li Dazhao, as assistant librarian at Peking National University, I had rapidly developed towards Marxism, and Chen Duxiu had been instrumental in my interests in that direction too."[37] To be sure, Li had organized a "Marxist Research Society" at the end of 1918 that secretly met in his office. It is quite conceivable that Mao Zedong attended several of the informal discussions there. If so, Marxism made little impression on him at the time. What clearly did influence him was anarchism.

Anarchist ideas, brought to China by students returning from study in Tokyo and Paris, had played a major role in radical Chinese intellectual life since the turn of the century. The writings of Kropotkin and Bakunin in particular were widely read. Mao Zedong was deeply impressed by Kropotkin's theory of "mutual aid" and his proposals for combining mental and manual labor. It was this anarchist ideal that inspired Mao's participation in the work-study program in Hunan in 1918. Although Mao did not accompany his friends to France, he continued to correspond with anarchist journals during his first stay in Beijing in the winter of 1918–19. When he returned to Hunan in March 1919, his work as a labor organizer was performed largely through anarchist associations. He later recalled: "I read some pamphlets on anarchy, and was much influenced by them. . . . I often discussed anarchism and its possibilities in China. At the time I favoured many of its proposals."[38]

Many of the anarchist ideas that Mao found attractive during these years were to intermingle with an overlapping cluster of populist beliefs then being expounded by Li Dazhao – conveyed to Mao through Li's writings and possibly also through his discussion groups. This anarchist-populist strain included a belief in the "advantages of backwardness" and a growing appreciation of the potential political importance of peasants, ideas which were to influence the way in which Mao was soon to receive and reinterpret Marxism.[39]

Socialism and the advantages of backwardness

Mao's six-month stay in Beijing had been less than happy, partly because of the material hardships imposed by living in an expensive city on a minimal salary, partly because of his marginal place in the intellectual and political life of Beijing University. The immediate reason for his departure from the capital was word that his mother was gravely ill. He returned home, pausing along the way to bid farewell to friends who were leaving for France under the work-study program. Mao arrived in Hunan in early April, accepted a position as a history teacher in a primary school in Changsha, and plunged into a flurry of political activities. Thus he was not in Beijing on May 4, when a dramatic incident set off a rapid train of events which were to decisively transform the character of Chinese intellectual and political life. On that day in 1919, 3,000 university students demonstrated in Beijing to protest the cynical decision of the victorious Allied powers to turn over to Japan as war booty the colonial territories that had been wrested from the decaying Qing empire by Germany. Outraged by the hypocrisy of the Western powers, who proclaimed that World War I had been fought to promote democracy and national self-determination, the student demonstration sparked a movement that signaled the birth of a modern nation. The movement quickly spread to virtually all of China's major urban centers and several dozen smaller cities as well. Students were joined by their professors and teachers, by merchant associations, and in some places by industrial workers and the urban poor. During the months of May and June, Chinese cities, which had long seemed politically inert, were caught up in a wave of demonstrations, strikes, marches, economic boycotts, and sometimes violent clashes between protesters and the police.

The massive wave of anti-imperialist nationalism that swept China in the late spring and summer of 1919 was the immediate political result of that day's uprising – but the term "May Fourth" was soon enshrined to characterize nearly a decade of "Westernizing" and anti-traditional cultural and intellectual transformation in the years that preceded and followed. And those who came to political and intellectual maturity during that era, including Mao Zedong, were proud to call themselves members of the illustrious "May Fourth generation."

The demonstration, and the events surrounding it, brought profound changes to the intellectual and political perspectives of the New Youth group. The image of a progressive West that would instruct China in the principles of modern democracy and science was shattered by the hypocritical behavior of the imperialist powers. Disillusionment with the West, in turn, eroded belief in Western liberalism, stimulating intense interest in socialism. For socialism had the great attraction of being a Western ideology – thus reaffirming the intelligentsia's Westernizing inheritance and its alienation from traditional Chinese values – while at the same time it was critical of the West in its existing capitalist (and imperialist) form. To become a socialist in the May Fourth era was a way to reject both foreign imperialism and traditional Chinese culture simultaneously, to be a modern Chinese nationalist without falling back on old Chinese values.

Mao Zedong had left Beijing seven weeks before the demonstration of May 4. But the powerful nationalist and anti-imperialist currents unleashed by the incident soon reached Changsha, plunging Mao into a whirlwind of political and intellectual activities. He founded the "Hunan United Student Association," which organized merchants and workers to boycott Japanese goods. He revived the New People's Study Society, which had become moribund after the departure of many its leaders for France. And he planned and raised funds for a "Cultural Bookstore" to make available to Hunanese the Western literature that had been popularized by the May Fourth movement.

Among Mao's notable contributions to that movement in Changsha was the founding of the *Xiang River Review*, a weekly periodical that first appeared on July 14, 1919, and gained a measure of national attention. The "Manifesto" in the inaugural issue featured Mao's first published response to the Russian Revolution. In welcoming "the great call for 'world revolution'" and "the liberation of mankind," Mao borrowed from the tidal imagery employed by Li Dazhao in "The Victory of Bolshevism." "No force can stop a tide such as this," Mao declared. "Those who ride with the current will live; those who go against it will die."[40]

But the great tide that Mao saw sweeping the world was not socialism. In contrast to Li Dazhao's celebrated article of six months earlier, neither the terms "socialism" nor "Bolshevism" appeared in Mao's "Manifesto." Rather, it was "democracy" that Mao called "the basic ideology" of resistance to oppression. Moreover, he insisted that the battle for democracy must take the form of a "bloodless revolution," eschewing bombs and chaos. "We must accept the fact that the oppressors are people, are human beings like ourselves . . . [if] we use oppression to overthrow oppression . . . the result [will be] that we still will have oppression."[41]

There was little in Mao's "Manifesto" to suggest a receptiveness to Bolshevism. Nor was there any hint of any populist celebration of "the wisdom of the masses." Indeed, Mao Zedong took a rather dim view of "the popular masses," whom he described as "simple untutored folk" who are "extremely parochial."[42] Indeed, he repeated the iconoclastic New Youth diagnosis that the fundamental problem of China resided in grave deficiencies in traditional culture: "The real danger lies in the total emptiness and rottenness of the mental universe of the entire Chinese people. . . . They superstitiously believe in spirits, ghosts, in fortune-telling, in fate, in despotism. There is absolutely no recognition of the individual, of the self, of truth."[43]

Mao took a more sanguine view of the Chinese people in his essay "The Great Union of the Popular Masses." Published in three parts in the *Xiang River Review* (July 21 and 28, August 4), it includes the first hint of the populist strain that was to loom so large in Mao's thought. In 1919, the populist impulse appeared in anarchist form. The "great union" that Mao proposed was based on the belief that the overwhelming majority of the Chinese people constituted an organic entity with great revolutionary potential. Differences among the people were not class distinctions but rather differences in occupation and social function. All that was needed was for the "small democratic unions" representing workers, peasants, students, women, policemen, professional groups, and even chambers of commerce to spontaneously join together in a "great unity" to achieve liberation.[44]

The Russian Revolution, vaguely, provided a model for this "great unity." But the Russian upheaval was not the "victory of Bolshevism," as Li Dazhao had proclaimed. Its real leader was the anarchist Kropotkin, who, with fellow believers in the "morality of mutual aid," Mao declared, "want to unite the whole globe into a single country, unite the human race into a single family."[45]

Mao was not alone in believing that the Russian Revolution was an anarchist victory, an illusion shared by many anarchists, in China and elsewhere. While Mao's understanding of the October Revolution soon was to change, one anarchist-populist theme announced in his article on the "Great Union" was to endure – a belief in "the advantages of backwardness."

The notion that backwardness, although a condition to be overcome, is a source of moral virtue and political vitality had been a prominent theme in the thought of Chinese intellectuals since the 1890s. China, by virtue of the very condition of its pre-capitalist backwardness, could forge its own path to socialist modernity (or the realm of "Great Harmony") without repeating all the social evils associated with Western capitalism.

In China, the notion of the advantages of backwardness was derived from anarchist writings. But it is an idea in Western intellectual history most closely associated with Russian Populism. The origins of the notion are to be found in the mid-19th-century writings of Alexander Herzen, the ideological founder of Russian Populism. Herzen believed that the advanced capitalist countries of Western Europe were too corrupted by their "overmaturity" to realize their own socialist ideals. It was backward Russia, precisely because of the moral and social virtues inherent in its backwardness, that would pioneer the socialist future by "bypassing" capitalism.[46]

Whether described as "populist" or "anarchist," his belief in the "advantages of backwardness" was to become a powerful strand in Mao's thought, with enormous consequences for the making of the Chinese Communist Revolution and its post-revolutionary history. The embryo of that notion appears in the final paragraph of "The Great Union of the Popular Masses":

> Our Chinese people possess great inherent capacities! The more profound the oppression, the more powerful the reaction, and since this has been accumulating for a long time, it will surely burst forth quickly. . . . The reform of the Chinese people will be more profound than that of any other people. The great union of the Chinese people will be achieved earlier than that of any other place or people.[47]

Mao's prediction that a backward China would soon leap to the forefront of modern civilization took its immediate inspiration – and much of its language and imagery – from the writings on the Russian Revolution by Li Dazhao, published in 1918. Li had argued that the very backwardness of Russia – and China by implication – contained the seeds of creative rebirth and extraordinary progress. Whereas economically advanced countries such as England and France "have reached a period of maturity in civilization" and thus "no longer have the strength to advance any further," Russia was comparatively slow in its progress and thus possessed "surplus energy for development."[48] And backward Russia's imminent revolutionary leap forward foreshadowed backward China's even more dramatic rebirth.

The notion of "the advantages of backwardness" had great nationalist appeal, supporting the hope that an impoverished China would rapidly transform itself into a powerful and modern nation-state. And both nationalism and a belief in the advantages of backwardness were involved in Mao Zedong's generally sympathetic view of Germany during and after World War I. Most New Youth intellectuals looked to the economically advanced Western countries – France, England, the United States – as models of modern science and democracy. But some members of that group sympathized with Germany. Among them was Li Dazhao, who in 1916 praised Germany as an "emergent nation," whereas the Allied powers were mostly nations in decline. Mao Zedong also took a generally positive view of Germany and sympathized with Germany's plight at the end of World War I. "Of all the peoples of the world," he wrote, "the spirit of the German people is richest in 'greatness.' A spirit of 'greatness' alone can overcome all difficulties."[49]

Mao sensed a certain affinity between Germany and China. Like China, Germany had been a relatively backward land in comparison to Western Europe. Mao admired Bismarck's success in unifying and rapidly modernizing a politically fragmented and economically backward land.[50] The swift rise of Germany to wealth and power was, in a sense, a demonstration of "the advantages of backwardness" – and a model for China to emulate.

Miss Zhao's suicide

In August 1919 the warlord-controlled Hunan provincial government confiscated the fifth issue of the *Xiang River Review* and banned its further publication. The journal had enjoyed a brief but influential life. Mao's writings had won a substantial readership in Changsha and drew praise from leading New Youth intellectuals in Beijing, including Hu Shi, the liberal follower of John Dewey, and Li Dazhao, the convert to Communism. Although it survived little more than a month, Mao's provincial journal had gained him a measure of national prominence that had eluded him while he was in Beijing.

After the suppression of the *Xiang River Review*, Mao's writings appeared in various student publications and in Changsha's leading newspaper, the *Dagongbao*. He wrote articles on contemporary political and social issues, ranging from the strikes sweeping post-war Europe to the student movement in Hunan. But none were written with greater passion than the ten articles he composed on the oppression of women, published in the *Dagongbao* in November 1919.

Among May Fourth intellectuals, Mao Zedong was far from alone in advocating women's emancipation. In a movement that sought to uproot oppressive traditions, women stood out as the most persecuted victims of old customs. Many iconoclastic intellectuals of the time, mostly men, felt the need to write on what was called "the women question." But Mao Zedong's articles were unusual for their power and emotional intensity. Perhaps personal experiences were partly responsible for the passion that pervaded his essays. Mao had just emerged from a month-long period of mourning for his mother, with whom he had enjoyed a close relationship and whom he felt had been unjustly treated by his father. Mao also harbored bitter memories of his own arranged marriage, when at the age of 14 his father betrothed him to a 20-year-old woman, with whom he refused to live but who remained in the family household as his father's concubine. And during the time he lived in Beijing, he had fallen in love with Yang Kaihui, the daughter of his one-time ethics teacher. They were to marry – unrestrained by ancient customs – during the winter of 1921.

The initial article was prompted by a tragedy that took place in Changsha on November 14, 1919. A 23-year-old woman, whose family had arranged for her marriage as a "second wife" to an elderly merchant, was being solitarily conveyed to her new home. When the bridal sedan chair arrived, the young woman was discovered dead, lying in a pool of blood. She had cut her throat with a razor.

In the first of ten articles he was to feverishly write over the next two weeks, Mao attributed the suicide of Miss Zhao to "the rottenness of the marriage system, and the darkness of the social system, in which there can be no independent ideas or views and freedom of choice in love."[51] In response to an editorial writer who suggested that Miss Zhao was "weak and negative" in choosing suicide rather than any other form of escape, Mao enumerated the "iron nets" of social convention and sexual discrimination that had entrapped her.[52] And in reflecting on the historical reasons for the social dominance of males, Mao put a rare emphasis on economic factors – the advent of settled agriculture and a new emphasis on work, with which there "arrived the terrible age in which women became subjugated to men."[53]

On "the women question," at least, Mao remained very much in the original May Fourth spirit, lauding the social progressiveness of the West in contrast to a backward China mired in ancient and barbaric traditions. Yet while Mao praised the enlightened family system of the Western countries, he attributed the oppression of women to "capitalism." "The slave's work of [women] making tea and cooking is a result of capitalism," he declared, "there is a tight bond between old men and capitalism, and the only good friends of love are young people."[54]

It is of course incongruous that Mao should have praised the capitalist West for achieving a relatively egalitarian system of gender relationships while at the same time blaming "capitalism" for pre-capitalist China's sexual inequalities and generational contradictions. Mao's use of "capitalism" as a general term of opprobrium and a timeless evil was probably derived from the anarchist literature he then was reading, writings that tended to treat capitalism in moral rather than historical terms. And this anarchist influence contributed to Mao's reluctance, long after his conversion to Marxism, to fully accept the Marxian faith in the historical progressiveness of capitalism.

In the months following the controversy over Miss Zhao's suicide, Mao Zedong's hostility to traditional Chinese culture and history, growing since the May Fourth demonstration, became more intense. The young woman's chilling death had vividly illustrated the human costs of adhering to ancient social customs. Mao did not become as virulently hostile to tradition as many other New Youth intellectuals – such as Lu Xun, who had dismissed the whole of Chinese history as little more than 4,000 years of cannibalism.[55] Yet Mao had moved closer to the radical mainstream of May Fourth iconoclasm and no longer refrained from sweeping condemnations of the Chinese past. On one occasion he wrote that every Chinese dynasty for four millennia "was based on one condition alone, massive killings and bloodshed."[56]

Mao Zedong's increasing hostility to tradition was accompanied by a growing attraction to socialist ideas. For Mao, as for many Chinese intellectuals, the appeal of Western socialist doctrines was closely bound up with alienation from traditional Chinese values and opposition to the Western imperialist threat. To become a socialist was a way to satisfy both needs. Socialism, inherently iconoclastic, reinforced an intellectual's rejection of traditional culture and also reaffirmed the May Fourth Westernizing inheritance – but at the same time it rejected the West in its contemporary capitalist and imperialist form. Socialism thus had enormous appeal to Chinese intellectuals in an era that was both culturally iconoclastic and nationalistic, one in which modern intellectuals assaulted old Chinese traditions and also sought to defend China against the assaults of foreign imperialism.

Socialist ideas and terminology appear with increasing frequency in Mao's writings after mid-1919. Mao's interest in socialism was initially inspired by anarchism, not Marxism. The anarchist writings which had so greatly impressed Mao while he was Beijing continued to fascinate him after his return to Changsha. He championed such anarchist ideals as combining work and study, integrating mental with manual labor, and Kropotkin's concept of "mutual aid." His bitter critiques of the Chinese family system in his articles on "Miss Zhao's suicide" were filled with anarchist imagery of authoritarian institutions stifling human freedom. He worked together with anarchists in organizing a Hunanese labor union in 1920. And the Cultural Book Society opened the first of its eventual seven bookstores in September 1920. The writings of Kropotkin were among its best-sellers in the autumn of 1920.[57]

The anarchist preference for "federalism" and small-scale organization also influenced Mao's role in the curious movement to establish an independent "Republic of Hunan" in late 1920. While the Hunanese independence movement soon faded, leaving few traces, Mao's participation in the abortive venture reveals an anarchist-type antipathy to large-scale organization. He declared:

> For the past four thousand years, Chinese politics has always opted for grand outlines of large-scale projects with big methods. The result has been a country outwardly strong but inwardly weak; solid at the top but hollow at the bottom; high-sounding on the surface, but senseless and corrupt underneath.[58]

And implicit in the articles Mao wrote on Hunanese independence was the belief that socio-political change could best be accomplished by moral example, a belief that Western anarchism shared with Chinese Confucianism.

In the summer of 1920, when Mao was engaged in the provincial movement for Hunanese independence, he also was drawn – perhaps incongruously – to the internationalist message of the Russian Revolution. The impact of the October Revolution, and Mao's reception of its accompanying Marxist-Leninist doctrine, is considered next, in chapter 2.

2

Communism and Marxism

Conversion to Communism

"By the summer of 1920," Mao Zedong recalled some 15 years later, "I had become, in theory and to some extent in action, a Marxist, and from this time on I considered myself a Marxist."[1] Yet, while Mao may well have imagined himself a Marxist in mid-1920, his knowledge of Marxist theory was meager – and it was to remain cursory for many years.

Mao's lack of familiarity with Marxist theory was quite typical of China's early converts to Communism. While many Chinese intellectuals had been drawn to Western socialist ideas in the first decades of the 20th century, Marxism, which had become the dominant socialist theory in Europe, was not among the doctrines that attracted significant Chinese interest. The reasons are not obscure. Marxism, especially in its orthodox pre-Leninist form, was a doctrine that addressed itself to the workers and intellectuals of the advanced capitalist countries. It was a doctrine that presupposed – as essential preconditions for effective socialist action – a modern industrial economy and a mature urban proletariat. Marxism had little relevance for intellectuals living in a largely agrarian land with little modern industry and only a tiny industrial working class. To Chinese intellectuals, Marxist theory somberly counseled that they must passively wait on the historical sidelines while capitalist forces of production slowly did their work, creating in due course the material and social conditions for socialism. It was not an appealing prospect. Thus the socialist theories that attracted Chinese intellectuals were anarchist and utopian doctrines which set no historical preconditions for socialism; instead they relied on moral appeals to what was assumed to be a naturally good human nature. It was not until the impact of the Russian Bolshevik Revolution – coupled with the transformation of Chinese intellectual and political life brought about by the May Fourth movement – that Marxism began to have a significant influence.

Mao Zedong's first comments on the Russian Revolution, in the summer of 1919, reflect the continuing influence of anarchist ideas. In hailing the Bolshevik victory, Mao borrowed Li Dazhao's tidal imagery of a year earlier. But the irresistible wave of global transformation that Mao dimly perceived was more reformist than revolutionary – and its "basic ideology," he informed his readers, is "democracy."[2] He interpreted the Russian Revolution not only as a democratic but also as a peaceful, anarchist-type revolution, a view shared by many anarchists at the time. In describing the political currents within the Revolution, he disparagingly noted that there is "one extremely violent party" whose leader is "a man named Marx who was born in Germany." But, as he approvingly emphasized:

> There is another party more moderate than that of Marx. It does not expect rapid results, but begins by understanding the common people. Men should all have a morality of mutual aid, and work voluntarily. As for the aristocrats and capitalists, it suffices that they repent and turn toward the good. . . . it is not necessary to kill them. The ideas of this party are broader and more far-reaching. They want to unite the whole globe into a single country, unite the human race in a single family. . . . The leader of this party is a man named Kropotkin, who was born in Russia.[3]

Mao Zedong's first response to the Russian Revolution, then, was to reject extremism and violence in favor of moderation and "mutual aid." At the same time, he rejected Marx (whom he believed to be one of the competing revolutionary leaders in Russia) in favor of Kropotkin and his vision of an anarchist utopia based on peaceful cooperation and moral example. The absence of revolutionary fervor in Mao's initial reaction to the Russian Revolution is striking.

During 1920 Mao Zedong was increasingly drawn to the Russian Revolution – but he accepted the Bolshevik message only gradually and without the revolutionary passions that animated many converts to Communism. In March of that year he wrote to a friend that he considered "Russia to be the number one civilized country in the world" and proposed organizing a delegation to visit Russia within the next two or three years. But at the same time he acknowledged a degree of political confusion: "To be honest, I still do not have a relatively clear concept of all the various ideologies and doctrines."[4]

The prelude to Mao Zedong's conversion to Bolshevism came in November 1920 when he joined the "problems and isms" debate, which marked the split of the New Youth intellectuals into vaguely "liberal" and "Marxist" camps. The controversy had been launched by Hu Shi, a disciple of John Dewey, who, alarmed by the growing influence of socialist doctrines, argued that intellectuals should devote their energies to the hard work of studying concrete social problems rather than parroting "fanciful [and] good-sounding isms." Socialist and anarchist theories advocating "fundamental solutions" were irrelevant to Chinese conditions and also hindered efforts to solve real social problems. Li Dazhao, the most prominent New Youth intellectual to embrace the Bolshevik Revolution, was the first to challenge Hu Shi. Li argued that a mass movement inspired by a common ideology (or "ism") was necessary to achieve a fundamental political transformation, which in turn was the essential prerequisite for the solution of concrete social problems.[5]

Mao Zedong at first seemed to favor Hu Shi's reformist position. In September 1919, influenced by Hu's call for "more study of problems," he organized "The Problem Study Society" in Changsha, listing 71 practical social, political, and educational issues to be investigated.[6] By late 1920, however, he recognized the need for "a total solution" rather than what "some people call piecemeal solutions, which are, in fact, halfhearted." And he echoed Li Dazhao in arguing that to change China required not only a group of resolute people, "but even more than that, it requires an 'ism' that everybody holds in common."[7]

The "ism" that Mao had in mind was Communism. Within a week of declaring his support for a "total solution" and a common ideology, Mao was firmly committed to the message of the Bolshevik Revolution. In a letter to his close friend Cai Hesan, who was in France under the work-study program, Mao embraced the two principles that Cai (already a convert to Marxism) had proposed as essential preconditions for those who wished to organize a Communist party in China. One was a commitment to internationalism and a rejection of patriotism. The second was the acceptance of the concept of the dictatorship of the proletariat, which, as it was understood in China at the time, meant that the first task was the seizure of state power.

Mao Zedong was enthusiastic in embracing internationalism as the guiding principle of the embryonic Communist movement. He observed that most members of the New People's Study Society (who were to constitute a good portion of the early membership of the CCP) "incline toward cosmopolitanism" and shun patriotism:

> they reject the pursuit of the interests of one group or nation while disregarding the happiness of all mankind. . . . each of us is a member of the human race . . . [and we do not want to belong] to some meaningless country, family, or religion and become slaves to these. . . . All socialisms are international in nature and should not have any patriotic coloration.[8]

These internationalist sentiments may seem surprising in light of the nationalist resentments that were so centrally involved in Chinese conversions to Communism. Yet internationalism was very much a part of the appeals of Marxism in the early years following the Russian Revolution. And Mao Zedong, by no means the least nationalistic member of his generation of revolutionary intellectuals, was clearly attracted to internationalist ideals at the outset of his Communist career.

Mao accepted Cai's second principle – the dictatorship of the proletariat – with less enthusiasm, indeed with some reluctance. He agreed in principle with critics of Bolshevism who preferred social transformation by peaceful means. But he no longer thought it realistic. He noted that Bertrand Russell, who recently had lectured in Changsha, favored socialism but opposed "the dictatorship of workers and peasants," instead urging educational methods. "This is all very well in theory," Mao wrote, but "in reality it can't be done." Education, Mao noted, required money – and money, the schools, and political power were all in the hands of capitalists. He now regretfully acknowledged that he had become skeptical about Kropotkin-style anarchism and its vision of achieving a socialist reordering of society through moral example and mutual aid. He concluded that it might be necessary to seize political power on the model of a "Russian-style revolution," which he characterized as a "terrorist tactic" and "a last resort when all other means have been exhausted."[9]

Mao Zedong's conversion to Communism was something less than a passionate response to "the messianic message" of the Bolshevik Revolution. His acceptance of Communism, more than three years after the October Revolution, had been a rather reluctant process growing out of his loss of faith in the efficacy of anarchist-inspired methods of peaceful change during 1920.

Once having accepted Bolshevism at the beginning of 1921, albeit as "a last resort," Mao plunged into Communist organizational activities in Hunan. The building of the organizational and ideological foundations of the Chinese Communist Party was already well under way in various parts of China, although on a tiny scale. In Beijing, Li Dazhao (who had abortively introduced Mao to Marxism in early 1919) established a secret Society for the Study of Marxist Theory in March 1920, the embryo for a Communist party "small group" organized in the autumn of 1920. A similar Marxist study society was founded in Shanghai by Chen Duxiu in May 1920. Chen, the editor of the *New Youth* magazine and the former Dean of Letters at Beijing University, had fled warlord-controlled Beijing to the relative safety of the French concession in Shanghai at the end of 1919. Shortly thereafter, the most prominent figure in the Westernizing New Culture Movement announced his conversion to Marxism.

Chen Duxiu had a considerable influence on Mao Zedong's abandonment of anarchism in favor of Communism. Although the doctrine that eventually came to be known as "Maoism" resembled Li Dazhao's voluntarist and populist reinterpretation of Marxism, Chen Duxiu's more orthodox version of the Bolshevik message was initially more important in Mao's conversion. In the summer of 1920 Mao visited Chen in Shanghai to discuss the few Marxist writings he had read. He later recalled that "Ch'en's [Chen's] own assertions of belief had deeply impressed me at what was probably a critical period in my life."[10]

Probably even more influential were the letters Mao received from Cai Hesan, then in France. Cai's fluency in French allowed him to read the writings of Marx and Engels in French translation as well as the literature now being published in revolutionary Russia. By contrast, Mao Zedong was confined to the smattering of Marxist writings that had been translated into Chinese. By mid-1920 Cai had become a sophisticated student of Marxism and he was also convinced of the validity of the Leninist revolutionary model. He conveyed his enthusiasm to Mao, and his many letters undoubtedly contributed to Mao's growing sympathy for the Bolshevik Revolution. By the beginning of 1921 Mao Zedong's conversion to Communism was unambiguous. He abandoned his anarchist beliefs as unpractical (although not without some regrets), proclaimed himself a Marxist and threw himself into Communist organizational activities. He convened the inaugural meeting of the Socialist Youth League (later renamed the Communist Youth League) on January 13, 1921, and simultaneously established a Communist "small group" in Changsha, consisting of five members.

By the time Mao organized the embryonic Hunan branch of the Communist Party, small Communist groups had been established in Beijing and Shanghai and in a half-dozen other cities – as well as among Chinese students studying in Paris and Tokyo. The early Communist groups largely drew their membership from the left-wing student organizations generated by the May Fourth movement. In Changsha most of the Hunanese who became Communists in 1921 were members of the New People's Study Society, which had been organized by Mao and Cai Hesan in 1918.

The Hunan Communists merged into a national organization in July 1921, when 12 delegates from the various "small groups" secretly gathered in Shanghai to formally establish the Chinese Communist Party. The First CCP Congress was quite unremarkable – save for the circumstances in which it convened. The 13 young Chinese delegates, guided by a senior

Comintern advisor, the Dutch Communist Hans Sneevliet (known under the pseudonym "Maring"), secretly gathered in the back room of a small store in the French concession of Shanghai. They slept in a nearby girls' boarding school, vacated for summer recess. Fearing a police raid, the delegates interrupted their meeting after several days, individually fleeing Shanghai by train to conclude their deliberations on a houseboat on a lake near Hangzhou.

The congress itself was otherwise uneventful. The ultra-centralist Leninist principle of "democratic centralism" became the basis of Party organization; the Chinese Communists formally joined the Moscow-governed Comintern and agreed to accept its dictates in accordance with the principle of "proletarian internationalism;" and Marxism was proclaimed the guiding ideology of the new Party, its mission being to organize the urban working class to seize state power and establish a "dictatorship of the proletariat."

Neither Chen Duxiu nor Li Dazhao, the two most important figures in the early Chinese Communist movement, attended the meetings that came to be celebrated as the First Congress – a gathering that appears far more important in retrospect than it did at the time. Chen, however, was elected Secretary-General of the newly established Party *in absentia* and Li was informally recognized as the Party's leader in north China. Mao Zedong attended the First Congress as the representative of the Hunan Communist group, and thus could claim in later years to have been one of the founding members of the CCP, although his contribution to the discussions at the initial meeting seems to have been very modest. Some thought him a bit uncouth. A delegate from Beijing recalled in his autobiography:

> Mao Tse-tung [Mao Zedong], who had not yet shaken off his rough Hunanese ways, was the pale-faced scholar, a youth of rather lively temperament, who in his long gown of native cloth looked rather like a Taoist priest out of some village. His fund of general knowledge was considerable, but he did not seem to understand much . . . about Marxism. . . . A good talker, Mao loved an argument, and while conversing, he delighted in laying verbal traps into which his opponents would unwittingly fall by seeming to contradict themselves. Then, obviously happy, he would burst into laughter.[11]

The founding of the Chinese Communist Party

The founding of the CCP did not seem a significant political event in a country ruled by rapacious warlords, its cities under the sway of foreigners. The number of Communists was tiny. The delegates to the First Congress could claim to represent only 57 members in all, scattered across the world's most populous land. There were perhaps another 50 Communists in various parts of the vast country not formally represented. And there were several hundred members of the Socialist Youth Corps, which became an auxiliary of the CCP. Four years later Communist leaders could claim only modest progress in recruitment: there were barely a thousand Party members in 1925.

Not only were they few in number, but the founding members of the Chinese Communist Party had little knowledge of the Marxist doctrine that presumably was to guide their political activities. Mao Zedong was quite typical of the early Chinese Communists. Like most members of the first generation of Chinese Communists, his political conversion to Bolshevism came well before he had any real intellectual commitment to Marxist theory. His education in Marxism proceeded gradually, carried out in the course of the practical political struggles into which he thrust himself. It was not until the late 1930s that he was to feel the need – and the confidence – to attempt to make his mark as a Marxist theoretician.

The origins of Chinese Communism, then, were strikingly different from the origins of Communist parties in Western Europe and Japan in the years immediately following World War I. Communist parties in the West were based on the left wings of older Social Democratic movements whose leaders were well versed in Marxist theory. They had been Marxists for many years, often for decades, before the Russian Revolution – and they viewed the Bolshevik message through Marxian lenses. Both their enthusiasm for the Bolshevik experiment, and their doubts about it, were molded by Marxist categories of thought and their experiences in Marxian Social Democratic politics.

But in agrarian China, the Communist movement – unlike Communism in Europe, Russia, and Japan – could not draw on an existing Marxist intellectual tradition or the membership of an older Social Democratic party. There were no Chinese Plekhanovs or Lenins, no socialist leaders who had spent many years studying Marxist texts before committing themselves to a course of political action. The Chinese Communist Party was organized by two professors and their student followers who embraced Bolshevism more because of their disillusionment with Western liberalism and democracy than because of Marxian intellectual convictions. It was only after they accepted the political message of the Russian Revolution that they undertook to learn its doctrinal foundations – and to adapt (in their different ways) that doctrine to the particular conditions of the Chinese historical environment. It is a striking feature of the origins of the Chinese Communist Party that its founders became politically committed to Communism well before they became intellectually committed to Marxist theory, indeed, in most cases well before they acquired any significant knowledge of Marxism. The general phenomenon is well depicted in the intellectual-political biography of Mao Zedong, whose somewhat reluctant decision to embrace the Bolshevik Revolution was made on practical political grounds – at a time when his knowledge of Marxist theory was virtually non-existent.

One consequence of the absence of a Marxian social democratic tradition was that there was no older socialist party from which the new CCP could draw its membership. The great majority of the early Chinese Communists – as in the case of Mao Zedong – came from the amorphous student movement. The leaders of the party were young, politically inexperienced, and ideologically insecure. These characteristics made the early CCP leaders less burdened by Marxist orthodoxies – and perhaps more willing than their Western counterparts to revise Marxist theory to suit unanticipated historical conditions. But they also made for a lack of confidence that fostered dependence on the Moscow-based Comintern, which increasingly presented itself as the sole repository of political truth.

Mao Zedong began his Communist career in rather orthodox Marxist fashion. From the winter of 1920–1 until early 1923 Mao devoted himself to organizing urban workers into trade unions. Both in his actions and writings he was fully in accord with the Marxist belief that the cities were the centers of modern revolutionary activity and that the urban working class was the agent of the socialist future. Such elemental Marxist principles were conveyed to the early Chinese Communists by the basic Marxist writings they were reading and translating, reinforced by the directives of the Comintern, and enshrined in the program adopted at the First Congress of the CCP.

In the early 1920s Mao Zedong had no doubts about the political primacy of the cities over the countryside. He was not, at the beginning, an advocate of rural revolution. Indeed, even before his conversion to Marxism, his political focus was on the cities. In promoting the movement for Hunanese autonomy in 1920, he assumed that the minority of urban dwellers would lead the countryside to the desired goal:

The 30 million [rural] people are too scattered. Our road is long and those endowed with consciousness are few. It would be too late to wait for thirty million people to wake up. . . . the responsibility has inevitably fallen on the shoulders of our 300,000 citizens [*shimin*, literally, "towns-people"] of Changsha.[12]

For the young Mao, the countryside was not a repository of revolution-ary energy but an idyllic place for urban intellectuals to recuperate from their mental labors. In a letter to a friend in the autumn of 1920, he com-plained that intellectuals suffered from a "psychological inertia" which resulted in "studying without rest" and consequent exhaustion. Mao therefore announced: "Now I have decided that for every two months of living in the city, I will spend one week in the countryside. This trip to Pingxiang is for the purpose of a rest."[13]

Mao Zedong's image of the countryside as the place where urban intellectuals retreated to rest occasionally stands in striking contrast to the views of Li Dazhao. In February 1919, when Mao was employed as Li Dazhao's assistant at the Beijing University Library, Li published an extraordinary series of four short articles entitled "Youth and the Vil-lages." Li passionately urged young Chinese intellectuals to abandon the corrupting life of the cities and settle in the countryside "to spread the principles of humanism and socialism," emulating the heroic example of Russian Populism in its "go to the people" movement of the 1870s. China's liberation, Li believed, was dependent on the liberation of the peasantry. But the peasants would not achieve liberation by themselves. It was the mission of young intellectuals to go to the countryside to educate and enlighten the peasants – and to merge with them. By settling in the villages, the youth would enjoy the purity of rural life while avoiding the fate of "sinking into the mire of the city and becoming treacherous people."[14]

Mao Zedong was not among the young Chinese intellectuals who responded to Li's populist appeals. Although he lived in a rural area during his childhood, he had become an urban intellectual. Since early 1911, when he was 17 years old, Mao Zedong had lived in cities. The greater part of his education as well as his early political experiences had taken place in Changsha, Beijing, and Shanghai. The roots of the anti-urban biases that were to become a prominent feature of "Maoism" are not to be found in the thought of the young Mao. He assumed, as a matter of course, that the political and intellectual life of China was lodged in its great cities. China was primarily an agrarian nation, as the young Mao sometimes noted in passing, but he had little to say about the vast country-side and its enormous peasant population.

Mao and the urban working class

In view of his urban orientations, it is hardly surprising that Mao Zedong at first embraced the orthodox Marxist view of the supremacy of the town over the countryside in the making of modern history. And, once having accepted the Bolshevik Revolution, he did not hesitate to adopt the Marxian faith in the urban proletariat as the social agent of modern revolution. Nor did he delay in acting on that belief. From the time of his conversion to Communism in early 1921 until February 1923, Mao's political efforts were mainly devoted to the organization of workers in Hunan. He did so in his capacity as head of the Changsha branch of the Communist Party's Labor Secretariat, a body established shortly after the First Congress to provide the new party, consisting mostly of intellectuals, with a "proletarian base."

But Hunan had little modern industry and thus few proletarians, at least in the Marxian sense of that term. Such modern industries as there were in China were concentrated in such foreign-dominated treaty ports as Canton and Shanghai. Hunan province, with a population of over 30,000,000, had no more than 100,000 workers – and the majority of these labored in handicraft industries and other traditional occupations. Thus, Mao perforce devoted much of his time attempting to organize trade unions among workers who labored in a pre-industrial society – barbers, masons, carpenters, tailors, rickshaw pullers, and shoemakers. Such workers in China's traditional economy were grouped in officially controlled guilds. The guilds brought greater benefits to the bureaucracy than to the workers, and many workers were receptive to the appeals of trade union activists.

Mao was not the first to attempt to organize workers in Hunan. He was preceded by a number of young anarchists who had organized the Hunan Workingmen's Association in 1920. Although Mao was critical of the anarchist labor group for promoting "trade unionism" instead of class consciousness, he worked closely with them – and convinced several of his anarchist associates to join the Communist Youth League.

Trade union organization was a perilous activity in warlord-ruled Hunan. Two young anarchists associated with Mao in labor organization were beheaded by the local militarist, and Mao himself barely escaped arrest on several occasions. Nevertheless, by cooperating with the anarchists, and building on their work, Mao achieved a measure of success in organizing traditional workers as well as those in the tiny modern sector of Hunan's economy. The latter included textile mill laborers, miners, and railroad workers. In the autumn of 1922 Mao was instrumental in establishing a modern-type trade union, the All-Hunan Federation of Labor Organizations, to replace the now banned Workingmen's Association. At its height, the federation consisted of some 20 unions, with a combined membership of over 30,000, a third of Hunan's small working class.

The new unions staged several successful strikes – notably ones by textile workers and miners – despite repressive political conditions in warlord-controlled Hunan. Moreover, the Federation of Labor Organizations established a network of evening schools for workers. And "workers' clubs" (a euphemism for trade unions, which were banned by the provincial authorities) offered innovative educational and recreational programs for workers.

The most modern sectors of the Hunanese working class consisted of the tin and coal miners in the Anyuan area (north of Changsha) and the workers on the strategic Hankou–Canton Railroad which ran through Changsha. Mao initiated the organization of the Anyuan miners and railroad workers in 1921, but then turned the task over to Li Lisan, a young Communist recently returned from France, and the 22-year-old Liu Shaoqi, who had studied in Moscow. Successful (if sometimes bloody) strikes by Communist-led miners and railroad workers in late 1922, which resulted in *de facto* recognition of the unions and a doubling of wages, marked the high point of the Hunan labor movement.[15]

In January 1923 the CCP Secretary-General Chen Duxiù, impressed by the relative success of the Hunan labor movement, asked Mao to become a member of the Party's ruling Central Committee in Shanghai. But before Mao left Changsha for Shanghai, the slaughter of striking railroad workers in central China dramatically transformed the prospects and the policies of the CCP – and terminated Mao's brief career as a workers' organizer. The "February Seventh Massacre" was ordered by Wu Peifu, the dominant warlord in north China, with whom the Communists had been uneasily allied since 1921. In one brutal blow the warlord army destroyed the most powerful and militant workers' movement in China. Dozens of workers were killed, Communist organizers were arrested and sometimes executed, and the fragile proletarian base of the CCP in the northern provinces was suddenly shattered. It proved the signal for the suppression of radical and labor organizations throughout China. In Hunan, warlords and business interests joined forces to crush the small labor unions which Mao and others had painstakingly organized.

The February Seventh Massacre profoundly altered the outlook and policies of the Chinese Communists. The suppression of the radical working-class movement in north China, built over several years but destroyed almost overnight, cast doubt about the feasibility of a working-class revolution in a pre-industrial China ruled by rapacious warlords. As a result, many Chinese Communists became receptive to a new political strategy that Moscow had been promoting since 1922 – an effort to forge an alliance between the Communists and the Guomindang (GMD), the Nationalist Party headed by the veteran revolutionary Sun Yat-sen, to carry out what was called "the national revolution."

The new strategy, eventually imposed by the Soviet Union on the fledgling Chinese Communist Party through the agency of the Comintern, was born in Europe. The failure of proletarian revolutions in the industrialized countries of the West left Bolshevik Russia isolated in a hostile capitalist world. Lenin and other Soviet leaders, no longer seized by expectations of an immediate world revolution, were now concerned with the sheer survival of the revolutionary regime in backward Russia. It was a situation that dictated a search for allies more substantial than the tiny Communist parties of China and other Asian lands. Moscow now looked to anti-imperialist forces in colonial and semi-colonial lands that could offer significant political and military support in the here and now, political groups and leaders labeled "bourgeois nationalists."

In China "bourgeois nationalists" included warlords of various political persuasions who found it expedient to temporarily ally themselves with the Soviet Union, offering political support of often dubious value in exchange for financial and military aid. But the Soviet search for Chinese allies focused on Sun Yat-sen's Nationalist Party. In 1922 Moscow informed the Chinese Communists that the Chinese revolution was still in its "bourgeois-democratic" phase, a political stage corresponding to an early period of capitalist development. A socialist revolution was not yet feasible. Moreover, the main agency of China's "bourgeois-democratic revolution" was the Guomindang, with whom the Chinese Communists were instructed to cooperate in a common front against foreign imperialism and domestic feudalism.

For Mao and most Chinese Communists, it was a disheartening message. They had became Communists with the expectation that a world revolution was more or less imminent. And most were engaged in organizing the working class to carry out what they assumed would be a socialist revolution in China. Now they were told that the world revolution was indefinitely postponed, that the Chinese revolutionary movement was capitalist rather than socialist in nature, and that the CCP would play a secondary role for the foreseeable future.

The February seventh Massacre made the Chinese Communists more receptive to the Comintern policy of seeking an alliance with the Nationalist Party. When Mao Zedong joined the Central Committee in Shanghai in the spring of 1923, he too had lost his faith that the urban proletariat would be the agent of revolution in China. He had spent almost two frenetic and dangerous years organizing workers in Hunan. But he now concluded: "All of Hunan Province is in the stage of handicraft industry."[16] The implication was that China, or at least Hunan, did not have a modern industrial proletariat, and that his work as a union organizer had been of little political value. Nor did he think Hunanese peasants held much revolutionary potential: "The thinking of the small peasants has changed little. Their political demands are simply for honest officials and a good emperor."[17] For the next three years, Mao, under the general direction of Chen Duxiu, was to devote his energies to working with the Guomindang to bring about the "national revolution."

The national revolution

The term "national revolution" was a euphemism for the Marxist-Leninist concept of a "bourgeois-democratic revolution," designed to appeal to the nationalist sentiments of followers of Sun Yat-sen and at the same time assuage Communist disappointment over the postponement of the socialist revolution. Bourgeois revolutions had a strong nationalist component in their original European historical settings, from which the Marxian concept was derived. A "bourgeois-democratic revolution," typically, created unified modern nation-states out of the politically fragmented territories left over from the feudal era and established national markets. These centralizing accomplishments, in turn, facilitated the development of modern capitalism, the defining feature of a bourgeois revolution.

In China, the nationalist content of the "bourgeois" phase of the revolution perforce was greater than it had been in Europe. For China required not only national political and economic unification but also national independence from the foreign imperialist impingements that had been strangling the country for nearly a century. Shared nationalist and anti-imperialist sentiments constituted the bond that brought the GMD and the CCP together in the Russian-manufactured alliance. It was thus not entirely inappropriate to refer to the joint enterprise as a "national revolution."

The alliance forged to carry out the national revolution was a most unusual one – a tripartite arrangement between the Soviet Union and the two Chinese parties, Nationalist and Communist. In return for Soviet financial aid, arms, and military advice, the GMD agreed to a united front with the Chinese Communists – but not as an equal partner. Rather, Communists were permitted to join the GMD as individuals to participate in the "national revolution" under the auspices of the Nationalist Party, which had established a fragile government (dependent on the support of a local warlord) in Canton.

Many Chinese Communists, including the CCP leader Chen Duxiu, opposed the Comintern strategy. Not only were they disappointed that the socialist revolution had been indefinitely postponed in favor of a perhaps prolonged "bourgeois" phase, they were reluctant to recognize the GMD as the leading force in the "national revolution," in which they were to participate only as individual members of Sun Yat-sen's party. But some Chinese Communists, mostly those of strongly nationalistic predispositions, welcomed the new strategy. Among them was Mao Zedong.

Mao Zedong was one of the most active Communist members of the Nationalist Party; he occupied a variety of high official positions in the GMD political apparatus and he was among the more ardent supporters of maintaining the Comintern-fashioned alliance to carry out the "national revolution." Yet, ironically, it was in the course of his activities as an official of the Guomindang that Mao discovered the revolutionary potential of the Chinese peasantry – and began to take part in organizing the rural social revolution that was to break apart the Communist-Nationalist alliance.

The Comintern-imposed alliance with the Guomindang was formally accepted by the Chinese Communists – although with considerable reluctance on the part of many – at the Third CCP Congress, held in June 1923. Mao Zedong, who had just been elected to the CCP Central Committee based in Shanghai, underscored his enthusiastic support for the alliance with an article lauding the bourgeoisie as the most important class in the national revolution. "This revolution is the task of the people," he wrote, "but because of historical necessity . . . the task that the merchants should shoulder in the national revolution is more urgent and more important than the work that the rest of the Chinese people should take upon themselves."[18]

It is strange that Mao should have found the bourgeoisie to be the crucial social class in China's "national revolution." He had devoted his first two years as a Communist to organizing urban workers and he was shortly to discover the peasantry as the true revolutionary class. Perhaps he took literally the Comintern insistence that the Chinese revolution was in its "bourgeois-democratic" stage and assumed that the actual bourgeoisie was its natural leader. Whatever the reasons, Mao was a most active and enthusiastic Communist member of the GMD, at the time the older revolutionary party was being reorganized along Leninist lines with the assistance of Comintern advisors, who were also beginning to provide Sun Yat-sen with a modern army. Mao rose rapidly in the Nationalist Party apparatus while continuing to carry out his growing responsibilities at CCP headquarters in Shanghai. He attended the Guomindang's First National Congress, held in Canton in January 1924, where he was elected an alternate member of the GMD Central Executive Committee. He was charged by both parties with the task of maintaining the united front.

It was an arduous – and ultimately impossible – assignment. Faced with growing tensions between (and within) the two parties, Mao's initial enthusiasm for the alliance began to fade. He was accused by fellow Communists of having sacrificed their interests in his efforts to accommodate the Nationalists. And as the most visible Communist in the GMD, he was attacked by right-wing Nationalist Party leaders as an agent of Communist subversion.

The tensions and hostilities generated by the Guomindang-Communist alliance were deeply discouraging. Mao, who had embraced the united front with tremendous enthusiasm in 1923, grew increasingly pessimistic – and then depressed. The depression was unrelieved by the general political situation in China in 1924. The urban workers' movement was mostly quiescent, having yet to recover from the shock of the February seventh Massacre. Mao's hope that the bourgeoisie would lead the "national revolution" proved transitory. Such faith that he had in Sun Yat-sen as leader of the "national revolution," already waning, was further undermined when Sun traveled to Beijing at the end of 1924 to negotiate with a reactionary government installed by the northern warlords. The Communist Party, suffering defections and lethargic recruitment, had fewer than a 1000 members. And Mao had yet to discover the political potential of the peasantry, which in any case was hardy visible from Shanghai.

Complaining of a "mental ailment" and overwork, Mao gradually withdrew from his political posts during the fall of 1924, retreating entirely from the political arena that December. Together with Yang Kaihui and their two sons, he left Shanghai and returned to Hunan, first living in Changsha and then retreating even further to his native village of Shaoshan. He did not attend the Fourth CCP Congress, which convened in Canton in January 1925, even though he was one of the Party's top half-dozen leaders. Although he had been a prolific writer and correspondent since his late teens, he wrote virtually nothing for almost a year.

Mao lived quietly in Shaoshan during the winter and spring of 1925, spending most of his time with his family and friends from his childhood, and reading the books he had brought to the village from Changsha. He slowly emerged from political seclusion only when he learned that peasants in the surrounding countryside were beginning to form unions, inspired by peasant uprisings in the neighboring province of Guangdong. Mao Zedong began to participate in peasant union activities in the spring of 1925. But he was by no means the organizer of the peasant movement in Hunan. It was a largely spontaneous movement of the peasants themselves – and no one was to emphasize its spontaneity more eloquently than Mao himself, when he later recorded his observations on the radicalization of the Hunan countryside.

It is impossible to trace the evolution of Mao's political thought as he gradually became involved with the peasant movement of his native province, for he wrote nothing during the spring and summer of 1925. Nor did he speak to anyone who was moved to record such conversations as they may have had. His return to political activism was less the product of his own intellectual evolution than of events taking place in the cities of Shanghai and Canton, where Mao had been politically engaged for almost two years – and from where he had fled at the end of 1924.

Return to politics

The great revolutionary upsurge of 1925–7 was ignited by what came to be celebrated as the "May 30th movement," the name derived from an incident that took place in Shanghai, the city that symbolized the foreign political and economic impingement. The murder of a Chinese factory worker by a Japanese foreman provoked a mass protest on May 30, 1925. The demonstrators were fired upon by British-commanded police in the International Settlement, killing a dozen workers and students. The deaths sparked a torrent of militant strikes, anti-foreign boycotts, and massive nationalist demonstrations in cities throughout south and central China.

The May 30th movement was fueled by an explosive combination of bitter nationalistic and social revolutionary grievances. Protests against the extreme economic exploitation characteristic of early industrial capitalism were intensified by the fact that the exploiting owners and managers usually were foreigners, armed and protected by special privileges gained by a century of Western and Japanese aggression. The combination of nationalism and social revolution was to remain the driving force of the Chinese revolutionary movement. Soon, under new historical and social circumstances, it was to find its personification in Mao Zedong.

The urban working-class movement was reinforced by the rise of an equally militant (and far more massive) peasant movement in the countryside in 1925. By the middle of that year peasant unions in Guangdong province alone had half a million members. Over the next two years the Guangdong associations mobilized more than 2,000,000 impoverished peasants and the movement spread rapidly to a half-dozen other provinces, including Hunan. The peasant risings greatly strengthened the Nationalist government in Canton, and enabled its Russian-trained army, led by Chiang Kai-shek, to launch the long-awaited "Northern Expedition" to unify warlord-torn China. The May 30th movement dramatically increased the power of the Chinese Communist Party as well, expanding its influence in the Nationalist Party and army and also enormously increasing the power of its own organization. The membership of the CCP, less than a 1000 at the end of 1924, grew to 20,000 by the end of 1925, and to almost 60,000 by early 1927.

Mao Zedong, re-energized by the popular activism of the May 30th movement and especially by the sudden upsurge of peasant radicalism in his home district around Shaoshan, threw himself back into the political maelstrom. In the summer of 1925 he organized peasant associations and peasant night schools in Hunan. Mao's political activities soon attracted the attention of the warlord dominant in Hunan province, who ordered his execution. Mao fled to Canton in the autumn of 1925 and reassumed his positions in both the Nationalist and Communist parties.

Mao was now back in the city that had become the main base of the surging revolutionary movement. But his mind was on the Hunanese countryside. He was soon to return to the rural areas, and it was there that "Maoism" was born.

3

Peasant Revolution

When Mao Zedong, under threat of execution, fled Hunan in the autumn of 1925, the great revolutionary upsurge of 1925–7 was well under way. Enraged by the incident of May 30, 1925, Chinese workers, concentrated in such treaty-port cities as Canton and Shanghai, joined in unprecedented numbers in a wave of strikes and nationalist political demonstrations, launching one of the most militant working-class movements in the history of the 20th century. The city of Canton was the political center of the revolutionary movement that quickly spread to the major cities and much of the countryside of south and central China during 1926.[1]

It was largely on the basis of the burgeoning popular movement that Sun Yat-sen had secured the power of the Guomindang in Canton. And it was the militant workers' movement, with the very considerable assistance of peasants from nearby Haifeng county, that enabled Sun's successors to proclaim a National Revolutionary government in mid-1925. Canton, thus, became the center of the Communist-Guomindang alliance, and it was on the nearby island of Whampoa that Sun's imported Russian advisors trained the officer corps of the Nationalist Army – and installed the Soviet-trained military officer Chiang Kai-shek as its commander.

The discovery of the peasantry

Despite the militant proletarian movement that thrived in Canton, Mao Zedong had little interest in the urban working class when he arrived in the "Red City" of Canton in the fall of 1925. Mao had devoted his first two years as a Communist to organizing workers in his native Hunan, under far less favorable conditions than prevailed in Canton, but he now all but ignored the successfully rebellious workers in favor of potentially rebellious peasants. No sooner had he resumed his positions in the CCP and GMD than he emphasized the need to organize "those broad peasant masses who constitute 80 percent of the population of Guangdong." In

January 1926 Mao published a detailed and remarkably astute analysis of rural China's social structure, denouncing "big landlords" not only as exploiters of the peasantry but also as "the real foundations of imperialism and the warlords," in short, as the main enemy of the national revolution.[2] The heretical implication was that the Chinese revolution mainly would be a rural revolution.

Early in 1926, Mao, then acting head of the GMD Propaganda Department, complained that "we have concentrated too much on city people and neglected the peasantry." And throughout the year he repeatedly emphasized that a peasant revolution was the key to success in the national revolution. It was the exploitation of the peasants by landlords, Mao argued, that financed the warlords, who in turn supported the compradore class as their "retainers."[3]

The decisive battles of the national revolution, then, were to be fought more in the countryside than in the cities. Mao thus proclaimed: "Every place in China must become like Haifeng." Haifeng was the rural county where Peng Pai, the son of a landlord who had "gone to the people," had been organizing peasants since 1922 and where, in 1927, he was to establish China's first (although short-lived) soviet government.

By 1926 Mao Zedong had set forth two interrelated propositions – both heretical in Marxist terms – that were to become critical features of the doctrine that would be canonized as "The Thought of Mao Zedong." First, he rejected the Marxist assumption that the triumph of capitalism definitively established the dominance of the city over the countryside in the making of modern history. Mao had little taste for Marx's triumphal assertion in the *Manifesto of the Communist Party*:

> The bourgeoisie has subjected the country[side] to the rule of the towns. It has created enormous cities, has greatly increased the urban population as compared with the rural, and has thus rescued a considerable part of the population from the idiocy of rural life.[4]

Secondly, Mao also rejected the central Marxist belief that modern history revolved around the two urban classes into which capitalism was progressively dividing society – the bourgeoisie and the proletariat. By 1926 Mao had come to be far more concerned with the struggle between landlords and peasants than the conflict between capitalists and workers. And he now believed that peasants, at least in China, were potentially more revolutionary than the urban proletariat.

Mao Zedong's discovery of the revolutionary promise of the peasantry reflected itself in a radically new understanding of 19th-century Chinese history. His great historical hero, from childhood well into his adult years, had been the Hunanese imperial viceroy Zeng Guofan, who had bloodily suppressed the great Taiping peasant rebellion in the mid-19th century. Mao had always portrayed Zeng as a morally upright Confucian statesman and had celebrated his restoration of social order. He now arrived at a far different historical assessment:

> The Taiping King, Hong Xiuquan, called on a broad group of unemployed peasants to rise up and make revolution, and this had great significance as a social revolution. . . . Everyone knows that the Qing dynasty overthrew him, but they don't know that the main military force which really overthrew him represented the landlord class. The one who contributed the greatest effort toward the overthrow of the Taiping Heavenly Kingdom was Zeng Guofan. At that time, he was the leader of the landlord class.[5]

In 1926, as the revolutionary movement grew in scope and social radicalism, Mao Zedong, curiously, was far more active in the leadership of the Guomindang than he was in the Communist Party. It was not simply because of his efforts to exert Communist influence in the party under whose banner the "national revolution" proceeded that Mao devoted himself to the affairs of the Nationalist Party. Rather it was because most Chinese Communist leaders were indifferent to the peasant movement. The intellectual roots of Communist distrust of peasants ran deep in the Marxist tradition. Karl Marx not only had written about "the idiocy of rural life," but also about the forthcoming disappearance of the peasantry under capitalist forces of production, the inability of peasants to articulate their own social interests, and the likelihood that they would play a reactionary political role and provide mass support for Bonapartist personality cults.

Leninist revolutionary strategy, growing out of conditions in largely agrarian Russia, provided a more meaningful, if still very limited, revolutionary role for peasants than original Marxism. The peasantry, according to Lenin, could serve as a substitute for a politically timid bourgeoisie and, in alliance with the proletariat, carry out the "bourgeois-democratic" phase of the revolution. In that alliance, the peasantry would be the junior partner, to be "led" by the proletariat, or more precisely, by a Communist party which presumably embodied "proletarian consciousness." Nonetheless, Leninist revolutionary strategy, however ambiguous on agrarian matters in many respects, emphasized that peasant participation was necessary in the making of modern revolutions, especially in economically undeveloped lands.

The views of CCP Secretary-General Chen Duxiu on peasants were closer to those of Marx than Lenin. "The peasants are scattered and their forces are not easy to concentrate," he wrote in 1923, echoing the orthodox Marxist assessment. The peasants' "culture is low," Chen maintained, "their desires in life are simple, and they easily tend toward conservatism. . . . These environmental factors make it difficult for the peasants to participate in the revolutionary movement."[6] Chen's image of peasants was one generally shared by Chinese Communist leaders in the 1920s. Most of those leaders had come from a Westernized intelligentsia whose members typically looked at peasants as simplistic, uncultured, and the carriers of all that was archaic in Chinese society and culture. Marxism reinforced that image.

While Mao Zedong was by no means the only – or the first – Chinese Communist leader to advocate a peasant-based revolution,[7] he did soon become the most formidable critic of the policies of the urban-oriented leaders of the Party, especially the policies of Chen Duxiu. His relationship with Chen became strained shortly after he arrived in Canton in the fall of 1925, following several months of detailed rural investigations and radical organizational activities. His difficulties with Party leaders originated over questions of agrarian policy, he later recalled:

> On the basis of my study and of my work in organizing the Hunan peasants, I wrote two pamphlets, one called *An Analysis of the Different Classes of Chinese Society.* . . . Chen Duxiu opposed [my] opinions which advocated a radical land policy and vigorous organization of the peasantry, under the Communist Party, and he refused [to publish them] in the Communist central organs.[8]

The hostility of Party leaders to his newly found faith in the peasantry led to Mao's growing estrangement – if not necessarily from Communism in general then certainly from the Chinese Communist Party in particular. This, in turn, resulted in his deeper immersion in the affairs of the Guomindang. The Nationalist Party, while partly a refuge for Mao, also offered positive appeals. For it was a party whose leaders, particularly those who constituted its left wing, demonstrated far more sensitivity to the plight of the peasantry and their political potential than their Communist Party counterparts – at least before the purge of radical GMD members carried out by Chiang Kai-shek in 1927. In the mid-1920s, the Nationalist Party, unlike the CCP, had established a variety of departments concerned with rural problems, including an institute to train peasant organizers. Thus, in 1926 and through the first six months of 1927,

Mao devoted most of his time and energies to the GMD and stood aloof from CCP politics. He occupied a large number of important Guomindang positions, including principal of the Peasant Movement Training Institute from May to October 1926.

But Mao's rise in the GMD hierarchy was cut short. For the Nationalist-Communist alliance, which had stimulated and led the massive popular movement that swept much of China in 1925–7, could not survive the successes of the radical social movement that had proceeded under its political auspices. Once exploited workers and impoverished peasants were politically activated, their increasingly radical demands could not be confined to the bourgeois limits of the "national revolution" that the Communists and Guomindang had brokered. Chinese workers struck at factories owned by Chinese capitalists as well as those owned by foreigners. And millions of rebellious peasants threatened the lands and privileges of Chinese, not foreign, landlords. The mass movement, in short, threatened property – and the propertied classes in both town and countryside placed themselves under the protection of the GMD, the party that now promised order. Or more precisely, landlords and capitalists fled into the arms of Chiang Kai-shek. And Chiang, for his part, turned his Soviet-built army to the task of destroying his Communist allies and crushing the radical trade unions in the cities and the peasant associations in the rural areas.

Chiang Kai-shek began with a brutal attack on Communist and workers' organizations in Shanghai in April 1927. From there the orgy of counter-revolutionary violence spread to other cities under the control of the Nationalist and warlord armies. But the greatest slaughter took place in the countryside, in the suppression of the peasant unions. The "White Terror" of the next few years was to take millions of lives, most of them in the rural areas. It is hardly surprising that the repression fell hardest on the peasantry. The peasant revolutionaries were not only far greater in number than the urban working class, they were also more socially radical. Factory workers in the cities could strike and demonstrate, which they did in heroic fashion, but peasants began to seize and redistribute land, directly threatening not only rural landlords but also their sons (who made up the bulk of the officer corps of the Nationalist Army) as well as the urban bourgeoisie who were heavily invested in the countryside as absentee landlords and mortgage holders.

More than any other factor, it was the social radicalism of the peasantry in 1926 and early 1927 that broke apart the Guomindang-Communist alliance and provoked the violent counter-revolution that began in the cities but took its greatest human toll in the countryside.

Mao Zedong played an important part in the upsurge of peasant radicalism that swept the Chinese countryside in late 1926. During his six months as principal of the Guomindang Peasant Movement Training Institute, he instructed many of the cadres who became organizers of peasant associations in the southern and central provinces in the wake of the Nationalist Army's Northern Expedition. Thereafter he undertook to investigate the desperate social and economic conditions of peasants in several districts of the provinces of Jiangsu and Zhejiang. For all their backbreaking labor, Mao observed, the peasants were left in "a condition of tragic misery. In addition to natural disasters, there are also the exorbitant taxes of the warlords and greedy officials, plus the heavy rents and high interest charged by landlords – layer upon layer of crushing exploitation. For this reason, many peasants are running away and becoming bandits." The graphic report Mao wrote on the basis of his investigations powerfully conveyed his empathy for the plight of the peasantry as well as a keen appreciation of their political potential.[9]

At the beginning of January 1927 Mao Zedong returned to Hunan to continue his study of agrarian conditions. His "Report on an Investigation of the Peasant Movement in Hunan," written after a month of intensive research in five counties, is an extraordinary document that announces many of the essential themes that were to go into the making of the doctrine that came to be known as "Maoism."

The "Hunan Report" and the birth of Maoism

The "Hunan Report," Benjamin Schwartz once observed, "might just as well have been written by a Russian *narodnik* as by a Marxist-Leninist."[10] Indeed, the lengthy document that Mao Zedong submitted to the CCP Central Committee in late February 1927 echoed many of the beliefs of the young Russian Populist intellectuals who went to the countryside in the 1870s to "merge" with the people, beliefs that romantically prized the revolutionary spontaneity of the peasantry.

Mao was not directly influenced by Populist ideas or by the heroic example of the Russian "go to the people" movement. He did not read Herzen and Chernysevsky, and he was only dimly aware of the *narodniki*. Mao no doubt was exposed to certain Populist notions that came under the aegis of Kropotkin's anarchism, writings that had so greatly influenced him in his pre-Marxist days. But the Populist strain in his thought was less the result of Russian intellectual influences than his own political experiences in the Chinese countryside in the summer of 1925, when a politically disenchanted Mao was regenerated by the spontaneous peasant radicalism he observed in his native province. In a sense, his Populist beliefs can be seen as the typical response of an alienated intellectual in an agrarian land experiencing the social disruptions of early industrialism and seeking a non-capitalist path of development.

Just as the Russian Populists placed their revolutionary hopes in what they assumed to be an inherently socialist peasantry not yet corrupted by capitalist relationships, so Mao looked to the elemental revolutionary energies of the Chinese peasantry. "The present upsurge of the peasant movement is a colossal event," he passionately wrote.

> In a very short time, several hundred million peasants in China's central, southern, and northern provinces will rise like a fierce wind or tempest, a force so swift and violent that no power, however great, will be able to suppress it. They will break through all the trammels that bind them and rush forward along the road to liberation. They will, in the end, send all imperialists, warlords, corrupt officials, local bullies, and bad gentry to their graves.[11]

Not only did Mao celebrate the revolutionary energies of the peasants, he did so in the belief that they were acting on their own, as an elemental tornado-like force that rose from the depths of their oppression. The peasants were not guided by political parties or dependent on the support of other social classes. Indeed, Mao's "Report" was remarkable for a Marxist in that it barely mentions the urban working class. Not even a ritualistic bow was made to "the leadership of the proletariat" or even to the Communist Party, presumably the incarnation of "proletarian consciousness." Mao quite explicitly defied Marxist-Leninist orthodoxy:

> To give credit where credit is due, if we allot ten points to the accomplishments of the democratic revolution, then the achievements of the city dwellers and the military rate only three points, while the remaining seven points should go to the achievements of the peasants in their rural revolution.[12]

Yet the spontaneity that Mao prized, Lenin had distrusted – and that distrust went into the making of the Leninist concept of the revolutionary party. The spontaneous movement of the masses, Lenin argued, was an insufficient condition for revolution. If left to itself, the spontaneity of the people would eventually result in an accommodation with the existing order. What was required to yield a revolutionary outcome was the imposition of the Marxist consciousness of the intelligentsia on the amorphous movement of the masses, channeling the diffuse revolutionary spontaneity of the people into effective political action. The embodiment of that all-important revolutionary consciousness was a highly centralized and tightly knit party organization presided over by a dedicated elite of professional revolutionaries.

In Mao Zedong's "Hunan Report" there is no suggestion that the spontaneous revolutionary strivings of the masses were to be disciplined by any political party. Mao assumed that the peasants themselves possessed the standards of political judgment that Marxist-Leninists attribute to the Communist Party. It was not the party that was to judge the revolutionary actions of the peasantry, but rather it was the peasants who were to judge the revolutionary sufficiency of the party. As Mao bluntly put it: "All revolutionary parties and all revolutionary comrades will stand before them [the peasants] to be tested, to be accepted or rejected as they decide."[13]

Mao Zedong was doubly heretical from the viewpoint of orthodox Marxism-Leninism. First, he departed from Marx (as well as Lenin) by identifying the peasantry rather than the proletariat as the main revolutionary class. Secondly, he defied Lenin by favoring the spontaneous revolutionary creativity of the masses over the organized revolutionary consciousness of the party. To be sure, Mao soon was to come to appreciate the efficacy of Leninist organizational principles and he was to be the leader of a party organized according to those elitist principles. But he never fully resolved the old Populist dilemma of the relationship between the "consciousness" of the intellectuals and the "spontaneity" of the masses in a purely Leninist fashion. His belief in the Communist Party as the organizational incarnation of socialist consciousness clashed with a persisting Populist faith (expressed in its most pristine form in the "Hunan Report") that true revolutionary creativity resided in the peasants themselves. The tension between these conflicting "Leninist" and "Populist" impulses became a persisting feature of "The Thought of Mao Zedong." And it was this unresolved tension that was in no small measure responsible for the ambiguous and sometimes hostile relationship between the person of Mao Zedong and the institution of the Chinese Communist Party.

From these unorthodoxies other heresies flowed. One was the inversion of the Marxist view of the relationship between town and countryside in the making of modern history. For Marx, and for Lenin as well, the dominance of the cities over the countryside was a necessary and progressive outcome of modern history. As part of this process, the peasantry qua peasantry would disappear under the pressure of capitalist forces of production. As Engels summed up the Marxist view: "Our small peasant, like every other survival of a past mode of production, is hopelessly doomed. He is a future proletarian."[14]

In 1927, his familiarity with Marxist literature still cursory, Mao Zedong was probably unaware of Marxian predictions about the fate of the peasantry, which he no doubt would have ignored in any case. However, he was well aware of the limitations that Marxist-Leninist theory placed on the political role of the peasantry, for these ideological restraints had been repeatedly set forth by CCP leaders and Comintern agents. But he disregarded the ideological orthodoxy. For Mao, the peasants constituted not only the overwhelming majority of the Chinese population but were the truly revolutionary class in Chinese society, politically more important than the city workers and the military put together.

The belief in the revolutionary primacy of the countryside and its inhabitants over the cities was not only an inversion of Marx (and Lenin) but it bred, over the years, a powerful anti-urban bias that was entirely foreign to the Marxist tradition. In the "Hunan Report" Mao's anti-urbanism was still muted and mostly implicit, but it found one of its first expressions in a hostility to urban educators who promoted foreign learning in ignorance of the needs of the peasants:

> See how the peasants who hitherto detested the schools are today zealously setting up evening classes. They always disliked the "foreign-style school." . . . I, too, used to identify myself with the general run of "foreign-style students and teachers" and stand up for it, feeling always that the peasants were "stupid and detestable people." Only in the 14th year of the Republic [1925], when I lived in the countryside for half a year, did I realize that I had been wrong and the peasants' reasoning was extremely correct. The texts used in the rural primary schools were entirely about urban things and unsuited to rural needs. . . . Now the peasants are enthusiastically establishing evening classes, which they call "peasant schools." . . . Before long, tens of thousands of schools will have sprung up in the villages throughout the province; this is quite different from the empty talk about "universal education," which the intelligentsia and so-called "educationalists" have been bandying back and forth and which after all this time remains an empty phrase.[15]

In this remarkable passage, Mao combines anti-urbanism and a hostility to intellectuals, themes common in Populist ideologies but ones alien to the Marxist tradition. His celebration of the "evening classes" that the peasants were establishing on their own initiative – contrasted to the "empty talk" of urban intellectuals – was to grow into a general distrust of intellectuals and a perception of the cities as dens of moral corruption and centers of political reaction. These strains in the "Hunan Report" went into the making of the intellectual preconditions for the Maoist strategy of revolution. It was a strategy – born partly out of necessity, partly out of conviction – that was to take the seemingly fantastic form of mobilizing the forces of peasant revolution in the countryside to "surround and over-whelm" the conservative cities.

Had it not been for the brutal counter-revolution of 1927, Mao Zedong's commentary on the Hunan peasant movement might well have cut short his career as a Communist. That report propounded two heresies that no Marxist-Leninist party could have tolerated. First, Mao had denied the cardinal Marxist belief that the urban proletariat was the principal agent of modern revolution. Secondly, he questioned the sacrosanct place of the Communist Party by attributing to the peasantry the revolutionary con-sciousness that Leninists insisted was embodied in the Party.

Were these not blasphemous enough, Mao had also challenged the authority of the Comintern and Moscow, where Stalin now reigned. As the Chinese revolutionary movement turned increasingly radical in the last few months of 1926, the Stalinist message from Moscow was to curb the "excesses" of the masses, particularly the peasantry, for fear of under-mining the Communist alliance with the Guomindang. The alliance had to persevere at all costs, Stalin insisted, even if those costs had to be borne by Chinese revolutionaries.

While most CCP leaders faithfully carried out Comintern policy, although often reluctantly, Mao dissented, passionately defending "the excesses" of peasant rebels. As he wrote in the "Hunan Report":

> turning everything upside down, they [the peasants] have even created a kind of terror in the countryside. This is what some people call "going too far." . . . Such talk may seem plausible, but in fact it is wrong. First, the local bullies, bad gentry, and lawless landlords have themselves driven the peasants to this. . . . the peasants keep clear accounts, and very seldom has the punishment exceeded the crime.[16]

And in a passage that was to be repeatedly quoted over the decades:

> a revolution is not like inviting people to dinner, or writing an essay, or painting a picture, or doing embroidery; it cannot be so refined, so lei-surely and gentle. . . . A revolution is an uprising, an act of violence. . . . All actions which have been labeled as "excessive" had revolutionary signifi-cance. . . . To put it bluntly, it is necessary to bring about a brief reign of terror in every rural area; otherwise we could never suppress the

activities of the counterrevolutionaries in the countryside or overthrow the authority of the gentry. To right a wrong it is necessary to exceed the proper limits.[17]

Counter-revolution

Mao Zedong's ideological heresies and his none-too-veiled criticism of the Comintern and Stalin threatened disciplinary action from the CCP, and perhaps his expulsion from the Party altogether. But the Party's reaction was cut short when Chiang Kai-shek turned against his erstwhile Communist allies in April 1927 and violently destroyed the radical mass organizations. In the cities the working class was terrorized into submission – and was to remain politically quiescent until the late 1940s. The greatest slaughters took place in the countryside, however. In Hunan province alone, more than half a million peasants perished under the military repression, and the peasant unions Mao had so enthusiastically celebrated in his report of February 1927 disappeared entirely.

During the early summer of 1927, as the White Terror was spreading from city to city and through much of the countryside, Mao Zedong advocated more radical agrarian policies. He did so in his capacity as a GMD agrarian official, although now as a spokesman for the left-wing faction of the Nationalist Party that had broken with Chiang Kai-shek and established a rival government in the city of Wuhan. Mao now set forth the militant slogan "land to the tiller" and advocated the confiscation and redistribution of virtually all landholdings of any substantial size, with the exception of land owned by families of "revolutionary soldiers."[18]

Yet in 1927 it mattered little what rural policies were proclaimed. The left-wing GMD government at Wuhan, with whom the Communists still cooperated, had neither the will nor the power to alter existing social relationships in the countryside. The Chinese Communist Party was even less receptive to Mao Zedong's radical proposals for rural revolution. At the Fifth CCP Congress, which convened in Wuhan in May 1927, a month after Chiang Kai-shek's coup in Shanghai, Mao's proposal for land redistribution was ignored by Party leaders. Mao later recalled that CCP Secretary-General Chen Duxiu

> did not understand the role of the peasantry in the revolution and greatly underestimated its possibilities at this time. Consequently, the Fifth [CCP Congress], held on the eve of the crisis of the Great Revolution, failed to pass an adequate land programme. My opinions, which called for rapid intensification of the agrarian struggle, were not even discussed.[19]

But it probably made little difference. Had the CCP pursued Mao's policy of radical rural revolution in May 1927 – or the calls of Trotsky and others for radical workers' revolution in the cities – it is unlikely that the Communists could have avoided the crushing defeat that they suffered in 1927, a defeat that very nearly extinguished the Chinese Communist Party. Fewer than 10,000 of 60,000 Party members remained at the end of that fateful year. Most of the relatively few Communists who survived were forced out of the cities, separated from the urban working class, and forced to flee to the more remote areas of the countryside. The ruins of the revolutionary movement set the stage for the rise of Mao Zedong to Communist leadership, although it was to prove a prolonged and some-times bizarre struggle that was not to be fully settled until the early 1940s. Mao had been arguing since 1925 that the peasantry was the main class in China's "national revolution." The Communists now had no choice but to turn to the peasantry, if only for survival.

The decisive blows against the CCP and the popular revolutionary movement had been struck by Chiang Kai-shek, beginning in Shanghai in April 1927. And the decisive factor, simply put, was that Chiang had an effective army and the Communists did not. That fact was not lost on Mao Zedong, who derived from the disasters of 1927 the elementary lesson that for the Communists to achieve political success in the modern Chinese historical environment they would have to have their own military force. From the recognition of that brutal fact came the oft-quoted maxim that "political power grows out of the barrel of a gun," a slogan Mao first set forth in the summer of 1927. It was hardly an original thought. Chiang Kai-shek knew and practiced the maxim well before Mao fully grasped it. Nor was it the case that other Chinese Communist leaders were oblivious to the political uses of military power. Chinese Communists attempted to gain as much influence as they could in the army that the Russian Com-munists had built for the Guomindang. But the notion that the CCP should have its own army did not come naturally to most of the intellectu-als who led the CCP. They had assumed, as did most Marxists, that the revolution would essentially be a political struggle and that a resort to armed conflict could be no more than a temporary expedient. It was left to Mao to make explicit the notion of a revolution based on military force, and to act in accordance with it. Over the next two decades the building of the Red Army was at the heart of Mao's revolutionary strategy.

The events of 1927 also made Mao distrustful of Moscow. The policies laid down by Stalin and imposed on the Chinese Communists through the agency of the Comintern had led the Chinese party to a nearly fatal defeat. On matters of Chinese revolutionary strategy he now followed his own judgment, even while paying ritualistic observance to the authority of Moscow. The rituals, however, did not disguise the fact, least of all to the immediate participants, that Mao's rise to power was to come in defiance of Moscow and in direct conflict with CCP factions backed by Stalin.

The birth of the Red Army

After the counter-revolution of 1927 Mao Zedong strongly urged the remaining Communists to retreat to the rural areas. By "going up the mountains," as he put it, "we can create a foundation for a real military force."[20] Here, in embryonic form, were announced the two essential features of the emerging Maoist strategy of revolution: first, the peasantry was to be the Communist Party's mass base; and, secondly, the Party was to build its own army.

Mao Zedong's insistence that the peasantry was the truly revolutionary class, at least in China, again brought him into conflict with the CCP leadership – and the Comintern. Mao did not shrink from the battle. Indeed, he seemed to invite it. At the Emergency Conference, a meeting of the Central Committee of the CCP held on August 7, 1927, to reassess Party policy in the wake of the disasters of the preceding spring and summer – and to blame the failures on Chen Duxiu – Mao was blunt in his critique of the CCP:

> The peasants want a revolution, [and] Party [members] close to the peasants also want a revolution, but the upper level of the Party is a different story. . . . yet the Party's guidance is not revolutionary; there really is a hint of something counterrevolutionary about it. I have established these views under the guidance of the peasants.[21]

Mao was not content simply to celebrate the revolutionary potential of the peasantry. He insisted on contrasting the spontaneous revolutionary strivings of the peasant masses with the conservatism of the Communist Party. Far from seeing the Party as bringing revolutionary consciousness to the amorphous movement of the masses, in Leninist fashion, Mao depicted the Party as an obstacle to the natural revolutionary yearnings of the peasants. At the same time, he portrayed himself as the repository of the wisdom of the masses, claiming (by no means as humbly as he perhaps intended it to appear) that he had arrived at his views about revolution "under the guidance of the peasants." Both of these propositions – the dichotomy between the revolutionary masses and the conservative Party, and the implicit claim to be the spokesperson for the peasant masses – were to be recurrent themes in Mao's long political career.

The views that Mao Zedong set forth in 1927 – the belief that peasants were the principal revolutionary class and the argument that the revolution could succeed only by employing organized military force – were ideas alien to the Marxist tradition. Even after Lenin's revisions of original Marxist doctrine, peasants were seen no more than an "auxiliary" force in the bourgeois-democratic phase of the revolution. And while Marxists generally assumed that a socialist revolution would necessarily involve violence – in the form of a popular armed insurrection, perhaps on the model of the Paris Commune of 1871 – the notion that a revolution could be the work of an army was a concept well beyond the imagination of most Marxists.

But the peculiarities of political conditions in China, especially after the catastrophes of 1927, brought home to most Chinese Communists the lesson that political success, indeed political survival, was dependent on the control of military force. Thus, in the summer of 1927, the Chinese Communists attempted to organize their own army, mainly around Communist-led units of the Nationalist Army that had defected. The scattered military forces that eventually were to be called the Red Army initially attempted to seize cities, with the aim of stimulating working-class uprisings. A series of desperate military adventures followed. The most ambitious was an ultimately failed effort of Communist-led soldiers to stimulate an insurrection on August 1 in Nanchang, the capital of Jiangxi province, an event that was to be later celebrated as the official birthday of the Red Army. Another involved the dispatch of Mao Zedong to Hunan province, where he hastily organized a military force of 3,000 men, mostly peasants, supplemented by unemployed Anyuan coal miners, vagabonds, and soldiers who had deserted the Nationalist Army. They proceeded to attack the provincial capital. But in Changsha, as elsewhere, the anticipated popular uprising did not materialize – for everywhere the urban workers, defeated and demoralized by the events of the spring and summer, had been terrorized into submission or had turned politically apathetic. Mao's loosely organized force was mauled by local warlord armies. At the end of September Mao gathered the 1,000 soldiers who remained of his defeated force – now known as the Red Army – and fled to the Jinggang Mountains, a remote bandit hideout bordering the provinces of Hunan and Jiangxi.

Jinggangshan, 1927–9

The prospects for revolution could hardly have been less promising than the conditions that Mao and his followers encountered in the Jinggang Mountains in October 1927. The desolate Hunan-Jiangxi border, sparsely populated by desperately impoverished peasants, was not only far removed from cities but it was also isolated from most of the rural population. Mao was forced to rely on displaced and wandering people, vagabonds, bandits, and beggars. Such social groups Marxists traditionally categorized as "lumpenproletarians," portrayed as a politically dangerous class whose miserable conditions of life made them prey to reactionary political demagogues.

But Mao's view of China's vast army of urban and rural "lumpenproletarians" was not formed in an orthodox Marxist mold. Indeed, his search for a sanctuary in the Jinggangshan had been greatly assisted by his efforts to win the trust of two secret society leaders whose vagabond forces held sway over the remote mountain range and its sparse population. Essentially leaders of bandit gangs, their activities were tempered by a sense of social justice, and they shared with the Communists a hatred of landlords. In exchange for guns, they provided Mao's soldiers with food and information – and they soon joined the tiny Communist force, adding 600 men to the 1,000 soldiers Mao had brought to the barren area.

Mao soon came under criticism from urban Party leaders for recruiting "vagrants," thereby undermining the "proletarian" character of his small army. He defended the practice by observing that "workers and peasants are hard to come by" and that "the vagrants are after all particularly good fighters." But, most interestingly, he argued that lumpenproletarians could be transformed into revolutionaries through "political training" and ideological remolding.[22] For what was important for Mao was not social class but "class consciousness" – and the latter was not dependent on actual social class. "Proletarian class consciousness" could be acquired through practical experience, political training, and education, irrespective of social class.

Mao Zedong's definition of class in terms of "consciousness" rather than according to objective social measurements was in part a matter of necessity. There were, after all, few proletarians in Mao's small army and little prospect of recruiting urban workers. The Red Army, as it had come to be called, was dependent on desperately poor peasants, wandering people who had been driven from the land, vagrants, vagabonds, and sometimes bandits. But if there were no proletarians to lead, there was a "proletarian consciousness" that could be taught. Mao's faith in eventual revolutionary success was sustained by a voluntaristic faith in the power of consciousness to transform social reality in its own ideal image. The enormous emphasis on the power of ideas in the making of history was to remain one of the central features of Maoism. And the blurring of the distinction between "class" and "class consciousness" (born in the desperate days on the Jinggangshan) was to become one of the most contentious and perplexing issues in the history of Chinese Communist politics.

The 16 months in the Jinggang Mountains, from October 1927 to January 1929, involved a struggle for survival. A year after his flight to the mountains, Mao wrote a report to the Central Committee, including the comment: "[We] are acutely aware that the revolutionary tide is ebbing daily in the country as a whole. . . . So we are reduced to contending for the country in this cold atmosphere. We have an acute sense of our isolation."[23]

On the Jinggangshan, the Communists were able to fight off attacks from various GMD and warlord armies, but Mao's forces suffered heavy losses when they descended to the plains to seek supplies and recruits. Mao's Jinggangshan base was considerably strengthened when he was joined early in 1928 by Zhu De, a Communist military commander who had been wandering through southern China with several thousand troops since the defeat of the Nanchang uprising in August 1927. The combined force was called the "Fourth Front Army" and popularly known as the "Mao–Zhu" army, with Zhu De as military commander and Mao as political commissar. Other remnant Communist military forces, most notably several hundred soldiers led by Peng Dehuai (a regimental commander in the Nationalist Army who became a Communist early in 1928) gravitated to Jinggangshan. In all, together with new recruits, Mao's army numbered about 10,000 soldiers a year after he had fled to the mountains.

Jinggangshan itself, with its steep and craggy cliffs overlooking fog-shrouded narrow passes, was relatively secure. But it had little else to recommend it. Inhabitants were few and resources were scarce. There were only six villages in the area, Mao Zedong reported: "Formerly, all these places were dens of bandits and deserters. The population . . . is under two thousand and the rice production is less than 10,000 *shi*."[24] To seek recruits and acquire food and supplies, it was necessary to descend to the plains, but to do so was to risk battles with larger and better-armed GMD and warlord forces, inevitably causing heavy losses for the inexperienced troops of the Red Army. As Mao somberly noted:

> Ordinarily, soldiers need six months' to a year's training before they go into battle. Our soldiers, recruited only yesterday, have to fight today with virtually no training. Consequently, part of the middle- and lower-ranking cadres, as well as many soldiers, know very little about the art of war and rely only on their bravery. This is very dangerous.[25]

It bordered on the miraculous that Mao's tiny army survived at all. Surrounded on all sides by hostile armies, depleted by desertions and illness, primitively armed and ill trained, and suffering fearsome casualties, the prospects for the "Mao–Zhu" army in 1928 could hardly have been bleaker. Commenting on the primitive state of medical care, Mao wrote:

> After every engagement there are wounded. Because of malnutrition, cold and other factors, many officers and soldiers are ill. We have founded a Red Army hospital on the Jinggangshan, which employs both Chinese and Western medicine for diagnosis and treatment, but we are short of both medicine and doctors.[26]

Only a tiny percentage of those who experienced the ordeals on the Jinggangshan lived to follow Mao and Zhu in the perilous descent to the Jiangxi plains in January 1929. Yet the Red Army had won new recruits – mostly from China's enormous population of wandering people (*youmin*) – and had modestly increased its numbers. Mao attributed the survival of his military forces to what he called "democracy," by which he primarily meant egalitarianism:

> the reason why the Red Army can hold out despite such miserable material conditions and continuous fierce battles lies in its thorough implementation of democracy. The officers do not beat the soldiers; officers and men have the same food and clothing, and receive equal treatment; soldiers enjoy freedom of assembly and speech; over-elaborate formalities have been abolished; all financial transactions are completely open; and the soldier's representatives inspect the accounts.[27]

Mao may have championed the superiority of "spiritual" over "material" factors, but at the end of 1928 he concluded that deteriorating physical conditions necessitated abandoning Jinggangshan. The morale of his small army had been undermined. The Red Army hospital overflowed with sick and wounded soldiers. And the mountain fortress was surrounded by 25,000 Nationalist troops dispatched by Chiang Kai-shek, to whom the small Communist base seemed more a political nuisance than a military threat. For the Communists, the Guomindang blockade threatened economic strangulation, preventing Communist forces from descending to the plains where they had sustained themselves by requisitioning food and money from landlords.

The Jinggangshan had been, at best, a place for the remnant Communist forces to survive. Now, even survival was in grave doubt. Thus, at the beginning of 1929, preparations were made to abandon the base. Mao and Zhu De led the bulk of the Red Army, some 3,500 men, marching and crawling single file over huge boulders and jagged peaks, braving snowstorms and icy winds, and fighting rear-guard actions against pursuing GMD troops. The remaining 800 under the command of Peng Dehuai held out on Jinggangshan to guard 1,000 sick and wounded soldiers along with a small number of women and children.

Although they suffered heavy losses in the descent from the Jinggangshan – 600 soldiers were killed in one battle alone – the main force of the Red Army remained intact and eventually established a new base in southern Jiangxi. Peng Dehuai, who had been left to defend the Jinggangshan base, fared far worse. A week after Mao and Zhu departed, the mountain fortress was overrun by GMD troops, who outnumbered the defenders by 30 to one. Most of the sick and wounded were slaughtered. Fewer than 300 of the 800 soldiers whom Peng Dehuai had led to Jinggangshan survived the escape to the Jiangxi plains.

The Red Army, even with new recruits, Mao reported in April 1929, numbered only 3,600 men, sharing 1,100 guns between them.[28] But the Communists now found themselves in a heavily populated rural area with abundant material resources. In striking contrast to the barrenness of the Jinggang Mountains, southern Jiangxi was a relatively prosperous part of the countryside where social-class differentiations were clearly demarcated. Substantial numbers of peasants were attracted by the Communist promise of land redistribution and the egalitarianism of the Red Army. In the new environment the Mao–Zhu army flourished, winning local peasant recruits as well as deserters from the Nationalist Army. The main body of the Red Army grew into a formidable force of 40,000 soldiers by early 1930 and controlled substantial territories in southern Jiangxi, near the Fujian border.

The survival and growth of the Red Army, after its near extinction on the Jinggangshan, is one of the most remarkable chapters in the annals of 20th-century military and political history. Mao Zedong attributed the capacity of his tiny army of poorly armed and half-starved soldiers to remain a cohesive military force to a combination of political and tactical factors. The political basis of the Red Army's survival against overwhelming odds, Mao suggested, was adherence to a common ideology – which imparted a sense of mission and purpose that other armies in warlord-torn China lacked. But he especially emphasized the importance of "simple rules of discipline" that Red Army soldiers were required to observe, and which brought peasants "everywhere to volunteer to help the revolution." Most of these were quite prosaic, but no less politically efficacious because of that. After the descent from the Jinggang Mountains, Mao enumerated eight such rules to be added to the code of the Red Army soldier:

> 1. Replace all doors [used to fashion a bed] when you leave a house; 2. Return and roll up the straw matting on which you sleep; 3. Be courteous and polite to the people and help them when you can; 4. Return all borrowed articles; 5. Replace all damaged articles; 6. Be honest in all transactions with the peasants; 7. Pay for all articles purchased; 8. Be sanitary, and especially establish latrines a safe distance from people's houses.[29]

These rules of behavior, which by all accounts were in fact largely observed during the revolutionary years, distinguished the Red Army from the predatory practices for which most Chinese armies of the time were notorious. For the peasants, who bore the brunt of the depredations of rampaging military forces, the Red Army stood in striking contrast to other armies and served to greatly reinforce the appeals of Communist land redistribution policies. Respect for the peasant population, demonstrated by what Mao called "simple rules of discipline," contributed greatly to the remarkable expansion of the Red Army in late 1929, now able to draw recruits from a populous rural society.

Yet peasant support for the Red Army presupposed the military viability of that army, an army constantly confronted with the overwhelming numerical and technological superiority of Nationalist and warlord forces. The survival of the Red Army owed a great deal to the innovative tactics that Mao Zedong began to employ in the Jinggang Mountains and which were developed more fully in southern Jiangxi. Maoist military doctrine is typically described as a form of guerrilla warfare. Indeed, Mao himself declared that "ours are guerrilla tactics," and these tactics included the classical four-line slogan adapted from ancient Chinese military strategy and recited by Communist troops defending the Jinggangshan base: "The enemy advances, we retreat; the enemy camps, we harass; the enemy tires, we attack; the enemy retreats, we pursue."[30]

But Mao's conception of guerrilla warfare, particularly as it evolved in southern Jiangxi around 1930, was quite different from what is commonly understood by that term. He ignored a directive of the CCP Central Committee ordering the Red Army, in the interests of self-preservation, to be broken down into small and more or less autonomous guerrilla bands. "The Central Committee," Mao replied in April 1929, "asks us to divide our forces into very small units and disperse them over the countryside." However, Mao objected: "we have tried this [guerrilla tactics] many times, but have failed every time." The failures, in turn, were attributed to the "weak leadership and organization" that inevitably results from the division into small units and the danger that such units will be "crushed by the enemy one by one." Rather than dividing the Red Army into guerrilla bands to compensate for its numerical and technological inferiority, Mao drew the opposite conclusion: "The more adverse the circumstances, the greater the need for concentration . . . because only thus can we have internal unity to resist the enemy."[31]

Rather than guerrilla warfare in the conventional sense, Mao advocated what he called "protracted warfare." Instead of what he disparaged as "roving guerrilla actions," Mao favored "luring the enemy deep" into Communist-controlled areas and "concentrating our forces to destroy the enemy one by one."[32] Such tactics presupposed that the Red Army would have great flexibility and mobility (usually identified with guerrilla-type warfare); it was also understood, however, that in any given battle Red Army forces would ideally be relatively concentrated while enemy forces would be dispersed.

It is remarkable that the Red Army, between October 1927 and January 1929, did not degenerate into "the roving bandit gangs" that Communist officials in Moscow and Shanghai sometimes suggested they were becoming. Yet even in the most perilous times, Mao was successful in enforcing "civilian" control of military power, that is, in ensuring the subordination of the Red Army to the authority of the Communist Party. In a situation marked by almost constant warfare in what often seemed a totally hopeless enterprise, the distinction between Party and Army, between civilian and military authority, was rather murky. Mao, the political leader, was also deeply immersed in the details of military operations, and the lines between Party and Army were blurred. Nonetheless, Mao insisted on maintaining the distinction between the two, and on the whole was successful in keeping the Red Army, formally commanded by Zhu De, obedient to the civilian authority of the Party. It was an arrangement to be canonized by the Maoist maxim: "The Party commands the gun, the gun shall never be allowed to command the Party."

Finally, a crucial principle of Mao's strategy of "protracted war," only incompletely implemented on the Jinggangshan, was the establishment of strategically defensible and economically self-sufficient base areas. Self-sufficiency presupposed a substantial settled rural population from which recruits to the Red Army could be drawn and an economy adequate to support both the population and the needs of the Red Army. Such bases, Mao advised, were to be established in the more remote regions bordering several provinces, where central state control was relatively weak and where the Communists could best exploit divisions among their enemies.

The Jiangxi Soviet

Once established on the populous southern Jiangxi plains, the Red Army grew rapidly, attracting peasant recruits and deserters from warlord and local military forces. By 1930 Mao was sufficiently confident to proclaim a provisional Soviet government, consolidating a dozen smaller Communist-controlled areas with his own base area.

But Mao was still formally under the authority of the CCP Central Committee in Shanghai. This mattered rather little during the precarious days in the Jinggang Mountains, when communications with Shanghai were slow and erratic, and when Mao's struggle on the remote mountain seemed a hopeless adventure, attracting little notice among members of the Central Committee. But after the descent to the Jiangxi countryside and the expansion of Mao's forces, the CCP Central Committee and its new Comintern-installed leader, Li Lisan, were determined to assert their authority over the rapidly growing Maoist movement.

Li Lisan and Mao had known each other since their youth as activists in the May Fourth movement. Li had become firmly wedded to the Marxist faith in the urban proletariat as the true revolutionary class. "All the talk of 'encircling the city with the country[side]' or on relying on the Red Army to take the cities is sheer nonsense," he impatiently declared.[33] The success of the Chinese Revolution depended on reactivating the proletariat. Thus he ordered the Red Army centered in rural Jiangxi to attack cities with the aim of stimulating working-class uprisings.

The Red Army attacks, launched in the summer of 1930 against far larger GMD armies, proved disastrous. Troops commanded by Mao and Zhu De reluctantly participated in two of these adventures, an abortive drive to capture the provincial capital of Nanchang and an attack on Changsha. "There was no workers' uprising," Mao reported to the Central Committee to explain why he abruptly called off the attempt to seize Changsha after 12 days of fighting on the outskirts of the city.[34] Mao later learned that in the wake of the attack a GMD commander discovered that Mao's wife, Yang Kaihui, was still living in Changsha. She was arrested, interrogated, and, when she refused to denounce Mao, summarily executed. Their three children were rescued by friends and sent to live in Shanghai.

To some extent, Mao shared Li Lisan's revolutionary zealousness, if not necessarily his faith in the proletariat. In the spring of 1929 Mao foresaw a "revolutionary high tide" which would enable the Red Army to conquer all of Jiangxi province.[35] He was not opposed in principle to using peasant armies to seize cities, if militarily feasible. But his aim was to expand the power and resources of Communist base areas, not primarily to activate the proletariat. For Mao, the poor peasantry remained the true revolutionary class in China, as he had come to believe in 1926, and this faith was reinforced when urban workers, still demoralized by the defeats of 1927, remained politically quiescent when the Red Army launched attacks on cities in 1930.

The Red Army suffered heavy losses in attempting to carry out Li Lisan's instructions to seize major cities in the summer of 1930. Hardly had they recovered from the adventures at Nanchang and Changsha, than the Communists fell into an orgy of self-destruction in the murderous train of events surrounding "the Futian incident" of December 1930.

Futian

The rapid growth of the Red Army in Jiangxi province in 1929 was greatly facilitated by the incorporation of local Jiangxi Communist Party organizations and guerrilla forces. It was not an entirely harmonious union, however. The Jiangxi Communists had been operating independently since the break-up of the GMD-CCP alliance in 1927 and had gained considerable political and social influence, as well as a significant military presence, in the southwestern areas of the province by the time that Mao's beleaguered army found refuge there. It was Mao's attempt, in 1930, to place the indigenous Jiangxi Communist movement under the firm control of his own expanding political-military base in Jiangxi that led to the most bloody internal conflict in the history of the CCP.

Issues of both power and policy were involved in the events that issued from the Futian incident. The dispute between Mao and the Jiangxi Communist leaders stemmed, in large measure, from provincial and regional differences in what was not yet a unified national revolutionary movement. The soldiers of the main Mao–Zhu Red Army were mostly Hunanese. They were looked upon as outsiders by the local Jiangxi Communists, as soldiers of a "guest army" that soon would be moving on. But behind these elemental provincial antagonisms lay important differences in social interests and political orientations. Most of the Jiangxi Communist leaders were the sons of gentry-landlord or rich peasant families. This itself did not distinguish them from the leaders of the Maoist movement, many of whom also came from relatively prosperous families. Mao himself, of course, was the son of a rich peasant, by virtue of which he had been among the less than 1 percent of young Chinese of his generation to be afforded a university education. But Mao, and most other surviving Maoist leaders, had long cut themselves off from their families and localities. The Jiangxi Communists, by contrast, lived and worked in or near their home districts and retained deep social and political ties to local communities. These differing relationships to society in southern Jiangxi manifested themselves in controversies over two crucial issues. One was land reform. Mao was now (at least temporarily) advocating a radical land redistribution policy based on the number of family members that would have adversely affected the interests of "rich peasants." On the other hand, the Jiangxi leaders, more sensitive to local interests, favored a less egalitarian policy of land redistribution based on a family's labor power. A second controversy revolved around the military tactics to be employed to defend the Communist base in Jiangxi against the anticipated attack by Chiang Kai-shek's Nationalist Army. While Mao insisted on employing the tactic of "luring the enemy deep," which had enabled the Red Army to survive in the Jinggang Mountains against far superior enemy forces, the Jiangxi Communist leaders feared that the immediate result of doing so would be heavy loss of life and property in their home districts, even if the tactic proved to be militarily efficacious in the long run.

These disputes within the Communist base area in Jiangxi were reflected in differing attitudes toward the national Party leadership located in Shanghai, where the Central Committee was now headed by Li Lisan. Mao was bitterly hostile to Li and the "Li Lisan line" of using the Red Army to attack cities in the hope of stimulating working-class uprisings. The Jiangxi Communist leaders, on the other hand, generally supported Li Lisan, partly because his agrarian policies conformed with their own preferences, and partly because his military strategy of attacking cities precluded Mao's mobile tactics and implied instead a conventional defense of the Jiangxi base area. It also had the virtue of moving Mao's Red Army out of the base area, at least temporarily, thereby increasing the influence of the local Jiangxi Communist leaders.[36]

These issues, and the political struggles they generated, led to a deepening antagonism between Mao and the Jiangxi Communist leaders. While Mao had tenuously incorporated local Communist military forces into the Red Army, Jiangxi CCP groups had retained a *de facto* independence and remained in hostile opposition to the Maoists. In February 1930 Mao widened the rift, charging that "the local leading organs of the Party at all levels are filled with landlords and rich peasants, and the Party's policy is completely opportunistic."[37] The struggle between Mao and the Jiangxi Communists was complicated, and the hostility between them was exacerbated in the spring, when rumors spread through the Communist-controlled areas that the Red Army and CCP had been infiltrated by a secret GMD counter-revolutionary organization known as the "AB-tuan," whose name is usually taken to mean "Anti-Bolshevik League."

The AB-tuan was a right-wing faction within the Guomindang organized under the aegis of Chiang Kai-shek during the 1925–7 revolutionary upsurge. Its original purpose was to limit Communist influence in the GMD-CCP alliance through clandestine means. The league was particularly strong in southern Jiangxi, where after the GMD-CCP split in 1927 its principal task was to root out Communist influence in local GMD organizations. While the existence of a secret AB-tuan in Jiangxi is no longer in doubt,[38] it is most unlikely that it could have exercised the pervasive powers that both Mao and the Jiangxi Communists attributed to it. Nevertheless, Communist fears that their ranks had been infiltrated by AB-tuan agents grew in the late spring and summer of 1930, reaching frenzied heights toward the end of the year as Nationalist armies surrounded the Communist base area, preparing to launch an "encirclement and annihilation" campaign.

Mao Zedong was apparently not directly involved in the initial large-scale purges of real or alleged AB-tuan agents in the CCP and the Red Army. He and Zhu De had reluctantly obeyed the order of Li Lisan and the Central Committee to lead the Red Army to launch attacks on major cities. An abortive move toward the city of Nanchang at the end of July was followed by the failed attack on Changsha in Hunan province in late August and early September. While Mao and the main units of the Red Army were away from the base area, engaged in futile efforts to implement "the Li Lisan line," local Communist leaders took control of the southern Jiangxi Party organization, repealed Mao's radical land reform policies, announced their support for Li Lisan and his policies, and inaugurated a widespread purge of AB-tuan suspects, replete with summary executions. When Mao returned to Jiangxi in October, he regained command of the local Party organization and ordered an even broader purge of AB-tuan suspects. Some 4,400 officers and soldiers of the Red Army were arrested, many of them Jiangxi natives, and half of them were summarily executed, often on the basis of confessions and accusations obtained through torture. Soldiers in the 20th Red Army, a force made up of mostly Jiangxi men who had been left behind to defend the Communist base while the main units of the Red Army were engaged in the hopeless adventure of attacking Nanchang and Changsha, mutinied when the purge reached them in early December. The rebellious soldiers attacked the old imperial *yamen* (local administrative office) in the small market town of Futian, where some of the victims of the purge had been imprisoned. The rebels killed 100 Red Army soldiers guarding the *yamen*, freed some 20 prisoners, issued a manifesto denouncing Mao Zedong as a "Party emperor" and appealed to Zhu De and Peng Dehuai to join them in opposition to Mao. Zhu and Peng quickly reaffirmed their loyalty to Mao and condemned the rebels. But "the Futian incident," coinciding as it did with the Nationalist Army's assault on the Communist base area, set the stage for even wider and more bloody purges.

The Communist attacks on urban centers in 1930, although they failed, had alarmed the Guomindang. Chiang Kai-shek, vowing to eliminate the "Communist bandits" once and for all, sent 100,000 soldiers against the Jiangxi base area in an "encirclement and extermination" campaign. Mao Zedong and Zhu De, with less than half that number under their command, employed the now well-tested tactic of "luring the enemy deep," turning back the Nationalist armies in January 1931.

As Mao Zedong was successfully defending the Jiangxi base against Chiang Kai-shek's first "extermination" campaign, he seemed to agree with most Communist leaders that the purge of suspected counter-revolutionaries had been excessive. Arrests and executions of AB-tuan suspects in the Party and Red Army continued during the early months of 1931, but at a less frenetic pace. The purge seemed to be winding down. Then in April, as 200,000 GMD troops were encircling the Communist base in preparation for a second "extermination" campaign, the purge was resumed with renewed fury. The impetus now came from the new Party Central Committee in Shanghai, consisting of young Chinese Communists who had been trained at Sun Yat-sen University in Moscow to do Stalin's bidding in China. Known as the "returned student faction" (or, more colorfully, as the "28 Bolsheviks"), they were still mostly in their early or mid-twenties when they were dispatched to Shanghai to take over the CCP Central Committee. Their leader, Wang Ming (Chen Shaoyu), became the CCP's new General Secretary, replacing the now disgraced Li Lisan, who was exiled to Moscow for "study."

The political and policy differences between Wang Ming and Li Lisan were negligible, save that Wang was even more slavish in his obedience to

Stalin than Li had been. It is unlikely that Mao Zedong was impressed by this, but he did have reasons to temporarily ally himself with Wang Ming in renewing the purge of alleged AB-tuan elements. For it was in the political interests of both to purge the Party organization of Li Lisan's supporters, which included the local Jiangxi Communists with whom Mao had openly clashed since February 1930. It was now the tendency, among Maoists and the new Central Committee alike, to conflate the AB-tuan with "Li Lisanism." As a result, a great variety of both Mao's and Wang Ming's political opponents within the CCP could now be branded enemy agents, and treated accordingly.

Thus the purge that resumed in April 1931 – just as the Nationalist Army, 200,000 strong, launched Chiang Kai-shek's second "extermination" campaign against the Communist base in Jiangxi – was more widespread and indiscriminate than ever, consuming many thousands of loyal Communists on vague suspicions that they were AB-tuan infiltrators or other counter-revolutionaries. Mao Zedong certainly participated in the purges, probably directing his energies to bring about the demise of supporters of Li Lisan, which included most of the original Jiangxi Communist leaders who had founded the base area. But the witch-hunt was not simply a Maoist affair. As the leading historian of the origins and aftermath of the Futian incident has observed:

> The question of specifically who presided over the fierce wave of "counter-revolutionary suppression" that spread through the soviet areas during the latter half of 1931 is rendered considerably less important, however, by the fact that the purges soon became so widespread, decentralized, and paranoid that for a time they were largely beyond the control of any of the top leaders.[39]

The ferocity of the purges began to abate in the fall of 1931, after Mao led the Red Army in successfully resisting the third "annihilation and extermination" campaign, which Chiang Kai-shek had launched in July, throwing 300,000 soldiers against the Communist base. The defeat of the Nationalist forces, along with the Japanese invasion of Manchuria in September 1931, was to provide the Communists with respite from major GMD attacks until the spring of 1933.

The terrible purges of real or alleged counter-revolutionaries in 1930–1 were in large measure the result of a collective hysteria that enveloped the Communist base area when it was surrounded by the Nationalist Army during Chiang Kai-shek's first three "extermination" campaigns. Few participants in the tiny revolutionary movement in Jiangxi believed that they would survive the imminent onslaughts of enemy armies, far superior both in numbers and military technology. They were well aware of the waves of the counter-revolutionary White Terror, which had swept over the land unimpeded since 1927 and had already taken millions of lives in a pitiless civil war. A pervasive fear of death provided fertile ground for the spread of rumors in the CCP and the Red Army that their ranks were filled with spies and traitors – and the besieged Communists struck out against each other in a frenzied witch-hunt against suspected enemy agents. It was to reinforce a Stalinist tendency in the CCP to attribute internal dissent to "counter-revolutionary elements" who had infiltrated the Party from without.

Mao Zedong and others certainly used the fears and confusion that enveloped the Jiangxi base in 1930 and 1931 to purge their political opponents in the CCP and pursue their own political ambitions, which they no doubt believed to be in the best interests of the revolution. It has long been known that it was during these years that Mao greatly expanded his influence in the Chinese Communist movement.[40] But while Mao no doubt aimed to win control of the CCP, he was notably unsuccessful in the attempt. Hardly had the purge of "counter-revolutionaries" begun to wane, when Mao's power in the Communist base in Jiangxi began to be undermined. In the summer and autumn of 1931 the Party Central Committee, under increasing police pressure in Shanghai, moved its headquarters to Jiangxi, or more precisely to the small southern Jiangxi market town of Ruichin near the border with Fujian province, which had been made the capital of the newly proclaimed Chinese Soviet Republic. Mao Zedong was the Chairman of the Republic, which was soon to claim a population of about 5,000,000. But Mao's authority was quickly eroded by the "returned student faction," whose members dominated the Central Committee. The young Moscow-trained Chinese Communists were hostile to Mao personally and opposed both to his military and agrarian policies. Mao remained Chairman of the Soviet Republic, but it soon became a mostly titular position. He was duly consulted over economic and military matters, but he no longer had any real power in either the Party or the Red Army.

Yet Mao retained the personal loyalty of many Communists, especially officers and soldiers of the Red Army. This had less to do with the purges that preceded and followed the Futian incident than with the tactical brilliance he demonstrated in leading the Red Army to fend off Chiang Kai-shek's first three "encirclement and extermination" campaigns. Mao's support among Communists was also enhanced by his reputation as the Party's foremost expert on rural affairs. Since 1925, when he discovered the peasantry as the true revolutionary class, he had immersed himself in painstaking investigations of rural social and economic life. It was this passion that resulted in his appointment as principal of the Guomindang's Peasant Movement Training Institute during the revolutionary upsurge of 1926 and which produced the document that announced the birth of Maoism, the "Report on the Peasant Movement in Hunan." Thereafter, wherever his revolutionary activities took him, even during the perilous days in the Jinggang Mountains, he seized every opportunity to carry out first-hand investigations of the conditions under which rural people lived. One of the most impressive of these many accounts was a remarkably detailed study (several hundred pages in length) of the socio-economic conditions of the inhabitants of Xunwu county in southern Jiangxi province and Xunwu City, its administrative center. The investigation was conducted with the assistance of 11 local informants during a ten-day period in May 1930 when Mao's Fourth Army was camped in the area, several months before the ill-fated attacks on Nanchang and Changsha. Mao's report meticulously recorded virtually every aspect of the social and economic life of the county, from the number of butchers and barbers to the origins and prices of hundreds of commodities. He discussed in great detail the intricacies of mortgages in the area, the multitude of taxes, the degree of literacy, and the status of women, among dozens of other topics. And he paid special attention to rural social divisions, enumerating ten distinct social groups ranging from large landlords to hired hands and vagrants.[41]

Mao of course used the data in the Xunwu report and other rural investigations to support his agrarian policies against those of his Party opponents. But for the most part the Xunwu report reads more like a sociological study than a political treatise. Mao encouraged others to engage in similar social investigations. Immediately following the writing of the Xunwu report he set forth the soon to be ubiquitous maxim: "Without investigation there is no right to speak."[42]

The fall of the Jiangxi Soviet

By the time Chiang Kai-shek launched the fourth extermination campaign in the late summer of 1932, Mao Zedong's authority in the Chinese Soviet Republic had been largely undermined by the "returned student faction," whose members had now fully reestablished themselves (and the Party Central Committee) in Jiangxi. Accused of "rightist deviations" and a "peasant consciousness," among other heresies common during the

Stalin era, Mao found his power in the base area was whittled away, and his functions in such official positions as he still held were largely reduced to ceremonial duties. The Party apparatus was controlled by the youthful Moscow-trained zealots. While Zhu De remained commander of the Red Army, Zhou Enlai had replaced Mao as the army's political commissar. But Zhu and Zhou largely retained the mobile tactics that Mao favored, and the Red Army once again decisively defeated the Nationalists in a long and drawn-out campaign.

This was not to be the outcome of the fifth campaign, which began in October 1933. Chiang Kai-shek mobilized nearly a million troops, out-numbering the Red Army by more than ten to one, and further maxi-mized the Nationalist advantage by employing mechanized artillery and an air force of 400 bombers and fighter planes. Chiang also hired two German generals who devised a new blockhouse strategy to crush the Communists. In early 1934 Chiang methodically tightened the ring of 14,000 blockhouses that surrounded the ever shrinking Chinese Soviet Republic. Prospects for the survival of the Jiangxi base were not enhanced by the abandonment of Mao's tactics of mobile warfare in favor of a more conventional defense. The strategy of the Red Army was now dictated by the Comintern advisor Otto Braun, a German Communist who had been trained at a military academy in Moscow and was known in China by the pseudonym Li De. It was a strategy based on conventional methods of positional warfare – and it inevitably failed to halt the Nationalist advance. Yet it is unlikely that Mao's mobile tactics would have been successful in the end, for the numerical and technological superiority of Chiang Kai-shek's army was now overwhelming.

Mao Zedong was later bitterly critical of Braun's tactics – although without claiming that his own would have saved the Chinese Soviet Republic. "It was a serious mistake," he later charged, "to meet the vastly superior Nanking forces in positional warfare, at which the Red Army was neither technically nor spiritually at its best." [43]

During the summer of 1934 the dwindling Communist base in Jiangxi began to crumble before the relentless Guomindang offensive. Plans were made to escape the Nationalist encirclement. In mid-October, the bulk of what remained of the Red Army – about 60,000 soldiers, along with 30,000 Party functionaries and bearers – managed to slip through Nationalist lines to embark on an extraordinary year-long journey whose route and destination had yet to be decided. Few of the approximately 90,000 who joined the migration were to survive. Mao Zedong was among those who fled, but the original plans for what came to be celebrated as the Long

March were made by Otto Braun, Bo Ku (the leader of the "returned student faction"), and Zhou Enlai. It was during the Long March, however, that Mao was to gain a measure of mastery over a much-shrunken CCP. And the legend of the Long March was to become intimately involved with the making of the legend of Mao Zedong.

4

Nationalism and Social Revolution, 1935–49

The Long March

When plans for the exodus from Jiangxi were being made in the summer of 1934, Mao Zedong had been stripped of all real power in the CCP by the Russian-supported "returned students," even though he retained the now empty title of Chairman of the Chinese Soviet Republic. His views ignored by most Party leaders, Mao retreated to a Daoist temple in the country-side, where he lived quietly with his second wife Ho Zizhen and their two-year-old son. Isolating himself from the top leaders of the Jiangxi Soviet, save for Zhou Enlai, he confined himself to local social and politi-cal affairs. Mao joined the flight, linking up with the long procession of retreating Red Army soldiers on October 18, 1934. He had little choice. He would have been executed by the Guomindang had he remained in Jiangxi. Ho Zizhen also joined the exodus, one of the 20 or so women who embarked on the retreat, mostly wives of Party leaders who served as nurses. The two-year-old child perforce was left behind in the care of friends.

The disasters that befell the fleeing Communist army early on the Long March soon thrust Mao back into the center of Party politics. Over-whelmed by the difficulties of managing a military force constantly on the march in the rural hinterlands, the authority of the urban-oriented leaders over the Red Army began to wane, and was further undermined by their military inexperience. A fierce five-day battle with a large GMD force dispatched to block their crossing of the Xiang River resulted in the loss of nearly half the Red Army barely a month after their departure from Jiangxi. Now many Red Army officers and political cadres once again began to look to Mao Zedong. He was remembered as a military genius, the builder of the Red Army facing seemingly impossible condi-tions on the Jinggangshan, and an innovative tactician who successfully resisted Chiang Kai-shek's first three "encirclement and annihilation" campaigns.

In the renewed battle with the Moscow-installed Chinese Communists, the political terrain of the Long March favored Mao. In a Communist movement now more than ever confined to remote parts of the country-side, Mao had great advantages over the young urban-oriented leaders favored by Stalin. Physically, emotionally, and politically, he had immersed himself in rural life for a decade. The political experience of the "returned students," by contrast, had been molded in Moscow and Shanghai. They were ill-prepared for life – and for political life – in a backward rural environment, much less with a fleeing military force pursued by far larger armies.

When the Long March halted at the town of Zunyi in impoverished Guizhou province in early January 1935, a rump session of the CCP Polit-buro (attended by six of its 12 members) put Mao in effective control of what remained of the Red Army. Although the internal Party struggle was to continue until the early 1940s, the 41-year-old Mao was now the dominant leader in the Party and sufficiently in control of the army to pursue his own policies and the tactics of mobile warfare he favored. The grip of the Comintern finally had been loosened and Mao had gained a degree of supremacy in the Chinese party in defiance of Stalin. It was an event unprecedented in the history of Communist parties in the Stalinist era.

In early 1935, however, Mao's triumph was more about sheer physical survival than political power. The Red Army had been reduced to a demoralized force of 30,000, barely a third of the number that had fled Jiangxi three months before. And the most difficult part of the journey lay ahead – across the raging rivers, forbidding mountains, and dangerous marshes of western China. It was the only route to the sanctuary that the Communists now decided to seek in the barren northwest province of Shaanxi, where a small Communist base had survived since the early 1930s.

It was to take another nine months for the Red Army to reach Shaanxi, and that was to prove the most perilous portion of the incredible year-long journey. In Mao's account, the Red Army traveled

> across the longest and deepest and most dangerous rivers of China, across some of its highest and most hazardous mountain passes, through the country of fierce aborigines, through the empty grasslands, through cold and through intense heat, through wind and snow and rainstorm, pursued by half the White armies of China, and fighting its way past the local [warlord] troops. . . . at last [we] reached northern Shensi in October, 1935.[1]

By any standard of historical and human judgment, the Long March stands as one of the most remarkable sagas of human courage and endurance in world history. It was, as Edgar Snow wrote in 1937, "an Odyssey unequaled in modern times."[2]

Few of those who embarked on that torturous 6,000-mile journey in October 1934 survived the ordeal. Only 8,000 half-starved soldiers remained when Mao led the main force of the Red Army into northern Shaanxi in the fall of 1935, finally finding sanctuary just south of the ancient Great Wall. Of the approximately 86,000 men (and 20 women) who marched out of Jiangxi in 1934, most were now dead – victims of the many battles fought along the way, of the persistent GMD aerial bombardments, the relentless outbreaks of illness, and the perils of an unremittingly harsh landscape of craggy mountains, icy gorges, raging rivers, and lethal swamplands. Among the dead left along the circuitous route to Shaanxi were many of Mao Zedong's closest friends and comrades, and one of his two younger brothers, Mao Zetan, killed in one of the many battles. And the child who was left behind in care of a sympathetic peasant family in Jiangxi was never to be found.

The awareness among the survivors of the Long March – that they lived while so many others died – lent a sacred character to their revolutionary mission and inspired an extraordinary sense of dedication to complete it. While there is little to suggest that Mao Zedong was tormented by the guilt that survivors often bear, he did feel the need to vindicate the sacrifices that so many had made by rededicating himself to the revolutionary cause. He was certainly acutely aware of his own defiance of death while so many of those around him were killed. In an interview with Edgar Snow in 1965, Mao, recounting the losses of close comrades and family members, noted some of the many times he had barely eluded what seemed certain death. He found it "odd" that he had survived and remarked that "death just did not seem to want him."[3]

The consciousness of having defied death undoubtedly contributed to Mao's growing sense of infallibility, and his perception that he was a leader destined to lead his followers to the completion of their revolutionary mission. The fact of survival became a matter of enormous psychological significance for Mao, and indeed for all "the veterans of the Long March." It was also a matter of enormous political consequence. Survival against such heavy odds was taken as testimony not only to the validity of the Revolution but also to the wisdom of its leader and his policies. Indeed, the cult of Mao was born out of the harsh and extraordinary experiences of the Long March, for Mao now began to be surrounded by a certain mystique and looked upon as a prophet and savior.

In celebrating the personal heroism of the veterans of the Long March, later Chinese Communist accounts hail it as a great victory, heralding the triumph of 1949. Victory did not seem so likely at the time, however. Mao Zedong later candidly acknowledged the gravity of the defeat:

> all the revolutionary bases except the Shaanxi-Gansu Border Area were lost, the Red Army was reduced from 300,000 to a few tens of thousands, the membership of the Chinese Communist Party fell from 300,000 to a few tens of thousands, and the Party organizations in the Guomindang areas were almost all destroyed. In short, we paid a severe penalty, of historic proportions.[4]

The military weakness of the Communists in the fall of 1935 was exacerbated by the barrenness of the remote territory where they were now confined. Northern Shaanxi was one of the most backward areas of China, its infertile land capable of supporting only a small and impoverished population. Nonetheless, however unfavorable the circumstances, the tiny Communist base in northern Shaanxi survived. The Red Army fought off attacking GMD and warlord armies and gradually expanded the sparsely populated areas under its control. At the beginning of 1937 the Communists were sufficiently secure to move their capital 50 miles southeast, to the obscure town of Yan'an, recently evacuated by Nationalist troops. An ancient city, founded some 3,000 years ago, Yan'an declined over the centuries as Chinese civilization moved south. It was a poor, dusty, and remote frontier town of about 10,000 inhabitants when the Communists made it their capital in January 1937. At the time, the Red Army numbered about 50,000 soldiers and the Communists governed a poverty-stricken area in the northwest which supported an almost entirely rural population of barely 1,000,000 people.

Yet, from these unpromising circumstances the Communist movement grew with extraordinary rapidity over what later came to be celebrated as the "Yan'an decade." During that most crucial period, the CCP, now marching under an unambiguous Maoist banner, mobilized the support of tens of millions of peasants in the countryside of north China as well as substantial popular support in the cities. By 1945 the Red Army had grown to a regular military force of over a million dedicated soldiers, supported by armed peasant militias of part-time fighters and part-time farmers numbering several million. The CCP could claim an active membership of 1,200,000. Such was the organizational basis for the Communist victories in the massive battles that marked the final stage of the civil war, fought between 1946 and 1948. In January 1949, exactly 12 years after the Communists moved their headquarters to Yan'an, Mao Zedong stood atop the Gate of Heavenly Peace in Beijing to proclaim the founding of the People's Republic of China.

How did a tiny and ill-equipped army isolated in the barren and sparsely populated loess lands of northern Shaanxi, an army and political movement chronically on the verge of extinction, mobilize such enormous popular support? How, in little more than a decade, did Maoists come to power in the world's most populous land and carry out the most thoroughgoing social revolution in modern history?

Maoism and nationalism

War and revolution are intimately associated in modern history, and nowhere did this relationship find clearer and more dramatic expression than in China. For it is difficult to imagine how the Maoist victory of 1949 could have come about had it not been for the Japanese invasion of 1937, its impact on Chinese society and politics, and especially the ability of the Communists to capture the banner of Chinese national resistance to foreign aggression.

A modernizing and militaristic Japan had threatened China for nearly half a century before the full-scale invasion of 1937, beginning with the aggressive War of 1894–5 and the colonization of Taiwan, seized by the Japanese as war booty. Japan emerged as the most aggressive of the imperialist powers threatening China in 1915 when it presented the infamous "21 Demands," which sought to make the whole of China a Japanese colony. The actual colonization of the Chinese mainland began in 1931 when the Japanese army took over Manchuria, establishing the puppet state of "Manchukuo." The Japanese imperial army followed with increasingly provocative incursions into north China, culminating with the full-scale invasion launched in the summer of 1937.

Between 1932 and 1937 the GMD undermined its nationalist credentials by its reluctance to confront the growing Japanese threat. It was necessary to defeat the Communists and achieve national unity before facing the Japanese, Chiang Kai-shek explained. Thus, the GMD followed a policy of appeasement, retreating before the relentless Japanese advance while devoting the greater part of its considerable military power to various "extermination and annihilation" campaigns against the Communists. It was an unpopular policy which cost the Nationalist Party much of its nationalist legitimacy.

In the meantime, the Communists were fortifying their nationalist credentials, appealing for a united front of all patriotic Chinese to protect the nation from Japanese aggression. In 1932, as Chairman of the Chinese Soviet Republic in Jiangxi, Mao issued a declaration of war against Japan, a purely symbolic gesture at a time when the Red Army was weak and isolated in a province some 2,000 miles distant from the Japanese army in Manchuria. But once the Communists had established a secure base in northern Shaanxi, Mao Zedong's calls for national unity to resist Japan became far more credible and politically effective. The Yan'an base area was within several hundred miles of Japanese troops gradually moving south from Manchuria and Mongolia. On the eve of the full-scale Japanese assault, the Communists were geographically well placed to organize a movement of national resistance.

Hardly two months after the conclusion of the Long March, at a Politburo meeting in late December 1935, Mao Zedong called for a "national united front" of all the Chinese people to oppose Japanese imperialism. But excluded from the national alliance were large landlords, big warlords, high bureaucrats, and compradores – and their "political chieftain Chiang Kai-shek." These groups constituted no more than "a camp of traitors," and therefore were not to be counted as part of "the people."[5]

In proposing a broad united front, Mao placed special emphasis on the progressive political potential of the "national bourgeoisie." Implicit in this term was an economic distinction between a "compradore" sector of the bourgeoisie, economically dependent on foreign imperialism, and a "national" bourgeoisie, whose economic interests were domestically oriented and were thus opposed to imperialism. Yet what seemed a socioeconomic distinction really was one based on subjective political attitudes and behavior. The "national bourgeoisie" was defined by Mao not according to objective economic and social criteria but almost solely on the basis of its political willingness to join a Communist-led united front to oppose Japanese imperialism. This stood in striking contrast to the elaborate class distinctions, based on careful consideration of concrete socio-economic factors, that distinguished Mao's detailed social investigations. And it marked the appearance of a Maoist tendency to define class more on the basis of political attitudes than according to objective Marxian economic and social criteria.

To encourage the national bourgeoisie to participate in a popular national front against the Japanese, Mao vowed:

> During the period of bourgeois-democratic revolution, [we] will not
> expropriate private property other than imperialist and feudal private
> property, and far from confiscating the national bourgeoisie's industrial
> and commercial enterprises [we] will rather encourage their develop-
> ment. We shall protect any national capitalist who does not support impe-
> rialism or the Chinese traitors. During the stage of democratic revolution
> there are limits to the struggle between labor and capital. The labor laws
> of the people's republic will protect the interest of the workers but will
> not oppose the national bourgeoisie's making profits or developing
> national industrial and commercial enterprises . . .[6]

It might appear that Mao's discovery of the "national bourgeoisie" at the
end of 1935, and his encouragement of private industrial and commercial
enterprise, reflected a Marxist belief in the progressiveness of capitalism.
There is little reason to believe that this was the case. Since 1925 Mao had
ignored the cities and the modern social classes who inhabited them,
looking instead to the backward countryside and the pre-capitalist peasantry for the sources of revolution and progress. His interest in the bourgeoisie in the mid-1930s derived not from any new-found Marxian faith in
the progressiveness of capitalism but rather from a non-Marxian nationalism. The overriding need was to repel the Japanese invaders, a need that
brought forth Mao's populist concept of the Chinese people as a more or
less organic entity whose common interests submerged all social class
differences. Thus, all of the Chinese people were potentially part of the
"revolutionary" united front. Mao's embrace of the bourgeoisie in 1935
was motivated more by nationalist than Marxist considerations.

In a land so deeply impinged upon by foreign powers for nearly a
century, it was inevitable that the appeals and content of Marxism would
be closely bound up with nationalism. The combination of Marxism and
nationalism may be an unholy alliance, but it was one inherent in the
origins of Chinese Communism. It was an alliance that the Japanese invasion greatly fortified.

While all Chinese Communists were perforce nationalists – in the
sense that they were above all concerned with the fate of China in a world
of rapacious nation-states – some strove to reconcile their nationalist feel-
ings with the internationalist principles of their new Marxist creed. The
most notable effort was made by the first leader of the CCP, Chen Duxiu,
with whom Mao Zedong had so contentious a relationship in the
mid-1920s.

Chen Duxiu was the leading intellectual in the anti-traditionalist and
Westernizing New Culture movement of 1915–9, and his conversion to

Marxism had greatly inspired Mao Zedong's adoption of the doctrine in 1920. While Chen's turn to Bolshevism had grown out of nationalist disillusionment with the West, he was drawn to the more cosmopolitan and modernistic features of Marxism, embracing the emphasis on cities as the centers of progress and the urban proletariat as the international agent of liberation. His revolutionary hopes centered on China's urban workers, who, however few in numbers, were members of a social class formed in the cosmopolitan image of the advanced countries of the West.

By contrast, Mao Zedong, after a brief and frustrating effort to build a working-class movement in agrarian Hunan, came to look to the country-side for the sources of revolution and to the peasantry as the essence of the Chinese nation. After having discovered the revolutionary potential of the peasants in early 1925, he devoted himself to the countryside and its inhabitants, largely ignoring the cities and the proletariat. The peasants not only made up the overwhelming majority of the Chinese people, Mao repeatedly emphasized, but they were the carriers of the best and most progressive aspects of China's national culture. He therefore lauded the peasantry's "fine ancient popular culture that is more or less democratic and revolutionary in character."[7]

Marxists traditionally looked upon peasants as carriers of a culturally and politically conservative nationalism. The peasantry, as Trotsky said, "by virtue of its entire history and the condition of its existence, is the least international of all classes. What are commonly called national traits have their chief source precisely in the peasantry."[8] It was a view shared by Chen Duxiu, who saw the peasantry as the repository of China's perni-cious cultural traditions, the source of its economic backwardness and social stagnation. But, what Marxist internationalists such as Trotsky and Chen saw as a fatal deficiency in the revolutionary potential of the peas-antry was for Mao a major virtue. His nationalism drew him not to the foreign-dominated cities but to the peasants in the countryside as the truly revolutionary class and the embodiment of the nation. And this per-ception was to facilitate his mobilization of the peasantry on the basis of a program of national resistance to foreign invaders, defying orthodox Marxist views both on the political role of peasants and the place of nationalism in the making of modern revolutions.

There is little to suggest that Mao was troubled by the contradiction between Marxism and nationalism, or that he was even aware of the incongruity. As it was, the increasingly ominous Japanese threat fused Chinese nationalism with Communist political interests: "We cannot even discuss communism if we are robbed of a country in which to practice it," Mao observed in July 1936, in an interview with Edgar Snow.[9] The organization of a movement of nationalist resistance to the foreign invaders became a matter of political survival for both the Communists and the Nationalists. And effective resistance to the Japanese, it seemed to many, required cooperation between the two warring Chinese political parties.

Yet the differences between the Communists and the Guomindang seemed irreconcilable. The massacres that had accompanied Chiang Kai-shek's betrayal of the first united front in 1927 and the White Terror that followed were still fresh in the minds of the Communists. And a decade of civil war, with its various "extermination and annihilation" campaigns, had shed much more blood and exacerbated the particularly bitter hatreds that civil wars engender. Mao himself had lost many family members, friends, and colleagues during these years, as had most other Communists. Few were disposed to ally themselves with what they saw as a party of butchers and traitors. When Mao Zedong called for a "broad united front" against the Japanese invaders at the end of 1935, he proposed an alliance of social classes, not an alliance of political parties. The "national bourgeoisie" was now invited to join workers, peasants, students, and the petty bourgeoisie in a "national revolutionary united front" led by the Communist Party. Chiang Kai-shek was not invited to join the alliance; instead he was denounced as the "chieftain" of "a camp of traitors."

Yet powerful forces inexorably were bringing the two warring parties to some sort of an accommodation – however much they distrusted each other. The Japanese Army moving southward from Manchuria was becoming increasingly aggressive in north China, and it was clearly only a matter of time before it launched a full-scale invasion. As Mao Zedong warned at the end of 1935: "Now Japanese imperialism wants to convert the whole of China from a semicolony shared by several imperialist powers into a colony monopolized by Japan."[10] It was a fear shared by much of the Chinese population as well as by the leaders of the GMD.

For Mao and the Chinese Communists, pressure to once again ally themselves with the GMD came from Moscow as well as from the perils to the Chinese nation posed by the Japanese Army. From mid-1935 the Comintern demanded the establishment of "popular fronts" against German and Japanese fascism, both threats to the Soviet Union. The united fronts were to include such conservative nationalists as Chiang Kai-shek, for whom, in any event, Stalin had a certain admiration and with whom the Soviet Union had maintained relatively cordial diplomatic relations for a decade. While Mao hardly shared Stalin's benign view of Chiang, nationalist impulses as well as political self-interest encouraged him to seek an accommodation with the GMD against the foreign invaders. The forces favoring a new Communist/Nationalist alliance were reinforced by public opinion, articulated by students and intellectuals in the cities, demanding unity against the Japanese. By the summer of 1936 Maoist accusations that Chiang was a "traitor to the nation" largely ceased.

The spontaneous patriotic movement in the cities found dramatic expression in the very army that Chiang Kai-shek had stationed in Shaanxi to crush the Communists. The Northeast Army, originally a warlord force based in Manchuria, now led by the "young Marshall" Zhang Xueliang, had been incorporated into Chiang's Nationalist Army. Headquartered at the ancient capital of Xi'an in southern Shaanxi, its mission was to destroy the Communists now based in the northern part of that province.

But the troops of the Northeast Army, their Manchurian homeland under Japanese occupation since 1931, had little taste for fighting other Chinese. Mao wasted little time in appealing to the patriotic sentiments of the Manchurian troops, not refraining from such chauvinistic reminders that they, like the soldiers of the Red Army, were "descendants of the Yellow Emperor."[11] Mao's nationalist appeals fell on receptive ears. Negotiations between the Communists and envoys of Zhang Xueliang began in February 1936. Warfare between the Red Army and the Northeastern Army virtually ceased and fraternization between the two armies grew.

At the same time Mao, pressured by both Moscow and Zhang Xueliang, reluctantly began to seek to include Chiang Kai-shek in an anti-Japanese united front. Stalin, desperate to form anti-fascist united fronts to ward off a Japanese attack on the Soviet Union, insisted that only Chiang had sufficient prestige and power to make a Chinese united front effective. Stalin admired Chiang as a strong ruler, a powerful symbol of Chinese nationalism, and the Chinese politician most likely to effectively resist Japanese expansion. Zhang Xueliang had come to the same conclusion. Mao Zedong, isolated in barren loess lands of northern Shaanxi with an ill-equipped army that numbered barely 50,000 soldiers, had little choice but to seek an accommodation with his old foe, despite many misgivings.

But Chiang Kai-shek responded by launching fresh attacks against the Red Army, employing new forces in addition to such units of the Northeast Army that would obey his orders. Chiang also arrested "Third Force" intellectuals who advocated a united Chinese resistance to Japan. And he held, no less strongly than before, to the dogma that the Communists must be suppressed before effective resistance to Japan could be undertaken.

Chiang's continuing refusal to join with the Communists in a national resistance movement provoked popular outrage, especially among urban intellectuals and the Manchurian soldiers of the Northeast Army. These nationalist resentments found dramatic expression on December 12, 1936, when Zhang Xueliang, after considerable soul-searching, finally ordered the arrest of Chiang Kai-shek in Xi'an, where Chiang was visiting for the third time in three months, futilely attempting to organize a more vigorous "extermination" campaign against the Communists. The aim of the "young Marshall" was to hold Chiang prisoner until he agreed to call off the civil war and unite with all Chinese patriots, including the Communists, in a coalition government to lead the anti-Japanese resistance.

After two weeks in captivity, Chiang reluctantly agreed to unite with the Communists in a war of national resistance to Japanese aggression – although this oral agreement was by no means made explicit when Chiang was released on December 25, 1936. It was to take another eight months of negotiations, haggling, and political intrigues before an agreement on the precise terms of the second CCP-GMD united front was formally reached in September 1937 – two months after the Japanese attacked Chinese Nationalist troups on the Marco Polo Bridge near Beijing, an event that became the pretext for the full-scale invasion of China.

The Xi'an incident brought about further strains in Mao Zedong's uneasy relations with Stalin. Although obscured by the mystique of Moscow as the center of world revolution, to which Mao paid formal obeisance, hostility between the two Communist leaders had been simmering for a decade. The "Hunan Report" of 1927, with its not-so-veiled critique of Stalin's conservatism, was followed by a long and bitter struggle between Maoist and Stalinist factions in the CCP. It is therefore hardly surprising that Mao reacted with great nationalist sensitivity to any suggestion that he was subservient to Moscow, as was charged by the GMD and almost universally assumed in the West. Thus, when he was interviewed by Edgar Snow in July 1936, he replied sharply when asked whether a future "Chinese Soviet government would be comparable in its relation to Moscow to the present government of Outer Mongolia?" *"We are certainly not fighting for an emancipated China in order to turn the country over to Moscow!"* Mao exclaimed.[12]

The Japanese invasion

As the Communists and the Nationalists negotiated the final details of the second united front in September 1937, Japanese troops were pouring into China. It was the beginning of World War II in Asia, and although it was an invasion unaccompanied by a formal declaration of war, the greater part of the Imperial Japanese Army soon was stationed in China. Guomindang forces fled far to the west, where they established their wartime capital at Chongqing in Sichuan province.

The Japanese invasion radically transformed the balance of military and political forces in the temporarily suspended civil war between the Communists and the Nationalists. Although Japan's militarists loudly announced that their aim was to "save China from Communism," the invasion had the unintended consequence of creating the conditions that permitted the eventual triumph of the Chinese Communists. Japanese troops quickly occupied most of the major cities of China, thus depriving the urban-based GMD of their major sources of financial and political support. The invaders also destroyed the fragile and superficial administrative authority that the Nationalists exercised in the rural areas of north and central China. But the Japanese Army could not effectively control the vast Chinese countryside, where the great majority of the Chinese people lived and where the Communists were experienced in organizing peasants. During the brutal Japanese occupation, much of rural China became a political vacuum – and young peasant Communist cadres came to fill it, organizing peasants for patriotic resistance to the foreign invaders, promising agrarian reform, and making efforts to alleviate the economic hardships caused by the invasion and its brutalities.

The result was the spectacular growth of Communist power during the eight years of Japanese occupation. In 1937 the Red Army numbered 70,000 primitively armed soldiers. In the summer of 1945, when the Japanese Army surrendered, Mao's guerrilla forces had grown dramatically into a 1,000,000-strong regular army, supported by peasant militias numbering several million part-time fighters. The membership of the CCP had increased to approximately 1,200,000 by 1945, its cadres heading an underground resistance in the Japanese-occupied cities as well as organizers in villages across much of the north China countryside. By 1945 the Communists effectively administered rural base areas with a population of almost 100,000,000. The enormous expansion of Communist peasant support in the war of resistance against Japan was the basis for the striking Communist victories in the massive civil war with the GMD following

World War II. The crescendo-like succession of victories were to make Mao Zedong the ruler of the world's most populous land in 1949.[13]

Both the Japanese and Mao Zedong were essential to the victory of the Chinese Communist Revolution. The Japanese, by invading China, created a revolutionary situation in Chinese society, albeit unintentionally. But "revolutionary situations" do not by themselves produce revolutions. Revolutions presuppose revolutionaries – revolutionaries who appreciate the political potentialities of the situation in which they find themselves and are prepared to act upon those potentialities in accordance with the ends they seek. In China it was clearly Mao Zedong who had the keenest appreciation of the revolutionary conditions created in Chinese society by the Japanese invasion – and who possessed the will and strategic vision to exploit those conditions to achieve Communist power. It was not predetermined, of course, that Mao Zedong was to play this historic role. Conceivably, a good number of other revolutionary leaders might have done so. But it is less conducive to historical understanding to speculate on how a revolutionary movement might have had a different outcome had it been led by different leaders than to understand the intellectual and political predispositions of the leader who actually led it.

To understand how Mao Zedong transformed China's "revolutionary situation" into the greatest of twentieth-century revolutions, it is necessary to first take into account his radical reinterpretation of the inherited body of Marxist-Leninist theory – how, in effect, he discarded many of the basic premises of Marxism to create the ideological preconditions for revolution in an impoverished agrarian land.

Marxism and "The Thought of Mao Zedong"

Before the rise of Mao Zedong, no Marxist could have conceived of a socialist revolution relying almost entirely on the support of peasants, one in which the revolutionaries fought in the countryside and largely avoided the cities and their inhabitants, a revolution that took the form of warfare between contending armies, and one where the revolutionaries marched under a nationalist banner. Yet however incongruous with the Marxist teachings that Mao claimed to be his guiding ideology, such were the essential features of the Chinese Communist movement in 1937. The experience of the wartime years, and the civil war that followed, only served to deepen the rural, militaristic, and nationalist content of the Maoist movement as it approached victory in 1949.

Mao Zedong was not unaware of how far the practice of the Chinese Communist movement departed from the premises of Marxism and Leninism. He attempted to conceal the ideological heresies by constantly invoking such phrases as "the leadership of the proletariat" or "proletarian hegemony," by which he meant not the presence of the actual proletariat but rather the organized "proletarian consciousness" presumably embodied in the Communist Party. The substitution of "proletarian consciousness" for the proletariat had been implicit in Maoist ideology since the mid-1920s, when Mao began to look to the peasantry as China's truly revolutionary class. The Marxian tie between social class and political party had already become frayed with Lenin's concept of the vanguard party, which attributed the historical initiative to the Marxist "consciousness" of a dedicated intellectual elite, a consciousness that was to be imposed on the amorphous mass movement of workers. The link was torn asunder when Mao retained the intellectual elite but substituted the peasantry for the urban working class as the social basis of the party – yet still proclaimed its "proletarian" character. For Mao, it was sufficient that the leaders of the Party were guided by "proletarian consciousness" to ensure the proletarian nature of the organization, irrespective of its actual social composition.

What, then, are the distinctive features of "The Thought of Mao Zedong," as his works were to be canonized at the Seventh Congress of the CCP in 1945?[14] One will not readily find answers to this question in Mao's official writings, which tend to disguise his ideological heresies behind an orthodox Marxist-Leninist facade and a Stalinist veneer of "dialectical materialism." Rather, the nature of Maoism is revealed only by taking into account the implications of Mao's political practice for his theories, only by examining his writings in the historical context of his actions. By doing so, it becomes apparent that Maoism, far from being orthodox or "hardline" Marxism, as commonly portrayed, can better be understood in light of Mao Zedong's departures from the fundamental premises of Marxist theory. The first, and the most striking, of Mao's revisions is the substitution of the peasantry for the proletariat as the agent of revolution. In Marxist theory no belief is more fundamental than faith in the redemptive historic mission of the proletariat. It is a faith that is demanded by the Marxian analysis of capitalism, which teaches that the proletariat is both the product of capitalism and its negation. Capitalism produces its own "gravediggers" in the form of the proletariat, in Marx's well-known image. Mao was the first revolutionary Marxist to dispense with the actual modern working class, retaining the terms "proletariat" and "proletarian" but employing them to suggest a free-floating cluster of revolutionary values and ideas that were no longer the attributes of a specific social class.

Mao Zedong's indifference to the actual proletariat was accompanied by an inversion of the Marxist view of the relationship between town and countryside in the making of modern history. In original Marxism (and Leninism as well), historical progress is identified with the supremacy of the city, whereas the countryside is associated with stagnation and regression. The dynamics of modern history revolve around the activities of the two urban classes into which capitalism is increasingly dividing society – the bourgeoisie and the proletariat. This definitive dominance of the cities over the rural areas is a progressive development, an essential precondition for socialism and for the eventual abolition of the age-old antagonism between town and countryside.

While Marxists had always taken it for granted that the revolutionary forces of the city would lead the backward countryside, Mao, by contrast, believed that peasants should be mobilized to "surround and overwhelm" the cities. This notion was reinforced by a powerful anti-urban bias, the product of the modern Chinese historical situation. For Mao, the city was not the Marxian revolutionary stage, but rather a foreign-dominated stage where the imperialist impingement was most far-reaching. Cities were seen as the sources of alien influences, dens of moral corruption, and bastions of political reaction. Mao Zedong's anti-urbanism was one of the intellectual preconditions facilitating his pursuit of a rural-based revolutionary strategy; it was not simply the reflection of the peasant revolutionary movement he came to lead.

Mao Zedong's faith in the modern revolutionary capacities of the pre-modern peasantry was reinforced by a pervasive belief in "the advantages of backwardness." Since the 1890s the notion that China need not follow a Western path of development and thereby suffer the agonies of a capitalist regime had been a prominent feature of the thought of the modern Chinese intelligentsia. By taking advantage of the moral virtues inherent in its very condition of backwardness, China could leap forward to a socialist utopia.

The notion of "the advantages of backwardness" influenced the young Mao Zedong, as it did many young intellectuals of his generation. In his early "pre-Marxian" writings, Mao deplored China's backwardness – but at the same time saw it as a great reservoir of revolutionary energy and creativity. In 1919, when he was editing the short-lived *Xiang River Review*, Mao declared that "our Chinese people possess great intrinsic energy."

Although the people and their energies had been suppressed for "thousands of years," that condition of historic backwardness seemed to augur well for the political future, for what "has been accumulating for a long time . . . will surely burst forth quickly."[15]

The belief that backwardness is a revolutionary advantage defies the logic of Marxism and its image of economically progressive stages of development. Nonetheless, the belief became an integral part of Maoism, expressed in various ways over the revolutionary and post-revolutionary years. In an interview with Nym Wales in 1937, for example, Mao declared that in the world revolution, "the backward countries will be victorious first. America will probably be last."[16] And several months later he declared that "the Chinese revolution can avoid a capitalist future and can be directly linked with socialism without traversing the old historical path of the western countries, without passing through a period of bourgeois dictatorship."[17] The nationalist-infused claim that China had the unique ability to leap over the Marxian-defined stages of development carried within it the ideological embryo of the greatest disaster of Mao Zedong's long political career — the Great Leap Forward campaign of 1958.

The notion of "the advantages of backwardness" reflected a lack of faith in the objective forces of history. The Marxist notion that history moves through successive phases of development in accordance with the workings of objective economic laws demands a degree of patience with historical processes that few revolutionaries possess, especially in economically backward lands. Mao Zedong certainly did not possess it. In a country so impinged upon by foreigners and impoverished by a web of domestic and external forms of exploitation, Mao was unwilling to retreat to the political sidelines to wait for the forces of history to do their work. Such would have been the case even had he had more confidence in the "objective laws" of historical development than he did. His faith rather was in determined people who could impose their subjective will on objective reality and mold the course of history in accordance with the dictates of their consciousness. This voluntarist emphasis on the human will in the making of history was another belief that Mao derived, in part, from the anarchist literature he read in his youth, and one that was greatly reinforced by Chinese historical circumstances.

Mao Zedong's faith in the peasantry as the main revolutionary class in modern China, his belief in the "advantages of backwardness," and his extreme voluntarist emphasis on human will and spirit were prominent and abiding features of his political worldview. They could not, however, be easily reconciled with the tenets of the Marxist doctrine that he had embraced. But Mao's most fundamental departure from the premises of Marxism – from which all his other ideological unorthodoxies flowed – was on the issue of capitalism.

Maoism and capitalism

What distinguished Marxism from most 19th-century socialist theories was its acceptance of capitalism as a necessary and progressive stage of historical development. While Marx's analysis of capitalism was perhaps the most devastating critique of the system, he nevertheless saw a fully developed capitalism as the essential precondition for socialism. Capitalism created the material abundance on which a future socialist society inevitably must rest, while at the same time it produced the modern proletariat, the class destined to bring about universal human liberation.

The 20th-century Chinese historical situation was less than conducive to accepting the Marxist faith in the progressiveness of capitalism. Insofar as industrial capitalism developed in early 20th-century China, it did so largely under the aegis of foreign imperialism. Capitalism in China not only created (in extreme form) all the social evils associated with early industrialism in the West, but it did so mostly in areas under foreign domination, primarily the treaty ports. Thus, the perception of capitalism as an alien phenomenon, a universal response to early capitalist development in pre-industrial societies, was greatly intensified in China due to its foreign origins. Accordingly, many Chinese intellectuals identified capitalism with foreign imperialism, condemned both as external encroachments, and looked to indigenous sources for the socialist regeneration of the Chinese nation. These tendencies found their most powerful expression in the Maoist version of Marxism-Leninism.

In the years before his conversion to Marxism, the young Mao Zedong shared with most Chinese intellectuals of his generation a deep antipathy to capitalism. In the early May Fourth period, to be sure, he was attracted to various theories associated with Western capitalism – individualism, liberalism, and democracy. But however appealing these ideas, they did little to mitigate his hostility to capitalism as a social and economic system. He viewed capitalism simply as a form of oppression and exploitation, lumping capitalists together with "aristocrats" as enemies of the common people.[18] And he often used "capitalism" simply as a pejorative term for all types of exploitation and inequality, sometimes incongruously employing it to condemn traditional Chinese forms of sexual oppression.

He charged, for example, that "the slave's work of making tea and cooking is a result of capitalism."[19]

After his conversion to Marxism Mao Zedong could no longer characterize old Chinese traditions as capitalist. But he remained reluctant to accept the Marxist-Leninist message that capitalism was a necessary stage in a universal pattern of historical development. His interest in organizing workers and courting the bourgeoisie in the early 1920s was short-lived. In 1925 he had discovered the peasantry – and his revolutionary visions centered on the countryside for the following quarter of a century. In the "Hunan Report" of early 1927, where Mao set forth his vision of peasant revolution in its most pristine form, neither capitalism nor the modern social classes associated with capitalist forces of production are mentioned.

When he inevitably turned to the problem of capitalism in the 1930s, Mao generally pictured capitalism in China as insolubly bound up with foreign imperialism. This served to support the Maoist denial that China's socialist future was dependent on the social and material products of modern capitalism – or that the relative absence of capitalist forces of production was a barrier to the pursuit of revolutionary socialist goals. The "principal contradiction" in Chinese society was thus not between the social classes involved in capitalist relations of production, but rather, as Mao put it in 1939, between "imperialism and the Chinese nation."[20] It was a thesis that satisfied Mao's nationalist proclivities as well as the political needs of the anti-Japanese united front.

Nonetheless, Mao Zedong could not completely ignore Marxist-Leninist teachings on the progressiveness of capitalism in economically underdeveloped lands. Nor could he ignore Comintern demands on the necessity for a two-stage revolutionary process, with a "bourgeois-democratic" (or capitalist) stage preceding a socialist one. He attempted to satisfy the need to conform to ideological orthodoxy, or to appear to do so, and at the same time reinforce the national united front, by setting forth the theory of "New Democracy."[21]

Mao's treatise *On New Democracy* appeared early in 1940, as the Communists were rapidly expanding their army and territory by mobilizing peasants for guerrilla warfare behind Japanese lines in north China. It was as close as Mao was ever to come to accepting the Marxist proposition that socialism presupposes capitalism. He drew a clear distinction between the bourgeois-democratic and socialist stages of the revolution. In the initial "democratic" stage, the national bourgeoisie would play a vital role as part of a broad revolutionary alliance of four classes – which also included the proletariat, the peasantry and the petty bourgeoisie (intellectuals, students, small shopkeepers, and so forth). Moreover, Mao acknowledged a necessary historical link between capitalism and socialism, observing that the "objective mission" of China's new democratic revolution was "to clear the path for the development of capitalism" and thereby eventually forge "a still wider path for the development of socialism." And he observed that the bourgeois-democratic era would be lengthy. He took pains to criticize as "utopian" the "theory of a single revolution" and the notion of "revolution at one stroke." In light of China's backwardness, he wrote in 1947, "it will still be necessary to permit the existence for a long time of a capitalist sector of the economy represented by the extensive petty bourgeoisie and middle bourgeoisie."[22] A partly capitalist economy, similar to the mixed economy that had been advocated by Sun Yat-sen, Mao repeatedly suggested, would flourish for the foreseeable future.

Yet, however politically and ideologically useful the notion of "New Democracy" proved to be, it seems most unlikely that Mao Zedong envisioned a long-term course of development that proceeded mid-way between capitalism and socialism, as he seemed to have suggested. It is even more unlikely that he was converted to any real Marxist faith in the historical progressiveness of capitalism, much less to the Marxian insistence that the future socialist society must inherit the material, social, and cultural achievements of a fully developed capitalist regime. Through most of his revolutionary career he had found the promise of socialism not in the development of capitalism but rather in the masses of "the people" – that is to say, the peasants – who inhabited a pre-capitalist land. For the sources of revolution – and of socialism – he looked to those sectors of Chinese society and its population least influenced by capitalism. In this respect, Mao shared a 19th-century Russian-type Populist skepticism about the Marxist thesis that capitalism prepared the way for socialism. Like Herzen a century earlier, he believed it was precisely the absence of capitalist development that held the promise of socialism. As Mao later argued, the backward lands were less poisoned by bourgeois ideology than the industrialized countries of the West, where the bourgeoisie and their pernicious ideas had penetrated "every nook and cranny," thus stifling the revolutionary spirit.[23]

Mao Zedong's Populist rejection of the thesis that capitalism is a progressive stage in historical development and the necessary prerequisite for socialism had profound implications for the theory and practice of Marxism in China. From that rejection there flowed a faith in the peasantry as the truly revolutionary class and a relative disinterest in the proletariat; a perception of the rural areas as a source of moral purity and revolutionary energy while cities were dens of iniquity and centers of political reaction; and a skepticism about the workings of "objective laws" of history in favor of an emphasis on the powers of human will and consciousness. Whether these fundamental departures from the premises of Marxist theory still left Mao a "Marxist" in any meaningful sense is a question that deserves serious consideration. Here it is perhaps sufficient to note that Mao's departures from Marxian orthodoxies served well the needs of revolution in a pre-capitalist and largely peasant land, permitting a Marxist-led party to come to power by harnessing the forces of revolt in the countryside to "surround and overwhelm" the conservative cities.

Mao Zedong fundamentally departed not only from the premises of original Marxism but from Leninism as well. Mao was a master of political organization, political intrigue, and revolutionary strategy – and in these areas he may well have been a "natural Leninist," as he often has been characterized. But intellectually he was something other than a Leninist. Lenin had inherited the old Populist dilemma of reconciling the "spontaneity" of the masses with the "consciousness" of the intelligentsia and resolved it in decisive fashion – the Marxist "consciousness" of the intelligentsia was to be imposed upon the "spontaneous" movement of the masses in the form of a tightly knit and highly disciplined party organization. Mao Zedong never clearly defined the relationship between the organized consciousness of the Party and the spontaneous consciousness of the masses in a purely Leninist fashion. The problem of the relationship between "consciousness" and "spontaneity" remained a Populist dilemma that contributed to a growing tension between the leader of the Party and the institution of the Party. It was a tension that reinforced, even if it did not necessarily create, Mao's growing conviction that true "consciousness," the combined wisdom of both the masses and the Party, resided in his own person and thought. It was this belief in his own political and ideological infallibility – which Mao shared with his Party acolytes and many peasants in Shaanxi – that nurtured the extraordinary phenomenon of the cult of Mao Zedong.

The origins of the Mao cult

The cult of Mao was born in China's rural hinterlands in the mid-1930s, at first growing mostly spontaneously. In 1936 the American journalist Edgar Snow made his way to the remote Communist base area in northern

Shaanxi to interview the 44-year-old Mao. "There seems to be some basis for the legend of his charmed life," Snow wrote, "in the fact that, although he had been in scores of battles, was once captured by enemy troops and escaped, and has the world's highest reward on his head, during all these years he has never once been wounded."[24]

The belief that Mao led "a charmed life" partly derived from the heroic experience of the Long March, concluded only a year before that interview. For the survivors of that extraordinary year-long flight through the wilderness, and the many more who were inspired by the miracle of their survival, there emerged an almost religious faith in Mao as the prophet who would lead his followers to the promised land. It was an experience that lent a sacred character to the revolutionary mission and to Mao as its invincible leader.

But it was among the peasants living in the early Communist base areas, perhaps more than the veterans of the Long March, that the emerging Mao cult found its deepest roots. Edgar Snow's observations of 1936 offer hints of the peasant sources of the Mao cult. In conveying his first "subjective impressions" of Mao, Snow dismissed the suggestion that any individual could be the savior of China but nonetheless prophetically observed:

> Yet undeniably you feel a certain force of destiny in him. It is nothing quick or flashy, but a kind of solid elemental vitality. You feel that whatever extraordinary there is in this man grows out of the uncanny degree to which he synthesizes and expresses the urgent demands of millions of Chinese, and especially the peasantry – those impoverished, underfed, exploited, illiterate, but kind, generous, courageous and just now rather rebellious human beings who are the vast majority of the Chinese people.[25]

It was among the impoverished peasants of northern Shaanxi that the deification of Mao Zedong began in the late 1930s. As mentioned above, the Red Army, formally commanded by Zhu De, was popularly known as the "Mao-Zhu" army. Many peasants thought "Mao-Zhu" to be a single god-like person who would free the peasants from oppression and restore justice in the world. The "Mao-Zhu" myth soon became the Mao myth alone and it was to become increasingly infused with ancient peasant superstitions and traditional imperial symbolism. As with the great emperors of old, portraits of Mao, with sunbeams radiating around his head, began to appear in Yan'an. Mao Zedong did little to discourage those who were constructing a hero-worshiping cult around his name and person, however incongruous the phenomenon was with the Marxist beliefs he professed.

The popular cult of Mao Zedong which had grown spontaneously during the early Yan'an years was soon bolstered by official decrees. The Rectification campaign of 1941–4, which sought to achieve ideological unity and political centralization in the burgeoning Communist movement, established Mao Zedong's writings as the Party's orthodox ideology. In 1941, when the Rectification campaign was officially launched, the overwhelming majority of Red Army soldiers and Party cadres were relatively new recruits, having joined the Communists after the outbreak of full-scale fighting with the Japanese Army in 1937. Over that four-year period, the Red Army had grown more than five-fold, to approximately 400,000 regular soldiers, while the CCP could claim a membership of 800,000. Most new recruits were peasants from the northern provinces, where Communist forces now controlled substantial territories; some were students and intellectuals who had made their way to Yan'an from cities throughout China to join the Communist-led resistance to the Japanese invasion. One of the aims of the Rectification (or "thought reform") campaign was to indoctrinate the new recruits with basic Marxist and Communist ideas, in accordance with the Maoist belief that correct thought yields correct action. A closely related purpose of the Rectification campaign was to carry out Mao's call for the "sinification of Marxism," that is to say, the adaptation of both the substance and style of Marxism-Leninism to the peculiarities of the Chinese historical situation.

It was made clear from the outset of the campaign that "correct thought" was not Marxism in general but rather a "sinified" Marxism – and that the latter was Mao Zedong's specific interpretation of the inherited body of Marxist-Leninist theory. Five speeches that Mao had delivered over the previous year, on such topics as the reform of work habits and the need to eliminate such erroneous practices as "foreign formalism" (that is to say, the uncritical repetition of Soviet ideas) became required texts for study in the Rectification movement.[26] Passages from Mao's writings were now ubiquitously quoted in Yan'an's literary and political publications.

The acceptance (or in some cases the imposition) of a common ideology no doubt contributed to the discipline and political unity that were necessary for survival in the long and bitter struggle against the brutalities of the Japanese invaders – and then for success in the resumption of the civil war with the Guomindang that inevitably followed. But the laying down of Maoist ideological orthodoxies also contributed to an extraordinary concentration of political power in the hands of their author. Perhaps it was a case where the imperatives of a harsh revolutionary war coincided with the political needs of the revolutionary leader.

Mao Zedong did not limit his claims of absolute ideological supremacy to matters of revolutionary strategy and military tactics, realms where the efficacy of his ideas had already been demonstrated in practice. He also felt the need to establish his credentials as an orthodox and creative Marxist philosopher, perhaps to justify (or perhaps to obscure) his departures from Marxian orthodoxies in so many other areas. Just as Lenin and Stalin had felt such a need before him in their turgid and lengthy philosophical works on "dialectical materialism," in 1937 Mao presented his essays "On Practice" and "On Contradiction" as his contribution to Marxist philosophy. While these had the virtue of being much briefer and considerably more lively in style than Stalin's tedious tome on "materialist" philosophy, the originality of Mao's philosophical writings is questionable and their relationship to his innovations in revolutionary strategy rather tenuous. Nonetheless, during the Rectification movement, the two essays were celebrated as creative contributions to the development of the Marxist philosophical tradition, and were required reading for intellectuals and Party cadres.

The Rectification campaign also established Mao Zedong as the final arbiter on the form and content of artistic and literary expression. In the spring of 1942 Mao convened two meetings attended by the many writers, artists, and other intellectuals who had made their way to Yan'an to join the Communist Revolution and the resistance to the Japanese invaders. Invoking both Lenin and Lu Xun, modern China's most celebrated writer, Mao lectured his audience on their social and political responsibilities, demanding that writers give primacy to political over artistic criteria and insisting that "the duty of learning from the workers, peasants, and soldiers precedes the task of educating them."[27]

Mao's talks were less remarkable for what he had to say about literature and art than the fact that he had arrogated to himself, and to the Communist Party that he now totally dominated, the authority to judge what was acceptable revolutionary literature and what was not. The potential for political repression inherent in that claim stood in striking contrast to the socially liberating impulses that Yan'an had come to symbolize and which had done much to encourage many urban intellectuals and students to embark on the dangerous journey to join the Communists in the northwest. The repressive potential of the establishment of literary orthodoxies was apparent even as Mao spoke at the Yan'an Forum. Several months before the forum convened, on March 8, International Women's Day, the noted writer Ding Ling sharply criticized the Party's hypocritical treatment of women in Yan'an. She was dismissed as an editor of Yan'an's main newspaper, *Liberation Daily*, and shipped off to labor in the surrounding countryside for several months.[28] A more tragic fate befell Wang Shiwei, a young Communist writer and translator in Shanghai who had migrated to Yan'an in 1936. Although his satirical and iconoclastic writings had ruffled official feathers for years, it was in 1942 that he got into trouble for his critique of the new hierarchy of official ranks and rewards – "the three classes of clothing and five grades of food."[29] Wang was subjected to a quasi-trial of mass criticism and eventually jailed at a prison just outside Yan'an. He was executed when the Communists temporarily evacuated Yan'an in 1947, apparently on orders from the Communist General He Long – but contrary to Mao's instructions.[30]

It was ironic – but not illogical – that Chinese Communists were punished for expressing "Maoist" ideas. Mao Zedong, after all, had been a champion of sexual equality since 1919, when he had written the moving series of articles on Miss Zhao's suicide. And his antipathy to bureaucratic rank and privilege was well known. But it was one thing for Mao to set forth such ideas; it was quite another for others to do so in criticism of the Party that Mao headed.[31]

The canonization of Mao's writings in the Rectification campaign was a further step in the construction of the Mao cult, adding an aura of ideological infallibility to the political supremacy in the CCP that Mao already had achieved. It was also a reaffirmation of the Chinese Communist movement's independence from Moscow. The Chinese Party and its leader, it was implied, had their own version of Marxism-Leninism appropriate to Chinese historical conditions. Both leader and ideology in Yan'an now stood on an equal plane with their counterparts in Moscow. It was a barely disguised challenge to Stalin's claim to universal ideological and political authority in the international Communist movement, but not one to which Stalin could easily respond, for it came at a time when the Soviet Union was desperately struggling to survive the massive Nazi invasion.

The political potency of the cult of Mao Zedong was fully revealed in April 1945, when the CCP convened its Seventh Congress. As the long war of resistance to the Japanese invaders was approaching its triumphant conclusion, the leaders of a party which could now claim 1,200,000 members gathered to celebrate the leadership of Mao Zedong. His writings and speeches were proclaimed the sole guide for the Party in the future as well as credited for its successes in the past. All delegates to the Congress lavished praise on Mao, but few more ardently than Liu Shaoqi, now second to Mao in the increasingly hierarchical Party organization. Liu declared Mao not only "the greatest revolutionary and statesman in Chinese history" but also China's "greatest theoretician and scientist." And he hailed the canon of Mao's thought as a new and higher stage in a universally valid body of Marxist-Leninist theory.[32]

The construction of the Mao cult now began to embrace not only celebrations of Mao's thought but also his person. Snow had observed in 1936 that "the role of his personality in the movement was clearly immense," but as yet there was "no ritual of hero-worship built up around him."[33] But hero-worshiping began soon enough, partly spontaneously and partly under official auspices. Foreign visitors to Yan'an in the early 1940s observed that Mao was less informal and more remote, both physically and spiritually, even though he retained "the personal habits of a peasant," as Snow put it. Mao's portrait appeared on village walls and buildings in the expanding Communist-governed areas; some were life-size and others showed Mao's face illuminated by the rays of the sun in traditional imperial fashion. In books and songs, Mao came to be worshiped as "the Great Saviour" and "the star of salvation." The new Chinese Communist anthem "The East is Red" revered Mao in almost Christ-like fashion: "The East is Red, the sun rises, In China a Mao Zedong is born."

The growth of the Mao cult went hand in hand with the concentration of political power. In 1941, at the beginning of the Rectification movement, virtually all Party leaders (save Mao) were forced to make public "self-criticisms" of past political and ideological errors. It was not a conventional political purge in that Mao's opponents, past and present, were not punished and for the most part were allowed to retain their official positions. But the mandatory ritual of self-flagellation left little doubt about who was the supreme leader.

The unchallenged and virtually total control over the CCP that Mao Zedong achieved during the Rectification campaign was formalized at the Seventh Party Congress in April 1945. To the chairmanship of the Politburo, the Party's highest policy-making organ, Mao added the chairmanship of the Secretariat, the body through which the top Party leaders exercised centralized control over local Party organizations. Mao's political dominance was further augmented by fortifying his ideological monopoly. The new Party constitution adopted by the Seventh Congress formally proclaimed "the Thought of Mao Zedong" to be the Party's guiding ideology.

Civil war: the last phase (1945–9)

As Japan's defeat in the Pacific War approached, both the Communists and the Nationalists prepared to resume the only partly suspended civil war. The united front for resistance to the Japanese invaders had meanwhile remained largely on paper. Save for changing the name of the main force of the Red Army to the "Eighth Route Army" (theoretically part of the Nationalist Army) shortly after the Xi'an incident, Mao Zedong had no intention of repeating the mistakes of the mid-1920s. Communist military forces were not again to be placed under the command of Chiang Kai-shek. Thus, the "Eighth Route Army" (along with the smaller New Fourth Army, an amalgamation of Communist guerrilla units in central China) remained under the ultimate command of Mao Zedong. Not only did the Communist and Nationalist armies fail to sustain any meaningful degree of cooperation in resisting the Japanese, they fought each other, especially after a clash in January 1941, when a large GMD force surrounded and attacked the headquarters of the New Fourth Army in Anhui province, killing or capturing thousands of Communist troops in a fierce week-long battle. Both Mao and Chiang Kai-shek assumed full-scale civil war would resume once Japan was defeated.

During the long war years the power and popularity of the Communists had grown enormously as they organized effective guerrilla warfare against the foreign invaders in the rural areas of north China. Through a combination of nationalist and socio-economic appeals, and promises of security, the Communists had won overwhelming support among the peasantry of north China and considerable sympathy in the cities as well, especially among students and intellectuals. The flight of most of the Nationalist Army to far western China had allowed the Communists to break out of their impoverished sanctuary in northern Shaanxi and establish base areas in many parts of north and central China. In the spring of 1945 Mao Zedong claimed that 95,500,000 people lived in rural areas under Communist control. The Red Army had grown into a highly disciplined force of almost 1,000,000 dedicated soldiers, having increased 20-fold since 1937. And local peasant militias had been organized throughout the northern and central provinces.

Still, when Japan surrendered in August 1945, the GMD appeared to have the overwhelming advantage. Chiang Kai-shek's army numbered 4,000,000 soldiers, four times the size of the Communist forces. Moreover, the Nationalists, unlike the Communists, had a sizeable air force and were equipped with tanks and modern artillery. And the Nationalists had the support of the US, which provided generous amounts of money and arms.

The resumption of the civil war was delayed – and complicated – by Stalin in an act that Mao must have regarded as yet another Soviet betrayal. At the Yalta conference in February 1945 Stalin secretly assured Roosevelt and Churchill that the Soviet Union would not support the Chinese Communists and agreed that the Guomindang was the only political party capable of ruling China, a view the Soviet dictator repeated at the Potsdam conference several months later. In return for joining the war against Japan (and not supporting the Chinese Communists), Stalin was promised the return of the Chinese Eastern Railroad and Port Arthur, tsarist Russian concessions in Manchuria lost to Japan in 1905.

Stalin did not inform Mao Zedong of these "big power" understandings. Mao became painfully aware of the secret agreements only on the eve of the Japanese surrender in August 1945, when the startling news arrived that the Soviet Union had signed a treaty of alliance with Chiang Kai-shek's Nationalist government. The CCP could no longer expect to receive Soviet assistance when the civil war resumed, although US support for the GMD certainly would continue. Thus Mao was no longer able to resist Soviet pressure to seek a "coalition government" with the GMD – and one in which the CCP would now surely be the very junior partner. At the end of August Mao sullenly flew to Chongqing to meet Chiang Kai-shek, whom he had not seen since the days of the first GMD-CCP alliance in the mid-1920s. Mao must have reflected on his long and contentious relationship with Stalin. He could hardly have forgotten that in the great revolutionary upsurge of the mid-1920s, Stalin had condemned the "excesses" of the Chinese peasantry, whose revolutionary fervor Mao so eloquently championed. Stalin, too, had been the architect of the first GMD-CCP alliance, which had left the Chinese Communists defenseless against Chiang Kai-shek's Soviet-trained army in 1927. Stalin also had sponsored the young Chinese Communist leaders who had fought Mao since the late 1920s and who had removed Mao from power during the Jiangxi Soviet period, a struggle which had continued into the early 1940s. And now, on the eve of victory over Japan, with an indigenous Chinese Communist movement more powerful than ever and prepared to contend for national power, Stalin had once again betrayed a Communist party that refused to submit to his control.

Yet Mao could hardly afford to openly defy Stalin, however great his anger at the Soviet dictator must have been, for the Soviet Union was the only possible source of outside support to counter growing American political, financial, and military assistance to the Guomindang. Moreover, the mystique of Moscow's authority as the sacred center of world revolution remained powerful, inhibiting the open expression of views critical of the high priest of what was still called "the international Communist movement." For Mao Zedong in 1945 public defiance of Stalin remained unthinkable, even though at the recently concluded Potsdam conference the Soviet dictator had again said that the GMD was the only political party capable of governing China.[34] Thus Mao, dutifully if morosely, journeyed to Chongqing to negotiate with Chiang Kai-shek. He expected that the talks would prove fruitless, save to deflect accusations that he had not done everything possible to avoid civil war.

Mao Zedong spent six futile weeks negotiating in Chongqing, from late August to early October, meeting personally four times with Chiang Kai-shek. There was a superficial air of cordiality, but both were marking time, performing to appease public opinion in China and politicians in Washington and Moscow. Mao and Chiang were maneuvering for advantage in the final civil war that both assumed to be inevitable. Both believed, in their own fashion, that "political power grows out of the barrel of a gun."

With the breakdown of the talks and Mao's return to Yan'an on October 10, 1945, clashes between Communist and Nationalist military units increased in frequency and intensity. Sporadic fighting between the two Chinese forces had continued throughout the eight-year Japanese occupation. With the Japanese defeat in August 1945, Communist and Nationalist armies had raced to accept the surrender of Japanese troops – and to acquire arms and territory. When the Chongqing talks ended, warfare accelerated, especially in Manchuria where most remaining Japanese troops and stores of arms were located. Manchuria contained much of China's natural resources and a good part of its tiny modern industrial base. The US now became more directly involved in the Chinese civil war. Fifty-thousand American troops were dispatched to north China, where they occupied major cities which were then turned over to the GMD. And the US airlifted Nationalist troops to Manchuria to occupy strategic points before either Chinese or Russian Communists could reach them.

The policies of the Soviet Union in post-war Manchuria were ambiguous and often contradictory, reflecting Stalin's dual role as heir of imperial Russia's expansionist ambitions and his posture as the leader of an international revolutionary movement. In accordance with Allied wartime agreements, the Soviet Union declared war on Japan on August 8, 1945, just a week before the Japanese surrender, and Soviet troops occupied much of Manchuria, ostensibly to accept the surrender of Japanese troops. The Russians initially assisted the Chinese Communists in occupying territory and acquiring arms. Then, in November, as fighting between GMD and CCP forces accelerated, the Russians suddenly demanded that Chinese Communist troops abandon the major cities and lines of transportation in Manchuria within a week, threatening to send tanks to drive them out if necessary.

The Soviet withdrawal of support for the Chinese Communists reflected, in part, Stalin's fear of a rival Communist regime in China. Stalin had already told Mao, albeit indirectly, that the Chinese revolution had little hope of success and had advised the Chinese Communists to join the Nationalist government and disband the Red Army.[35] Soviet actions in Manchuria must have seemed to Mao yet another example of Stalin's duplicitous behavior. Nonetheless, Mao had no choice but to order Communist troops to withdraw from the cities and other strategic points. But the relations between Mao and Stalin, long strained, were further poisoned.

The strains were temporarily alleviated in the spring of 1946 when Soviet troops withdrew from Manchuria, turning over substantial quantities of captured Japanese arms to the Chinese Communists as they left. But the Russian departure was not complete; the Soviets retained their most prized Manchurian territories, the Pacific ports of Dairen and Port Arthur. The question of their return to China was one of the many problems in Sino-Russian relations that would confront Mao after 1949 – not to be resolved until after Stalin's death in 1953.

As Soviet troops were withdrawing from Manchuria, Nationalist and Communist armies were maneuvering to gain the advantage in the final battle that both Mao and Chiang expected. Although fighting between the two had never ceased, full-scale warfare had been delayed by the efforts of the United States to mediate a political settlement. To that end, General George Marshall, US Army Chief of Staff during World War II and now special envoy of President Truman, had arrived in China in late December 1945. But the truce Marshall managed to negotiate broke down completely in the spring of 1946, and by the summer China was rapidly sliding into massive civil war.

In 1946 the Nationalists enjoyed an overwhelming material advantage. The GMD armies numbered over 4,000,000, nearly four times the number of soldiers in the Red Army, which had been renamed the People's Liberation Army (PLA). The Nationalists had even greater superiority in military technology, including a substantial airforce, heavy artillery, and tanks. Of such modern weapons, the Communists had virtually nothing. Moreover, the GMD received many billions of dollars in US financial aid. The captured Japanese military supplies that the departing Soviet army in Manchuria turned over to the Chinese Communists in 1946 were minuscule in comparison. Nationalist generals boasted that they had at least a ten to one military advantage over the Communists. And on the eve of the outbreak of full-scale civil war, Stalin told Mao that the Chinese Communist cause was hopeless and advised him to seek an accommodation with Chiang Kai-shek.

Although Mao Zedong was now confident of a Communist military victory, he expected a prolonged struggle. In part, his confidence was based on evidence that corruption and demoralization afflicted the GMD, and made the Nationalist Army far weaker than it appeared on paper, an assessment shared by a good number of American military officers who had been assigned to Chongqing during the Pacific War. But in greater part, Mao's confidence in eventual victory was based on his faith in the decisive historical role of the human will and spirit, a long-standing voluntarist faith that had been greatly fortified by the extraordinary growth of the Red Army during the anti-Japanese war. As China was plunging into all-out civil war in the summer of 1946, he told an American journalist: "We have only millet plus rifles to rely on, but history will finally prove that our millet plus rifles is more powerful than Chiang Kai-shek's aeroplanes plus tanks."[36]

Mao Zedong, who took overall command of Communist forces during the three-year civil war, was at the height of his powers as a military strategist. Mao no longer counseled a reliance on the tactics of guerrilla warfare that had been so successfully employed against the Japanese invaders. He now emphasized what he termed "mobile warfare," the tactics he had largely borrowed from Sun Tzu, a military strategist of the 5th century BC. Those ancient tactics were adapted and developed on the Jinggang Mountains in the late 1920s, during the Jiangxi period, and on the Long March. They were now employed on a far larger scale, for the army that Mao commanded was no longer a small band of fighters struggling for sheer survival but a force numbering over a million soldiers. Nonetheless, many of the well-honed practices of earlier revolutionary eras remained – surprise, deception, rapid movements, unconventional maneuvers, secrecy of troop movements, and, as Mao especially emphasized, "concentrating a superior force to destroy the enemy forces one by one."[37] He also instructed the Red Army to refrain from attacking big cities, to aim to "wipe out the enemy's effective strength" rather than hold a particular place, and to avoid battles of attrition.[38] But perhaps most important was the old Maoist tactic of "luring the enemy deep," which was employed on a massive scale in the crucial battle for Manchuria.

With the end of World War II, Chiang Kai-shek was determined to establish control over the vast and strategically vital territory of Manchuria. As the Russian army withdrew in mid-1946, Chiang hurriedly dispatched more than a million of his best troops to occupy the former Japanese puppet state. Most were well equipped with new American arms and many were transported to the northeast by the US Airforce. They were the cream of the Nationalist Army.

The battle for Manchuria became, in part, a personal contest between Mao Zedong and Chiang Kai-shek. Mao drew up the battle plans for the Manchurian campaign, as he did for most of the more important military engagements of the civil war, which were then mainly carried out by the Communist Fourth Field Army under the command of Lin Biao, the most skilled of the PLA's generals. And Chiang Kai-shek, at a crucial point in the battle, assumed personal command of the Nationalist forces in Manchuria.

It was an unwise decision. By the time Chiang took over the Manchurian command, the Nationalist Army, its lines of supply and communication overextended, had been demoralized and put on the defensive by the brilliant maneuvers of Lin Biao's army. The GMD forces, as was their habit, were now concentrated on the railroads and around three cities in central and southern Manchuria – Changchun, Shenyang (then known as Mukden), and Jinzhou (Chinchow). The latter was the smallest of the three, but also the most strategically important, Mao recognized, for the town was essential both for supplying the GMD troops in Manchuria and for their retreat. Thus, in early September 1948 he instructed Lin Biao to concentrate his forces to capture Jinzhou, "leaving the [larger] enemy forces at Changchun and Shenyang alone."[39]

With the large GMD armies defending Shenyang and Changchun isolated, Lin Biao ordered most of his army to attack the town of Jinzhou, throwing 13 columns – several hundred thousand troops in all – in rapid succession against the 100,000 Nationalist defenders. The town was captured on October 15, with half of the Nationalist soldiers going over to the Communists. Belated GMD reinforcements were destroyed or dispersed. Changchun fell on October 19 and Shenyang on November 2. In all, the Manchurian campaign resulted in the loss of half a million of Chiang Kai-shek's best troops, many of whom deserted, joining the Communists. Lin Biao's Fourth Field Army nearly tripled in size as a result, growing to over 800,000 soldiers who were now well equipped with captured American arms. The Manchurian campaign illustrated, on a gigantic scale, the efficacy of classic Maoist military principles.

The Communist victory in the civil war was not, of course, primarily the result of Mao's military brilliance. A more important part was played by the overwhelming support of the peasantry, especially in the northern and central provinces, in large measure a response to Communist policies which attempted to alleviate the most pressing economic problems of the impoverished rural inhabitants. The participation of the peasantry in the revolutionary war against the Guomindang – whether as recruits for the Red Army or local militias, contributors of goods and money, workers in the self-sufficient economies of the blockaded Communist base areas, or providers of intelligence – was the essential condition for the conduct of what Mao termed "people's war." And the latter, in turn, was the precondition for employing the distinctive military tactics he had devised. However efficacious, these could not be successfully employed unless the army enjoyed genuine popular support, as Mao emphasized time and again.

The tie between the CCP and the poorer peasants had been strengthened during the last years of the civil war when the Communists adopted a radical land reform policy, redistributing the holdings of landlords and rich peasants. During the anti-Japanese war, in accordance with nationalistic united front policies, Mao had insisted on a very moderate, reformist land policy that emphasized the reduction of rents, limits on usury, and the promotion of cooperative methods of farming. In 1947, however, with civil war raging, Mao supported a radical agrarian policy that sanctioned the confiscation of the holdings of landlords and their distribution among the landless and land-short peasants. In large part, the radical agrarian policy – which proceeded under the egalitarian slogan "land to the tiller" – was a political response to the spontaneous social radicalism of the poorer peasants, who were the most numerous and ardent supporters of the Communists and who filled the ranks of the PLA.

The social radicalism that erupted into violent class conflict in the villages of north China in 1947 marked a major change in the appeals and nature of the Communist Revolution. During the eight years of the Japanese invasion and occupation, peasants (and others) flocked to the nationalist banner hoisted by Mao Zedong and a movement which promised to organize resistance against the foreign invaders and to bring some degree of stability to a war-disrupted economy. While Maoism was always a doctrine that combined nationalism with social revolution, an uneasy but powerful combination, during the wartime years Mao muted the social

revolutionary impulses in favor of national struggle and reformist economic measures. During the last phase of the civil war, however, it was
class struggle rather than nationalism that propelled the revolutionary
movement, foreshadowing the violent social revolution that was to mark
the nation-wide land reform campaign of 1950–2.

The unification of China

In the fall of 1948, Mao Zedong had optimistically predicted that the
Guomindang could be defeated by the summer of 1951.[40] Events moved
even more rapidly than he had anticipated. The victory in Manchuria in
early November 1948 proved decisive, demoralizing the GMD, giving the
Communists numerical superiority for the first time, and opening the
way for the conquest of north and central China. In less than four months,
from the beginning of the Manchurian campaign in October 1948 to the
conclusion of the north China campaign in January 1949, the GMD had
lost over a million and a half soldiers. And the PLA had expanded to a
regular force of over 2,000,000, supported by large peasant militias and
auxiliaries.

With the military and political situation hopeless, Chiang Kai-shek
sued for peace. But Mao was now uncompromising, insisting on punishment for war criminals – and, as he repeatedly charged, Chiang Kai-shek
was "China's No. 1 war criminal" as well as "Chieftain of the GMD bandit
gang and bogus president of the Nanking government."[41] Chiang, defeated
and demoralized, resigned the presidency of the Nanjing regime – although
he did not give up such military power as he still retained – and there was
a temporary lull in the fighting while other Nationalist leaders attempted
to negotiate a peaceful solution. At this point Stalin made yet another contribution to the increasingly hostile relationship between Mao and
Moscow. On the eve of the Chinese Communist victory, he advised that
the PLA should not cross the Yangzi and that the civil war conclude with
a Communist regime in north China and a GMD state in the south. The
ostensible purpose of this scheme was to avoid provoking direct US intervention. More likely, Stalin feared the challenge Mao would pose to
Moscow as the leader of a rival Communist regime in a united China. Mao
Zedong, in any event, once again ignored Stalin's advice and on April 20
ordered a general offensive to complete the conquest of the mainland and
unite all of China under Communist rule.

On September 21, 1949, ten days before he stood atop the Gate of
Heavenly Peace in Beijing to proudly proclaim the establishment of the

People's Republic, Mao Zedong celebrated the revolutionary victory with a speech to the Chinese People's Political Consultative Conference, a united front body established in 1946 in the failed effort to form a coalition government:

> Fellow Delegates, we are all convinced that our work will go down in the history of mankind, demonstrating that the Chinese people, comprising one quarter of humanity, have now stood up. The Chinese have always been a great, courageous and industrious nation; it is only in modern times that they have fallen behind. And that was due entirely to oppression and exploitation by foreign imperialism and domestic reactionary governments. For over a century our forefathers never stopped waging unyielding struggles against domestic and foreign oppressors, including the Revolution of 1911 led by Dr. Sun Yat-sen, our great forerunner in the Chinese revolution. . . . Ours will no longer be a nation subject to insult and humiliation. We have stood up.[42]

To his audience, Mao Zedong must have seemed more a Chinese nationalist than a Marxist revolutionary. And so it appeared to many in China and abroad at the time of the founding of the People's Republic of China on October 1, 1949.

Mao as revolutionary, northern Shaanxi, 1937

Mao as ruler, 1957

Mao Zedong in Power: Nationalism and Modernization, 1949–57

State, Party, and class

When Mao Zedong became the ruler of China in 1949 – unlike Lenin in Russia in 1917 – he did not count on the *deus ex machina* of world revolution to ensure the survival of a Marxist-led revolution in an economically backward land. The Chinese Communist Revolution had been an eminently national movement, largely isolated from international revolutionary currents. While Mao Zedong duly reaffirmed internationalist Marxist goals on appropriate occasions, he did so in ritualistic fashion. The Marxian principle that socialism was to be a world-wide movement in scope and spirit was not a belief that weighed heavily on the thought and actions of Mao Zedong.

The nationalist character and appeals of the Maoist revolution greatly facilitated the rapid consolidation of Communist power in China after 1949. The contrast between Mao in 1949 and Lenin in 1917 is striking. Lenin was the first Marxist to appreciate the revolutionary significance of nationalism in the colonial and semi-colonial countries. But while Lenin could appeal to the grievances of oppressed nationalities in tsarist Russia and elsewhere, he could hardly do so under the banner of Russian nationalism, which after all was the nationalism of the oppressor. Mao Zedong, on the other hand, had become the symbol of Chinese national resistance to foreign intrusions in the long struggle against the Japanese invaders. His image as a nationalist leader greatly broadened popular support for the Revolution, particularly among students and intellectuals in the cities where Communist organizational structures were weak or non-existent.

Mao Zedong also enjoyed other advantages that facilitated the rapid construction of the post-revolutionary regime. Unlike Lenin, Mao, after achieving power, did not face a hostile peasantry in a largely agrarian country. The Chinese Communists had achieved victory by winning enormous popular support in the rural areas – and many peasants continued to deify Mao Zedong as a "savior." Moreover, the Maoists had come to power not only with their own organizational forms and administrative methods, but with considerable experience in governing large populations in the rural base areas. Unlike the Bolsheviks in 1917, Mao and the Chinese Communists were not suddenly thrust into the unfamiliar role of rulers. Mao could not complain, as Lenin had, that the revolution was overwhelmed by bureaucratic structures and habits left over from the old regime.

Yet these advantages were greatly outweighed by China's extreme economic backwardness, which had inflicted on the Chinese people a whole century of deepening impoverishment. By the early 20th century China was known to the world as "the land of famine" and "the sick man of Asia," a backward country even by contemporary Asian standards. China's modern industrial sector was tiny, mostly concentrated in the foreign-dominated treaty ports and Japanese-controlled Manchuria. China's total industrial capacity at its peak (in 1936–7) was less than $\frac{1}{8}$ that of backward Russia's in 1917 and about $\frac{1}{50}$ (on a per capita measurement) of the advanced industrialized countries. Moreover, a good part of this meager industrial sector had been destroyed by a decade of war and civil war (1937–48). And that was compounded by the post-war Soviet looting of as much of the Manchurian industrial plant as the Russian Army could cart away. Industrial production in 1949 was barely half of what it had been in 1936–7. The politically victorious Chinese Communists inherited not only one of the world's most backward economies, but one that lay in ruins. Progress in the Mao era must be measured from this miserable starting point.

The first precondition for economic revival and development was the political unification of China. For more than a century traditional structures of central authority had been disintegrating under the weight of bureaucratic corruption, foreign aggression, civil war, peasant rebellion, the obscurantism of the old imperial regime, and warlordism. For lack of a viable central government, the Chinese people paid a terrible price at the hands of marauding warlord armies, the armed gangs of predatory landlords, foreign aggressors, rural bandits, and a vast criminal underworld in the cities.

It was perhaps Mao Zedong's greatest achievement that the revolution he led resulted in the unification of China under an effective central government. However harsh the rule of the new Communist state, the establishment of order and security brought enormous and immediate benefits to the great majority of the Chinese people. And the unification of China was the essential precondition for the modern economic revolution that has transformed China since the mid-20th century. In this sense, the year

1949 stands as a milestone in Chinese history comparable only to 221 BC, when the various feudal states of antiquity were united into an empire under the Qin dynasty. The imperial political system survived for two millennia, albeit with dynastic interruptions, and it was the foundation for the great accomplishments of traditional Chinese civilization.

The Maoist state was not simply the resurrection of the old imperial order. However politically sophisticated the traditional empire was, its bureaucratic apparatus was relatively superficial, its functioning dependent on the cooperation of local landed elites. The Communist state, by contrast, was a modern nation-state. It was far more powerful than its traditional counterpart, it penetrated society far more deeply, and its bureaucratic apparatus soon reached into even the most remote villages.

Mao Zedong's historical role as the unifier of China and the founder of a modern nation was lauded even by those who suffered under his rule. In 1980, as the then "paramount leader" Deng Xiaoping was constructing the post-Maoist order, he advised theoreticians who were drafting the official CCP critique of Mao to take into account the Chairman's merits as well as his failures. On one occasion, Deng observed that "it isn't only [Mao's] portrait which remains in Tiananmen Square; it is the memory of a man who guided us to victory and built a country."[1]

Three months before he stood atop the Gate of Heavenly Peace on October 1, 1949, to formally proclaim the establishment of the People's Republic, Mao Zedong described the new Communist state as a "people's democratic dictatorship." The essay in which this seeming oxymoronic term was elucidated is widely regarded as a seminal expression of the Maoist version of Marxism.[2] Seminal or not, the notion of a "people's democratic dictatorship" was less a creative contribution to Marxist theory than a reflection of the ambiguities and contradictions that mark its Maoist variant. The ambiguities are especially striking in Mao Zedong's treatment of the relationship between social class and political party.

The new government, according to Mao, was to rest on a coalition of the four progressive (or "democratic") classes that theoretically constituted the united front of the Yan'an era – the proletariat, the peasantry, the petty bourgeoisie, and the national bourgeoisie. However, this coalition of social classes would be under "the leadership of the Communist Party," Mao was quick to emphasize.[3] But "proletarian hegemony," he implied, can exist quite apart from the actual proletariat, although this heresy was rarely explicitly acknowledged in Mao's writings. After all, China's small proletariat had been a politically inactive class for more than two decades before the peasant soldiers of the PLA marched into the cities in 1949. Thus it is hardly surprising that at the time of the founding of the People's Republic, even with most of the cities under Communist control, less than 5 percent of the 4,500,000 members of the CCP were classified as members of the proletariat – and the great majority of these had been recently recruited in the months after the cities fell to the PLA.

Mao Zedong did not feel any urgent need to substantially increase the number of actual proletarians in China's proletarian party. The percentage of CCP members classified as workers grew only gradually in the years that followed, even as China was experiencing rapid industrialization and the urban working class was growing. In 1957, at the conclusion of the First Five-Year Plan, less than 13 percent of CCP members were workers, who were outnumbered by intellectuals. The overwhelming majority of Party members in the post-revolutionary period, just as during the revolution itself, were peasants.

Who, then, according to Mao, was the revolutionary class that would exercise "proletarian hegemony"? Clearly not the proletariat itself, a class which had waited passively in the cities to be liberated by an army composed of peasants. Nor was it the peasantry, the class that had actually carried out the revolution. However much Mao praised the revolutionary qualities of the peasants, at no time did he regard the peasants as a class, the bearer of "proletarian consciousness." That left only the Chinese Communist Party – as an institution above and beyond all social classes – as the vital revolutionary force that would guarantee China's transition through the "bourgeois" stage to its eventual socialist and communist destination.

In substituting a party for a class, Mao Zedong appeared a super-Leninist. It was Lenin, after all, who had argued that proletarian consciousness was an attribute of revolutionary intellectuals, the Marxian elite of professional revolutionaries who were to impose that superior political consciousness on the spontaneous movement of the masses. But however great the historical initiative Lenin assigned to the revolutionary intelligentsia, he took it for granted that the urban working class would constitute the mass base of the vanguard party. For Mao Zedong, by contrast, it was only necessary for the Communist Party to be guided by "proletarian consciousness," irrespective of the Party's actual social composition, to carry out its revolutionary mission.

Maoism thus marks a further deterioration of the organic relationship between party and class that is assumed in original Marxist theory. Not only did Mao separate "proletarian consciousness" from the actual proletariat, he failed to attribute it to any other social class or group. The question of where true consciousness resides thus became a most ambiguous matter in Maoist theory and practice. It was a question that loomed ever larger in the post-revolutionary years as Mao came to doubt the revolutionary sufficiency of the Communist Party itself, a suspicion that was to have turbulent and eventually cataclysmic political consequences.

Beyond the ambiguities surrounding Mao Zedong's claim to "proletarian hegemony," the notion of a "people's democratic dictatorship" was deceptive in several other respects. The "people" (broadly defined as the four classes who constitute the coalition) were to enjoy such democratic rights as freedom of speech, assembly, and association, according to Mao, while dictatorial measures were to be directed only against the reactionary classes. But nowhere does Mao mention the institutions through which "the people" might exercise their democratic rights. On the other hand, the dictatorial functions of the new state were made abundantly clear: "The state apparatus, including the army, the police and the courts, is an instrument by which one class oppresses another. It is an instrument for the oppression of antagonistic classes; it is violence and not 'benevolence.'"[4]

It is a Marxist axiom that "classes decide and not parties," as Trotsky once put it. But in China it was clearly the case that the crucial decisions were made by the Communist Party, not the classes that the Party claimed to represent. More precisely, power was lodged in a small group of CCP leaders, and to an extraordinary degree concentrated in the hands of one man. Mao Zedong had emerged from the long revolution with unchallenged control of the Communist Party and the PLA – and with enormous personal popularity as the leader of the anti-Japanese resistance, the unifier of the Chinese nation, and the liberator of the peasants. In a land where political and military power towered over society and its classes, it was inevitable that Mao would become the dictator of China. The personal concentration of power was symbolized by Mao's assumption of the chairmanship of the new government of the People's Republic while retaining the chairmanship of the Party. It was the Party that created and controlled the new civilian administrative apparatus, much as it traditionally had controlled the army. At the birth of the People's Republic, Mao Zedong dominated all three institutions – party, army, and government. And his power was augmented by the enormous popular prestige he enjoyed as the liberator of the Chinese nation. The acclaim nourished the still growing cult of Mao Zedong, which in turn further enhanced his power – and the mystique that surrounded his name and person. Rarely in history has so much power and prestige resided in a single person.

Yet the revolutionary success was not simply a political triumph for Mao. It was the victory of a leader who had identified himself with the oppressed classes of Chinese society, especially the peasantry, and who had derived his power from them. However much Mao craved personal power and popular adulation (and he certainly enjoyed both in abundant measure), he remained committed to the social and economic liberation of the peasantry – and to the destruction of the classes that had been privileged under the old regime. The monopolization of political power by Mao and the CCP was the most visible result of the Communist victory of 1949, but the political triumph also signaled a radical transformation of social relationships.

Yet, for the most part, Mao Zedong's policies during the early years of the new regime were ones that would have been pursued by any strong nationalist leader, Communist or not, in similar historical circumstances. Foremost among Mao's goals were the eminently nationalist demands for the unification of China under a strong central government and its independence from foreign impingements. In a land where traditional forms of authority had been disintegrating for over a century, political centralization was a universal demand. For lack of a viable central government, the Chinese people had paid a terrible price at the hands of warlord armies, corrupt bureaucrats, rapacious landlords, bandits in the countryside, and a vast criminal underworld in the cities. The Communist unification of China, while hardly the harbinger of the democracy Mao had promised, at least for "the people," nonetheless was an enormous advance. For the first time in generations, the Chinese people enjoyed the dignity of genuine national independence, an effective government, and a reasonable degree of physical security.

While the Communists' unification of China was a momentous historical achievement, the land that Mao Zedong now ruled was among the most wretchedly backward on earth, its long suffering and half-famished 500,000,000 inhabitants now further impoverished by decades of foreign invasion and civil war. Bandits roamed much of the countryside, land reform had yet to be undertaken in most rural areas, urban commerce and industry had declined during the wartime years and suffered further from the flight of many members of the urban bourgeoisie and technological intelligentsia, and unemployment was rampant in both town and countryside.

It was China's desperate economic situation and the new government's isolation in a hostile international arena that impelled Mao Zedong to seek assistance from the Soviet Union. On December 6, 1949, barely two months after the proclamation of the People's Republic, and even as fighting against remnant GMD forces continued, Mao boarded a special train in Beijing, embarking on the ten-day journey to Moscow. It was to be his first (and only) meeting with Stalin and the first time the 55-year-old Mao traveled beyond the borders of China.

Mao and Stalin

It no doubt was with considerable apprehension that Mao Zedong prepared to negotiate with the Soviet dictator. Stalin had come to personify the mystique of Moscow as the center of world revolution. And Mao had duly made his own contribution to Stalin's "cult of personality," publicly praising Stalin as "the savior of all the oppressed." Yet the relations between Stalin and Mao had been fraught with tensions for nearly a quarter of a century. As early as the "Hunan Report," published in March 1927, Mao had been implicitly critical of Stalin's injunction to curb "the radical excesses" of the Chinese peasantry. There followed in the 1930s Mao's long struggle with the Stalinist "returned student faction." Mao eventually achieved full dominance over the CCP, but he did so in direct defiance of the Soviet dictator – and it won for Mao Stalin's enmity. Stalin's fear of a Communist state not under his control drove him to desperate and foolish interventions. On the eve of the Maoist victory in 1949, Stalin advised the Chinese Communists to halt at the Yangzi and divide China into two states, one Nationalist, and the other Communist. Mao ignored – but did not forget – the suggestion. Nor had he forgotten that Stalin had clung to the Chiang Kai-shek regime as long as possible. In April 1949, when the GMD capital Nanjing fell to the PLA, the Soviet ambassador was the only foreign envoy to follow the Nationalists to their temporary capital at Canton, a reflection of Stalin's stubborn belief that a Communist movement beyond his personal control could not (and should not) come to power.

However much he felt required to praise Stalin's "revolutionary genius" in public pronouncements, Mao owed little to the Soviet dictator's "advice." "The Chinese revolution," he later remarked, "won victory by acting contrary to Stalin's will. . . . If we had followed Wang Ming's, or in other words Stalin's methods, the Chinese revolution couldn't have succeeded."

But when the revolution did indeed succeed, Mao recalled, "Stalin said it was a fake. We did not argue."[5]

But despite their contentious relationship, Stalin and Mao were dependent on each other. With the Cold War intensifying in Europe, Stalin had to ensure that the Soviet Union's long eastern border with China was secure. And China desperately required foreign military and economic assistance. Long before the Cold War precluded other sources of aid, Mao concluded that the Soviet Union was the most likely source of assistance – and the most desirable. A Communist China, he had decided well before the revolutionary victory, would necessarily "lean to one side." American support for the Guomindang during the civil war fortified Mao's determination to "lean" to the side of the Soviet Union.

But Mao, having resisted Stalin's efforts to control the CCP for over two decades, had no intention of now subordinating China to the Soviet Union. In this he defied not only Stalin but many Western observers who were convinced that Mao's China was part of a monolithic Communist world controlled by Moscow. The negotiations in the Soviet capital were difficult and prolonged, and often on the verge of collapse. "In 1950 I argued with Stalin in Moscow for two months," Mao later recalled.[6] Stalin drove hard bargains but Mao was alternately patient, stubborn, and angry. He remained in Moscow far longer than he had planned, for nine frustrating weeks before an agreement of sorts was hammered out. When Mao returned to Beijing in late February 1950, he could claim only a partial success. He did win a Soviet pledge of military assistance if China were attacked by Japan, or, by implication, the United States. In return Mao was forced to swallow his nationalist pride by acknowledging that Mongolia was a *de facto* Soviet satellite and also acquiescing in the continuing Russian occupation of Dairen and Port Arthur in Manchuria. In a separate pact on economic aid, Stalin offered only paltry sums in the form of interest-bearing credits. But however meager in purely economic terms, the accord did provide the Chinese a significant degree of access to Soviet scientific and technological knowledge. It was to prove essential to the success of the Maoist drive for rapid industrialization, which was to be launched in 1953.

Mao Zedong's only encounter with Stalin left him with a deepened distrust of the Soviet dictator. In public pronouncements, Mao continued to hail Stalin as "the greatest genius of our age" and he promoted the slogans that were ubiquitous during the early years of the People's Republic: "Learn from the Soviet Union" and "Let's be modern and Soviet." But privately Mao was critical of Stalin, sometimes to a petty and egotistical extent. For example, in 1958 Mao commented:

> Buddhas are made several times life-size in order to frighten people. . . . Stalin was that kind of person. . . . When Chinese artists painted pictures of me together with Stalin [in the early 1950s], they always made me a little bit shorter, thus blindly knuckling under to [Soviet] pressure.[7]

But Mao also touched on more serious political and ideological differences with Stalin – and on Chinese resentments over Moscow's influence in the People's Republic. One political manifestation of the latter was the purge of Gao Gang, the chief CCP leader in Manchuria, shortly after the death of Stalin in 1953. Mao believed Gao Gang was Stalin's agent in China, promoting Soviet political and economic influence in a region that historically had been a focus of Russian expansionism. In December 1953, the CCP Politburo, at Mao's insistence, ordered the arrest of Gao for having set up an "independent kingdom" in Manchuria and for conspiring to seize state power. Gao Gang, it was said, conveniently responded to the accusations by committing suicide. Although Stalin was not mentioned at the time, the purge of Gao Gang was aimed at eliminating Soviet influence in Manchuria.

However much he distrusted Stalin, in the early 1950s Mao was still convinced that Stalinist Russia was "a great and splendid socialist state." And he believed that Stalin, for all his faults, had pioneered the way to modernize a backward land and build a socialist society at the same time. Thus Mao was eager to borrow Soviet economic methods and techniques of central planning, which were at the core of China's First Five-Year Plan for rapid industrialization, launched in 1953. Even before the adoption of the Soviet model of economic development, Mao had established the new Chinese state largely on the basis of Stalinist political methods. As in the Soviet Union, the Communist Party totally dominated society, controlling not only all important economic, bureaucratic, and civic organizations, but – through a system of political commissars – the Army as well. Party control was reinforced by an elaborate network of secret police organizations. Despite his frequent warnings that "China has suffered a great deal from the mechanical absorption of foreign materials," Mao apparently did not object to the importation of Soviet political and economic methods – or even architectural styles. He had, after all, hailed Stalinist Russia as the model for both modernization and socialism.

When Mao returned to China in late February 1950, after his contentious meeting with Stalin, he lived and worked in a traditional house in a corner of the old "Forbidden City," not far from the Gate of Heavenly Peace. It was there, in a compound which once housed high officials of the Qing dynasty, that Mao for the first time since the early 1920s settled into a reasonably conventional family life – at least during the times he was not touring the vast country. When he was in Beijing, on average six months of the year, he lived with his third wife, Jiang Qing (a one-time Shanghai actress whom he had married in Yan'an), their daughter Lin Na and a daughter from his second marriage, Li Min. The largest room in the compound (where he lived until his death) became Mao's study, where the walls were lined with the thousands of books he had collected since his student days.

Nearby Mao's compound were the homes and offices of China's most powerful Communist political and military leaders (among them Zhou Enlai, Deng Xiaoping, Liu Shaoqi, Peng Dehuai, and all the members of the Party Politburo). Zhongnanhai, as this secluded and garden-like corner of the old imperial palace grounds was known, became the home and workplace for the most prominent members of a remarkable generation of revolutionaries, who were now transforming themselves into the rulers of the world's most populous land.

In the early 1950s China's Communist leaders stood united. While important decisions were ultimately made by Mao, he was careful at first to seek the advice and opinions of his colleagues. The first task, all agreed, was to establish firm Communist political and military control over the huge country, the essential prerequisite both for political survival and the reconstruction of a backward and war-wracked economy. Thus when Mao returned from Moscow in the late winter of 1950, he first turned his attention to building a viable state apparatus and training able cadres to carry out essential administrative functions. The task was daunting, and it had to be performed under conditions of extreme economic backwardness and in a vast land with only a primitive (and half-ruined) system of transportation and communication.

By the late spring of 1950 Mao Zedong was sufficiently satisfied with the progress made in consolidating Communist political power to prepare to embark on two perilous ventures. One was the nation-wide land reform campaign, scheduled to begin in June. The other was the invasion of Taiwan, where Chiang Kai-shek and the Nationalist Army had fled and where it was widely assumed that the final battle of China's civil war would be fought. That battle was to be delayed – and for far longer than anyone could have expected in 1950 – by the outbreak of war in Korea.

The Korean War

A tangled web of provocations and intrigues – woven by the regimes in North and South Korea, Washington, and Moscow – still obscure the origins of the Korean War. But it is clear that the North Korean dictator Kim Il Sung, encouraged by a wily Stalin (who took care not to commit Soviet military forces but hoped that China would be forced to become involved), launched a full-scale invasion to unify the Korean peninsula on June 25, 1950. Mao Zedong, although he sympathized with the North Koreans, not least because many Korean Communists had fought alongside the PLA in Manchuria against the Japanese and the Guomindang, did nothing to encourage the adventure. In fact, Mao apparently was not informed that the North Koreans planned to move in force against South Korea, an American military protectorate, until the very eve of the invasion. Mao hardly would have encouraged a war that portended grave dangers for China at a time when he was still striving to consolidate the new Communist state, when unemployment in the cities was rampant and bandits still roamed the countryside, when he had recently ordered the demobilization of much of the PLA, and when the best PLA units were being deployed on the southern coast for an invasion of Taiwan, apparently planned for that summer. It was not until massive American military intervention had driven the North Koreans back across the 38th parallel and General MacArthur's "march to the Yalu" directly threatened Chinese borders that Mao made the final decision to intervene.

PLA troops, officially known as the "Chinese People's Volunteers," began filtering into the northern part of Korea in October 1950. And then in late November, as MacArthur's troops rushed headlong to the Yalu, falling prey to Mao's old revolutionary war tactic of "luring the enemy deep," the PLA entered Korea *en masse*, inflicting on MacArthur's overextended forces one of the most humiliating defeats in US military history. Within two months, by January 1951, American forces had retreated from virtually all of Korea, and much of the south as well. For the next two years, Chinese and American armies fought a bloody war of attrition largely along the original boundary between North and South Korea.

It was a costly war for both sides, but particularly for the Chinese, who lacked an airforce and heavy artillery: 150,000 Chinese soldiers were killed in Korea and twice that number seriously wounded. Among the dead was Mao Anying, Mao Zedong's eldest son by his first wife Yang Kaihui, killed in a US bombing raid in late November 1950.

The war placed a heavy burden on the fragile Chinese economy, which had only just begun to recover from a decade of invasion and civil war. Although the Chinese received economic and military aid from the Soviet Union, it was considerably less than had been promised, and excluded air cover. The paucity of Russian assistance became yet another irritant in the relations between Mao and Stalin.

The Korean War also delayed the conclusion of the Chinese civil war. The outbreak of hostilities in Korea in June 1950 was the pretext for President Truman's order "neutralizing" the Taiwan Straits, thereby making Taiwan a *de facto* American military protectorate and prolonging the life of the rump Nationalist regime. The American intervention raised the threat of renewed civil war, with Chiang Kai-shek now enjoying active US military backing. Thus, less than a year after it was established, the People's Republic was threatened by that deadly combination of civil war and foreign invasion that had crushed so many revolutions. That threat, in turn, made the suppression of internal political opposition to the Communist regime ever harsher. In February 1951 Mao issued a draconian decree on "Regulations Regarding the Punishment of Counterrevolutionaries" that greatly intensified the repression of real or imagined opponents of the new regime. A period of terror took some 2,000,000 lives during the land reform and other mass campaigns that solidified Communist rule in the early 1950s. The term "counter-revolutionary" was broadly defined, and there were countless public executions.

While the economic and human costs of the Korean War were heavy, it yielded unanticipated political benefits for Mao Zedong. The threat of yet another foreign invasion of China, after a century of foreign aggression, rallied popular nationalist support behind Mao and the new Communist government. And perhaps more importantly, the early Chinese military victories – and the ability of Chinese soldiers (so long objects of ridicule in Western accounts) to fight the world's most powerful army to a stalemate – stimulated enormous nationalist pride that transcended conventional political boundaries. The Korean War, costly as it was in human life and economic resources, greatly fortified and expanded Mao Zedong's already powerful nationalist credentials and thus his personal political power.

Land reform

The nation-wide land reform campaign was launched in June 1950, on the eve of the Korean War, and ended just as the *de facto* Sino-American war was giving way to an uneasy truce roughly along the 38th parallel, where the hostilities had begun. Although the two events were more or less contemporaneous, they were essentially unrelated – save that the fears generated by the Korean War lent a harsher political cast to land reform than would have been generated by the campaign itself. As far as China was concerned, the Korean War was a fortuitous event, largely determined by secret decisions made in foreign capitals – Pyongyang, Seoul, Moscow, and Washington. The land reform movement, on the other hand, was a long-planned campaign that grew out of the social logic of the Chinese Communist Revolution. Its main aim was to destroy the gentry-landlord class, the ruling elite of Chinese society for two millennia, by confiscating their landholdings and distributing them among the poorer peasants.

Agrarian reform, in one fashion or another, had been undertaken in rural areas where the Communists had achieved military dominance since the Jiangxi days. During the anti-Japanese War of Resistance (1937–45) Mao greatly moderated land-reform laws in order to build the broadest possible united front, which was to include patriotic landlords. With the defeat of Japan and the resumption of the CCP-GMD civil war, Communist land policy turned radical in the northern base areas, as free rein was given to young peasant activists who had scores to settle with landlords and their "local bullies." The resulting violence was deemed excessive, not least because it disrupted agricultural production. Many cadres were accused of "indiscriminate killings" and their methods were denounced as "leftist deviations." Land reform was largely halted as more moderate guidelines were drawn up. When the campaign resumed in mid-1950 it was in accordance with Mao Zedong's long-standing insistence on safeguarding the economically efficient farms of middle and rich peasants so as to preserve the viability of the rural economy. While considerable violence was inherent in the very nature of land reform, exacerbated by the counter-revolutionary fears generated by the Korean War, on the whole the greatest agrarian revolution in world history was completed by the beginning of 1953 without major disruptions of China's vast and precariously balanced agricultural economy. Indeed, agricultural production increased substantially in the early 1950s – although the gains had less to do with agrarian social reform than with the restoration of political order, and the revival of trade and transport, after a decade of foreign invasion and civil war.

Mao intended the land reform campaign to serve a variety of political and economic purposes, but its main aim was to destroy the landlord class, the parasitic survival of the landed gentry elite that had dominated

Chinese society since the 3rd century BC. The landlord class was economically dispensable and socially undesirable. Chinese landlords collected rents and profited from usury but rarely engaged in productive
activities or even the organization of agricultural production. As the
anthropologist Fei Xiaotong summed up the matter: "The landlord cannot
find a way to eliminate the tenant and get income directly from the land
but the tenant can cultivate the land without the assistance of the
landlord."[8]

The distinction between productive and non-productive activities
loomed large in Mao Zedong's social and political thought, coinciding in
this respect with the Marxian view on the relative progressiveness of capitalism. Thus, the Agrarian Law prohibited the confiscation of land and
equipment used by landlords for the operation of private industrial and
commercial enterprises. But rather few Chinese landlords had turned to
capitalist-type production, and even fewer escaped the fury of the land
reform campaign by invoking Mao's distinction between productive and
unproductive economic activities. Once the agrarian movement was
launched by local Communist cadres, angry peasants seeking both land
and revenge made few distinctions between landlords who engaged in
quasi-capitalist activities and those who relied entirely on pre-capitalist
modes of rentier exploitation. Many landlords (and many more members
of their armed gangs) were executed in the violence and summary trials
that came as the land reform movement swept the countryside. Others
were dispatched to labor camps. But the great majority of the approximately 20,000,000 people classified as members of landlord families, most
of their holdings confiscated and distributed among poor peasant families,
were reduced to cultivators of small plots of soil – although they retained
the label "landlord," now an inheritable social and political stigma. China's
long-declining landed gentry, the longest-lived ruling class in world
history, had ceased to exist as a social class with the conclusion of the
Maoist land reform campaign in early 1953.

Land reform was propelled by powerful political as well as socio-
economic considerations. The Communists had won the overwhelming
support of poor peasants (about 70 percent of the rural population) by
promising "land to the tiller." That promise had to be honored if the Party
was to retain the support of the peasants.

Another political aim of land reform was to establish direct
Communist power within the villages. The traditional imperial state, as
its Guomindang successors, had ruled over the villages rather than within
them, relying on landlord-selected "village elders" to maintain order,

collect taxes, and exercise most judicial functions. The traditional bureaucratic apparatus was sophisticated but rather superficial in the rural areas. The Communist government was the first in Chinese history to establish central control of the natural village. This came about largely through the land reform campaign when young local, Maoist-inspired activists destroyed traditional village social and political relationships. These young cadres became the new leaders in the villages, and tied as they were to a pervasive Leninist party organization, they became the *de facto* representatives of the central Party-State in the villages. That penetration of central state power into virtually all the villages was the essential precondition for what was ultimately the most important result of the land reform movement – the industrialization of China.

The intimate relationship between land reform and industrialization was recognized by Mao Zedong at the outset, well before it became part of conventional academic wisdom. In June 1950, when the Agrarian Reform Law was formally promulgated, Mao hailed it not only as an "opportunity for emancipation" but also as "the basic condition for industrialization." "The peasants form the bulk of China's population," he continued. "It was with their help that victory was won in the revolution, and it is again their help that will make the industrialization of the country possible."[9] Mao Zedong was well aware, although he failed to candidly say, that the industrialization of China necessarily would involve the exploitation of the very peasants who had made the revolution and put him in power. He also knew that the land reform campaign, by firmly establishing Communist power within the villages, would enable the state to extract the agrarian surplus to finance industrialization.

Land reform brought a degree of social and economic equity to the villages and improved the life of the majority of peasants. But it did not result in a total social leveling. To be sure, large-scale landlordism was eliminated. Members of the landlord-gentry class who physically survived found their traditional political influence and social prestige shattered and their landholdings reduced to what they and their families could cultivate on their own, generally about 90 percent of the village norm. But significant economic distinctions – between poor, middle, and rich peasants – remained. "Rich peasants" who generally owned twice as much land as they could cultivate on their own – and who therefore hired laborers or leased land to tenants – were largely untouched by the land reform campaign.

The survival of middle and rich peasants reflected the relatively moderate character of Mao Zedong's agrarian policies (at least after the very early years in Jiangxi), which in the revolutionary years had brought forth accusations that he pursued a "rich peasant line." But Mao's concern was to maintain agricultural production in a society which lived on the bare margins of subsistence – and to subordinate egalitarian social policies to that overriding imperative. The farms of the middle and rich peasants were left largely intact because they constituted the most productive sector of the rural economy.

The destruction of the gentry-landlords as a class was the culmination of a great social revolution. But it was not a socialist revolution. Land reform was an eminently bourgeois revolutionary act, one which established conditions favorable for the development of rural capitalism. The immediate social result of the land reform movement was a system of individual family proprietorship, with peasant families issued official title deeds to their land and legally free to buy, sell, rent, and mortgage their properties. Moreover, significant semi-class socio-economic differences remained among the rural population.

Mao Zedong foresaw the essentially capitalist outcome of the land reform campaign, describing land reform as an "anti-feudal" measure, not a socialist one. He assumed, in accordance with the orthodox Marxian scheme of history, that an anti-feudal revolution would yield a capitalist-type economy. Moreover, his theory of "New Democracy" anticipated a lengthy period when significant sectors of the Chinese economy would operate on a capitalist basis. The bourgeois outcome of land reform was thus not inconsistent with Maoist theory. But it soon was to clash with Mao Zedong's impatience with the pace of history.

Land reform was one of the great accomplishments of the Maoist revolution, standing alongside (but dependent upon) national unification and national independence. The reform did not solve the economic and technological problems which had so long afflicted Chinese agriculture and impoverished the great majority of Chinese farmers. But it did alleviate some of the worst abuses that landlords, "local bullies," moneylenders, and corrupt officials had inflicted on peasants. It was an essential step in creating a viable agricultural economy that could provide an adequate supply of food for China's enormous population. At the same time, land reform was crucial for the industrialization of China. By tying the villages to a national political structure, the land reform campaign provided the essential mechanism for the state to extract a growing surplus from the countryside to finance its program for rapid industrialization, rather than to permit the surplus to be squandered by landlords and bureaucrats in traditional parasitic fashion.

Mao Zedong was primarily responsible for planning and implementing the nation-wide land reform campaign. Although land reform came to involve far more violence than he anticipated – once the pent-up anger of the peasants against their oppressors was released and encouraged – on the whole Mao was remarkably successful in keeping a balance between peasant social radicalism and the need to maintain production in carrying out the most crucial socio-economic movement of the post-revolutionary era.

It is one of the ironies of modern Chinese history that Mao Zedong, the leader of a party that aimed to abolish private property, presided over a bourgeois agrarian revolution whose social result was the establishment of a petty capitalist system of individual peasant proprietorship. It was an incongruity that resulted from the abortiveness of bourgeois revolutionary movements in modern Chinese history, most notably the failure of the Guomindang to deal seriously with China's rural problems and the plight of the peasantry. As it was, it fell to Mao to carry out what China's weak bourgeois movements had failed to accomplish.

Mao Zedong was well aware of the capitalist nature and limitations of land reform. As he later observed:

> To divide up the land and give it to the peasants is to transform the property of the feudal landlords into the individual property of the peasants, and this still remains within the limits of the bourgeois revolution. To divide up the land is nothing remarkable – MacArthur did it in Japan. Napoleon divided up the land too. Land reform cannot abolish capitalism, nor can it lead to socialism.[10]

Industrialization

In January 1953, as the land reform campaign was drawing to a close, the Maoist government announced China's First Five-Year Plan for industrial development. The inauguration of the industrialization drive was in accord with the slogan Mao had set forth in 1949: "Three Years of Recovery, Ten Years of Development." By 1952 Chinese industrial and agricultural production had in fact recovered, restored approximately to the levels of 1936–7, the highest of the pre-war years.

In the early 1950s Mao looked to the Soviet Union to learn how a socialist state could industrialize a backward land. Like its Soviet precursor of 1928–32, the overwhelming emphasis of China's First Five-Year Plan was on heavy industry – to the neglect of light and consumer goods industries.

The plan relied on the wholesale borrowing of Soviet methods, techniques, personnel, and highly centralized means of control. Yet the task was far more formidable in China than it was in Russia. In 1952 the Chinese industrial base was less than half the size of its tsarist Russian counterpart while China's population was four-fold that of Russia. Moreover, China's levels of literacy, scientific and technological knowledge, and transportation were far lower than those of tsarist Russia. Per capita agricultural output in China in 1952 was only about 20 percent of what it had been in the Soviet Union at the time Stalin launched the First Five-Year Plan in 1928, thus severely limiting what could be extracted from the rural sector to finance urban industrialization. Industrial pro-gress in the Maoist era must therefore be measured from this low starting point.

In light of Mao Zedong's many warnings against "the mechanical absorption of foreign material," it seems surprising that the Chinese should have embraced the Soviet model of economic development in so wholesale and uncritical a fashion – and that Mao should have taken the lead in doing so. Yet there was nowhere else to turn. During the Cold War years, no other industrialized nation was willing to provide significant economic or technological assistance to China. Mao Zedong believed that Soviet aid and advice were more desirable in any event. However contentious relations with Stalin had been over the years, Mao did not yet question the efficacy of the Stalinist strategy of development. In the early 1950s the Soviet Union was "the land of socialism," as Mao often said, and the economic model for China to emulate.

Although actual Russian economic aid proved far more limited than had been expected – making up only 3 percent of investment in the First Five-Year Plan – access to Soviet technology and methods of central planning were essential if the plan was to be successful. Between 1953 and 1957 Chinese industry grew at an annual rate of 18 percent, according to official statistics – or 16 percent, according to the calculations of most foreign economists. In any case China's industrial output more than doubled over the five-year period. Particularly impressive gains were made in such basic industries as steel, pig iron, and electric power. By 1957 China was producing small but significant numbers of trucks, tractors, jet planes, and merchant ships. The industrial working class had increased from 6,000,000 to 10,000,000 while the urban population grew from 70,000,000 to 100,000,000 over the five-year period.

Mao Zedong was soon to rebel against the political and social consequences of Soviet-style industrialization – although to rather little effect.

However undesirable the social effects, he was unwilling to abandon (or even seriously modify) "the heavy industrial push," which continued unabated throughout the political turbulence of the Maoist era. The First Five-Year Plan initiated a massive epoch of rapid industrialization and urbanization – though with particularly heavy human and environmental costs. Such costs throughout the world have been primarily borne by the poor. In China the agrarian surplus was extracted from an impoverished peasantry, a process of exploitation that was to be facilitated by the establishment of collective farms in 1956. The only justification for exploiting the poor, as Barrington Moore has written, is that without industrialization they would steadily become worse off.[11]

The stages of development

For Mao Zedong industrialization was the key for achieving his two most cherished visions: first, he sought the nationalist goal of making China "wealthy" and "powerful" in a hostile world dominated by highly industrialized countries; second, he sought to make China socialist, which, Marxist theory taught, presupposed a developed industrial economy. For Mao the two goals were inseparable. Socialism, as he had derived the concept from the May Fourth intellectual tradition, was the highest expression of Western modernity – but China was not destined to mechanically repeat the Western stages of development to achieve socialism. By virtue of its backwardness, Mao believed, China had accumulated the creative energies to "leap" to the very forefront of world civilization, avoiding the worst agonies of capitalist development. Indeed, it was China's national mission to achieve modern industrialism and modern socialism simultaneously – and to be the pioneer nation in doing so. As early as 1930 Mao predicted that "the revolution will certainly move towards an upsurge more quickly in China than in Western Europe."[12]

The implications of this messianic nationalist strain in Mao's thought did not fully reveal themselves until 1958, when Mao launched the ill-fated Great Leap Forward campaign. In the early 1950s the more utopian impulses in his revolutionary mentality were restrained by orthodox Marxian considerations. Marxism taught, as Mao well knew (but was reluctant to acknowledge), that socialism could be built only on the economic and social foundations of capitalism, only on the basis of a mature industrial economy. Marx had warned of the dangers of historically premature attempts to establish socialism, in situations where capitalist industrialization was not sufficiently developed to make possible the permanent abolition of private property. Such premature socialist revolutions would bring only a crude social leveling, which in turn would soon result in more extreme social inequalities and ever harsher forms of political despotism.

That Mao was aware of Marx's warnings about forcing the pace of history – albeit indirectly aware through secondary Soviet Marxist-Leninist literature – is suggested in his own frequent admonitions against the perils of "absolute egalitarianism." And his messianic impulses were further restrained by continuous Stalinist exhortations against the dangers of "skipping over" the necessary stages of historical development, presumably a Trotskyist heresy.

Yet Mao was more than a little ambiguous on the Marxian-defined "stages of history" and the material preconditions for socialism. On the one hand, he appeared to recognize that a socialist reordering of society presupposed a significant degree of industrial development. He predicted that it would take three five-year plans to achieve a minimal industrial base for socialism and half a century for China "to build a powerful country with a high degree of socialist industrialization."[13] But Mao's impatience with history did not allow him to sit back and wait until the industrial foundations for socialism were laid. His voluntarist faith that the will and energy of dedicated people formed the decisive factor in socio-historical progress made him believe that both socialism and its material prerequisites could be constructed simultaneously. Thus on October 1, 1953, on the fourth anniversary of the founding of the People's Republic, Mao announced that China was embarking on "the transition to socialism."

In the mid-1950s, socialism for Mao essentially meant state ownership or control of productive property, as it did in the Soviet Union. In the cities, what remained of privately owned industrial and commercial enterprises were *de facto* nationalized between 1953 and 1956. In the countryside, "the transition to socialism" at first meant the promotion of cooperative forms of work organization, the first step on what was then conceived to be a gradual and voluntary movement to collectivized agriculture.

But an impatient Mao Zedong became increasingly critical of the social and economic results of China's "socialist transition," especially in the rural areas. Not only was the agricultural sector failing to generate a sufficient surplus to meet the financial needs of urban industrialization, but the countryside after land reform was rapidly generating new inequalities. In mid-1955 Mao charged:

> As is clear to everyone, the spontaneous forces of capitalism have been steadily growing in the countryside in recent years, with new rich peasants springing up everywhere and many well-to-do middle peasants striving to become rich peasants. On the other hand, many poor peasants are still living in poverty for shortage of the means of production, with some getting into debt and others selling or renting out their land. If this tendency goes unchecked, it is inevitable that [class] polarization in the countryside will get worse day by day.[14]

Mao was not alone in his fears over the rapid growth of petty capitalism in the countryside. It was a concern shared by most Party leaders, who cautiously advised expanding the number of "semi-socialist" cooperative farms to include approximately one-third of China's 100,000,000 peasant households by the end of 1957. But for Mao the remedy favored by most Party leaders was woefully inadequate. He took matters into his own hands. On July 31, 1955, he bypassed formal Party channels and delivered a speech on agricultural collectivization to an informal gathering of regional leaders.[15] He demanded a more rapid pace of bringing peasants into cooperative farms (where private landownership was retained) and then into collective farming (where private property was abolished and peasants were remunerated according to work).

But it was not only the pace of radical agrarian change that was at issue. For Mao now implicitly raised the question of the relationship between the Communist Party and its supreme leader. He did so by attributing to the peasantry a spontaneous desire for radical social change, by presenting himself as the spokesman for the peasants, and by contrasting the radicalism of the peasantry (and their leader) with the conservatism of the Communist Party. He began his speech by declaring that while peasants were striving for socialism, Party members were "tottering along like a woman with bound feet," complaining that others are going too fast. "Yet as things stand now, it is the mass movement which is running ahead, while the leadership cannot keep pace with it."[16] Party officials who complained that the movement for establishing cooperative farms had "gone beyond the level of political consciousness of the masses" merely revealed their lack of faith in the peasantry.[17] It was the pessimism and inertia of Party leaders that was the real problem.

By so starkly contrasting the spontaneous radicalism of the peasantry with the bureaucratic conservatism of the Party, Mao Zedong placed himself above the Party and its rules. He could now presume to speak *to* the Party (as well as for it) as the acknowledged leader of the peasants. The tension between the institution of the Leninist Party and the leader of the Party, long in the making, was now evident.

Mao Zedong's speech of July 31, 1955, not only had enormous political implications, it also set off a massive and frenetic social movement that resulted in the virtually complete collectivization of the vast Chinese countryside within little more than a year. Poor peasants, still the majority of the rural population, demanded a general social leveling. Encouraged by Maoist-inspired local rural cadres, they rapidly amalgamated private farms into "agricultural producer cooperatives" – and then even more rapidly merged the latter into collective farms. Before the end of 1956 more than 100,000,000 peasant households, some 600,000,000 people in all, lived on collective farms where private property (save for small family plots) had been abolished and where peasants were paid (at least in theory) in accordance with the socialist principle of "to each according to one's work."

Mao initially believed that it would take a decade to collectivize the countryside. Now even he was astonished by the extraordinary speed, spontaneity and force of the movement that he had called into being. And he responded in a fashion that recalled the revolutionary imagery that had marked his celebration of peasant radicalism and spontaneity in the "Hunan Report" of 1927. He had then characterized the peasant movement as an elemental tornado-like force that would sweep away everything before it. Now, employing similar imagery, he described the collectivization movement as "a raging tidal wave" that had "swept away all demons and ghosts," attributing the success to his belief that the peasants were "filled with an immense enthusiasm for socialism." Just as in 1927 he had predicted that revolutionary peasants would wipe away all parties and intellectuals unwilling to join with them, so now he contrasted peasant radicalism with the conservatism of the Communist Party. It was a most unusual comparison for the leader of a Leninist party to make.

The success of the collectivization movement fortified Mao's belief in the radicalism of the peasantry, a class filled with "socialist revolutionary activism." At the same time, the swift success of the collectivization campaign reinforced his own conviction that he personally embodied the interests and hopes of the peasant masses. Mao's faith in the inherent socialism of the peasants – and his conviction that he alone was their true spokesman – were soon to find tragic expression in the adventure of the Great Leap Forward.

Leader and Party

The agricultural collectivization campaign of 1955–6 is one of the most striking examples in history of how, on rare occasions, the will of one man can generate a massive social movement. It was not of course the personal authority of Mao Zedong alone that brought about the collectivization of the Chinese countryside. It was the hundreds of millions of poor peasants who responded to Mao's socially radical appeals who brought about the radical transformation of rural China. Yet had Mao not delivered his July 1955 speech, it is most unlikely that the peasants would have acted on their own. They did so only under the guidance of a deified Mao Zedong, a reflection of the awesome concentration of power and prestige in the hands of a single individual.

The antagonism between Mao Zedong and the Communist Party – so starkly revealed in the collectivization movement – is also a dominant theme in that brief but crucial episode known as the "Hundred Flowers" (1956–7). The speech of July 1955 had left bitter resentments among many of Mao's colleagues. Mao, after all, had bypassed the Party's highest leaders and appealed directly to the peasants to launch a massive social movement, violating accepted Party procedures. Most Party leaders not only feared that the movement would end in economic catastrophe, but that the way it came about would undermine the Leninist foundations of the Communist Party and reinforce Mao Zedong's dictatorial tendencies. With the collectivization campaign already well under way, sullen Party leaders gathered in October to formally ratify the movement.

Political opposition to Mao and resentments over his highhanded actions remained, however, and Mao attempted to buttress his authority by turning to China's intellectuals for support. In a speech to the Politburo on agrarian policy (December 1955), Mao Zedong made an unusual and unexpected plea for intellectuals to play a more autonomous role in economic and political life. It was the beginning of the campaign that was to proceed under the slogan: "Let a hundred flowers bloom, let a hundred schools of thought contend."

In 1949 the Communists had come to power with the support, or at least the sympathy, of the majority of China's intellectuals. Intellectuals made up 15 percent of the membership of the Communist Party during the revolutionary years, a far greater percentage than that of urban workers, the class that the Party claimed to represent. Furthermore, intellectuals played a major and often heroic role in the revolutionary movement, particularly in the Communist underground in the

Guomindang-controlled cities. While the majority of intellectuals would have preferred their own democratic political organization, when ultimately faced with the stark choice between the Communists and the Nationalists, most chose the Communists as the lesser evil – and most were willing to cooperate with the new revolutionary regime.

Yet intellectuals did not fare well in the early years of the People's Republic. Their "class origins" made them suspect in a regime that had come to power on the basis of peasant support and had absorbed peasant suspicions of the cities and their inhabitants. Mao Zedong, although he had sprung from the urban intelligentsia, came to personify these anti-urban and anti-intellectual biases during the more than two decades he was immersed in the countryside. Thus, in the early 1950s, intellectuals were the main victims of the regime's determination to suppress dissent, subjected to constant "thought reform" and "ideological remolding" campaigns. The result was that many intellectuals who had greeted the new regime with great hope in 1949 became estranged and retreated to a state of passive compliance.

The disaffection of the intellectuals posed not so much a political threat to the regime as a danger to its economic plans. As industrial development proceeded, Communist leaders realized that continued progress required the intensive development of science and technology, and the expansion of education at all levels. Only the intelligentsia could provide these essential prerequisites for modern industrialization. Thus Party leaders made an unprecedented effort to win the support and cooperation of the intellectuals for the economic development of the nation. Mao Zedong's speech setting forth the "Hundred Flowers" slogan was among the first attempts to overcome the estrangement between the Communist regime and the intelligentsia. The following month, January 1956, Premier Zhou Enlai gave his address on "The Question of Intellectuals," which for the first time classified intellectuals as "part of the working class" engaged in socialist construction. The problem of the relation between the government and the intellectuals was not so much political or ideological, Zhou said, but rather technical; intellectuals were insufficient in numbers and scientific expertise, and suffered from a lack of adequate facilities and funding. As for political frictions between intellectuals and the state, these were primarily the fault of the Communist Party's "sectarianism" and "unreasonable" policies toward intellectuals. These deficiencies would be corrected, Zhou promised.

It is most unlikely that Zhou would have remarked on so sensitive a matter without Mao's approval. But these openings to what was to become known as the Hundred Flowers campaign were temporarily interrupted by Nikita Khrushchev's "secret" speech denouncing Stalin at the 20th Soviet Party Congress, delivered in Moscow on February 25, 1956.

China's Communist leaders may have been surprised by some of the more bizarre aspects of Stalin's personality and methods that Khrushchev revealed. But they were by no means wholly ignorant of Stalin's major crimes, even though they had chosen to remain silent about them. The problem for Mao and other CCP leaders was how to explain the extravagant praise they had lavished on the Soviet dictator over the years now that he had been officially revealed as a bloodthirsty tyrant. While Mao had been privately critical of Stalin, the public record was one that praised the Soviet leader as a great revolutionary genius and the pioneer builder of socialism.

The problem for CCP leaders was not simply personal embarrassment over years of panegyrics for a dictator who now stood condemned for his grisly record of crimes, which Khrushchev had so vividly, if selectively, described. Even more shocking was that Stalin's record posed grave moral and historical doubts about the Soviet "socialist" system that China was so zealously emulating.

Mao Zedong replied to Khrushchev's speech early in April, in a lengthy treatise ponderously entitled *On the Historical Experience of the Dictatorship of the Proletariat*. Mao agreed that Stalin had made "serious mistakes" in his later years. But he was critical of Khrushchev for blaming all the failures and evils on what Khrushchev termed "the wilfulness of one man" while attributing all Soviet achievements to the Party and to Leninism. Stalin, Mao insisted, was to be evaluated in the historical context of the international Communist movement, for his actions "bore the imprint of the times." Therefore Stalin was to be credited with the socialist achievements of the Soviet Union as well as held responsible for its defects. And since, in Mao's view, the achievements outweighed the defects, the historical picture Mao drew was generally favorable, although by no means uncritical. Among Stalin's accomplishments that Mao emphasized was the pursuit of industrialization and collectivization – precisely the policies that Mao was then pursuing in China.

The real dilemma that Khrushchev's speech presented for Mao – and one that was peculiar to Mao alone – was the issue of "the cult of personality." A major theme of the Soviet leader's speech, and his explanation for the crimes of Stalin, was the charge that Stalin had "placed himself above the [Communist] Party," and fostered a personality cult that had put him beyond criticism. Khrushchev's critique was directed against a now dead

Stalin, but for Chinese readers it seemed eerily pertinent to Mao Zedong, who was very much alive. Had not Mao "placed himself above the Party" when, only seven months before Khrushchev's revelations, Mao delivered his July 1955 speech launching the agricultural collectivization movement? And had he not been constructing a "cult of personality" for the better part of two decades?

Mao Zedong took up the delicate matter of the "personality cult" in his reply to Khrushchev's speech but his response was rather feeble and unconvincing. He repeated the standard Marxist argument that the cult of the individual was an expression of the "patriarchism" rooted in a "small-producer [i.e., peasant] economy." That it should manifest itself in a presumably socialist country, Mao wrote, was due to "poisonous ideological survivals of the old society" which "remain in people's minds for a long time." While it was natural for Stalin to be greatly honored for his contributions to socialism, it was unfortunate that he succumbed to backward ideological influences.

Mao's remarks implied that the problem of the "personality cult" was not a product of a socialist society but rather a hangover from the pre-revolutionary order. In any case, Mao was confident that the problem would not arise in China since the CCP, he claimed, "has incessantly fought against the elevation of oneself and against individual heroism." Moreover, the CCP continued to rely on the "mass line" and to maintain a tradition of modesty and prudence on the part of its leaders. Such were Mao's remedies for "the personality cult" – shortly before his own cult, already rather pervasive, was to burgeon in extravagant fashion.[18]

Chinese Communist Party leaders who feared Mao Zedong's growing power – and his violation of Leninist organizational norms – seized on Khrushchev's speech to curb Mao's increasingly arbitrary rule. These efforts came to a head at the Eighth CCP Congress which convened in September 1956, the first since 1945. The meeting was dominated by Liu Shaoqi and Deng Xiaoping, veteran leaders who were determined to prevent Mao from going beyond the Party's Leninist rules. They insisted on the principle of "collective leadership." To reinforce the point, they deleted from the Party constitution the phrase that the CCP was "guided by the Thought of Mao Zedong." Mao's power was further reduced when the Eighth Congress revived the post of General Secretary, which was occupied by Deng Xiaoping and permitted him to exercise considerable control over the Party organizational apparatus. Mao later was to complain, with considerable exaggeration, that his views were met with "indifference" by many Party leaders during 1956.

Yet Mao was doing more than complaining in 1956. After disposing of, or at least burying, the issues raised by Khrushchev's speech, Mao returned to the task of regaining the support of the intelligentsia, reviving the abortive campaign that he and Zhou Enlai had begun the previous winter. But while Zhou and other Party leaders were primarily interested in winning the cooperation of intellectuals for modern economic development, Mao also hoped to use the intelligentsia for political ends. By encouraging non-Party intellectuals to challenge the Communist Party from without, Mao believed he could shake up a Leninist apparatus that had grown stale, conservative, and rigidly bureaucratic – and create conditions which would allow him to more fully assert his personal ideological and political authority.

Mao resumed the Hundred Flowers campaign in May 1956, encouraging intellectuals and scientists to freely express and debate their ideas. Maoist ideologists sarcastically criticized Party cadres for their arrogance and ignorance, and castigated them for their heavy-handed suppression of the work of scientists and writers. Party officials resisted the new Maoist policy and intellectuals were suspicious. But by the summer of 1956 some intellectuals were emboldened to challenge CCP orthodoxies on art and literature that had been laid down during the Yan'an Rectification campaign, publish hitherto banned writings, and discuss long-suppressed democratic ideas. However, the first phase of "blooming and contending" was limited in scope and content. And Party leaders used the anti-Communist revolution in Hungary in November 1956, which had begun with intellectual dissent, as a pretext to end the Hundred Flowers movement entirely and punish the critics who had responded to Mao's invitation. The movement was once again revived, and on a far larger scale, as a result of Mao Zedong's remarkable speech "On the Correct Handling of Contradictions among the People," delivered in February 1957.[19]

Mao's speech began with the none-too-novel proposition that contradictions existed in a presumably socialist society and that certain of these contradictions could become antagonistic class contradictions between "the people" and their "enemies." Since Mao believed that contradictions were inherent in all phenomena from the time of his youthful encounters with philosophy, and had emphasized that notion in a Marxist idiom in his Yan'an writings, the restatement of the proposition could hardly have raised eyebrows. What was new – and politically explosive – was Mao's emphasis on the contradiction between the "leadership and the led" and his suggestion that on some issues Party leaders might be wrong and "the people" right. Only through open debate and the free struggle of ideas and ideologies, Mao said, was it possible to distinguish between correct and incorrect ideas – for "correct and good things have often at first been looked upon not as fragrant flowers but as poisonous weeds." Since it was entirely possible for the Party and its leaders to fall into error, it was important that they be subject to criticism from "the people" and "hear opinions different from [their] own," Mao emphasized. Intellectuals, as members of "the people," were thus invited to criticize the Communist Party and "exercise supervision" over it.[20]

Yet this seemingly democratizing invitation to "the people" to "criticize" Party officials and their policies had political implications that were far from democratic. If the people could now say what they believed, then how could their voices, and their collective voice, be heard in a vast land that lacked democratic institutions? If the people were free to speak, then who could possibly be their spokesman if not Mao Zedong himself? Mao, after all, was the leader of the people's revolution, the head of the people's government, and the Chairman of the Party that claimed to represent the interests of the great majority of the people. Moreover, Mao could assert special bonds to the masses that no other Communist leader could possibly claim. The political point and effect of Mao's speech on handling "contradictions among the people" was to free Mao from the Leninist discipline of the Party and enable him to criticize the Party from without, in his assumed role as the supreme spokesman for "the people."

Even more ominous for Party leaders was a second proposition advanced in that speech. While Mao agreed with official Party doctrine that class exploitation had been basically abolished in a now "socialist" China, he nevertheless maintained that "class struggle is not yet over." However, it was now no longer a class struggle between the proletariat and bourgeoisie as actual social classes, but rather a struggle between their respective ideologies, which had survived their original social class carriers. It was a struggle between ideas that would determine the future of China. As Mao declared: "the class struggle in the ideological field between the proletariat and the bourgeoisie will still be long and devious and at times may even become very acute. . . . the question whether socialism or capitalism will win is still not really settled."[21]

Mao Zedong's transmutation of class struggle into a struggle between class ideologies had grave political implications for his opponents within the Party, although most did not recognize the danger at the time. For if even the highest Party leaders were capable of error and thus subject to criticism from "the people" – and from Mao as the people's spokesman – then they were not immune to the infection of bourgeois ideas. And if class struggle was now more a matter of contention between class ideologies rather than actual social classes, then political and ideological conflicts within the Party could be seen as a "class struggle" between the "proletariat" and the "bourgeoisie." While this interpretation might have seemed fantastic at the time of the Hundred Flowers campaign, it was a prophetic pointer to the Cultural Revolution that Mao Zedong was to unleash within a decade.

"On the Correct Handling of Contradictions," although extraordinary in many respects, reflected many of the features that long had characterized the Maoist mentality. Among the persisting strains was the emphasis on the role of ideas in determining the course of history; a tendency to define class in terms of conscious political attitudes; and a belief in the value of struggle, particularly the need for ideological struggle to preserve the vitality of Marxism. "If correct ideas are pampered in hothouses and immunized against disease," Mao said, "they will not win out against erroneous ones." Alongside these familiar Maoist beliefs, one finds a sense of historical indeterminateness that was to become increasingly pronounced in the decade that followed. The question of "whether socialism or capitalism will win is still not really settled," Mao conceded.[22]

The aim of Mao's speech was to revive the Hundred Flowers movement, which had been suppressed by the Party apparatus in November 1956. But the reaction was not immediate. Party officials were resistant and intellectuals were fearful. But Mao persisted, encouraging intellectuals to voice their views and ordering Party organs not to interfere. Finally, a timid stream of criticism in March 1957 became a flood of bold critiques of Communist policies and methods during a remarkable six-week period in May and June. The critics ranged from scientists who pleaded for a realm of autonomy within their respective spheres of expertise to students and intellectuals who demanded true freedom of expression and launched fundamental attacks on China's one-party system. Mao Zedong was rarely criticized, but the officials of the Communist Party, high and low, were vehemently attacked for their repressive actions, their arrogance, and their incompetence. And the critiques were published in official newspapers (usually without official comment), on wall posters, in mimeographed pamphlets, and voiced at various organized and spontaneous meetings.

The "blooming and contending" of May and June was largely confined to intellectuals and students. Mao Zedong, despite his growing hostility to the intelligentsia, extended the Hundred Flowers appeal specifically to intellectuals; he did not invite "the masses" to participate. Few workers and peasants were to be found among the critics. The great majority of the people were either unaware of the movement or indifferent to it, although some intellectuals attempted to expose the hardships under which the peasants labored and to speak on their behalf.

Among the criticisms that poured forth in the spring of 1957, it is striking how many anticipated Mao Zedong's critique of post-revolutionary society. The critics charged that the Communists in power had abandoned their egalitarian revolutionary ideals and their tradition of "plain living and hard work" and were transforming themselves into a new ruling class increasingly separated from the common people. Once prized for sharing the hardships of the masses, Communist cadres now enjoyed (according to bureaucratic rank) a host of special material privileges – from servants, to "aristocratic" schools for their children. It was, of course, precisely this division between the "leadership and the led" that Mao had emphasized in his February speech.

Other eminently Maoist (or soon to be Maoist) themes appeared prominently during the period of "blooming and contending." Among them were critiques of the rapid growth of inequality in post-revolutionary China, especially the ever-widening gap between town and countryside and the chasm between relatively privileged workers and impoverished peasants. Other critics questioned the "socialist" credentials of the Soviet Union, and criticized China's "blind imitation" of Soviet methods. Mao Zedong was soon to express similar sentiments.

Yet Mao took the lead in suppressing the critics he had brought into being. An editorial in the *People's Daily* of June 8, undoubtedly published at Mao's direction, declared that "poisonous weeds" had sprung up among "the fragrant flowers." Right-wingers and counter-revolutionaries, it was charged, had abused the invitation to "bloom and contend" by attacking the Communist Party and "the socialist system." Official organs and forums, which for six weeks had been limited to reporting the criticisms of the Hundred Flowers intellectuals, now devoted themselves to denouncing the critics. Party officials turned on their critics and exacted retribution. Intellectuals who had accepted Mao's invitation to "bloom and contend" were forced to renounce their criticisms of the Party and to make abject public confessions. Some were sent to the countryside for "reform through labor." Many writers were expelled from their official positions and their works removed from library shelves. Fear and silence settled over the intellectual world and the universities.

Mao Zedong placed himself at the head of this heresy hunt, a massive purge that came to be called the "Anti-Rightist" movement. To justify the repression, Mao revised his speech of February 27, adding six criteria to distinguish between permissible and counter-revolutionary ideas in the official version published in mid-June. Mao Zedong's final twist of the screw was to turn the Communist Party's Anti-Rightist movement against the Party itself. In September 1957 Mao prevailed on the Central Committee to purge "rightists" within the Party. Over the next six months more than a million Party members (out of a total of about 13,000,000) had been expelled, reprimanded, or "sent down" to the countryside for reformation. In the witch-hunting atmosphere of the campaign, with Party officials fearful of being branded "rightists," Mao Zedong regained full control of the Party apparatus and sanction for the radical economic policies he was advocating. The stage was set for launching the Great Leap Forward.

Mao Zedong's betrayal of those he had urged to "bloom and contend" raises the question of why he inaugurated the Hundred Flowers campaign in the first place. Mao himself felt no need to explain why he began the movement or why he ended it, leaving only the official pronouncements of the time and the sometimes sketchy record of what actually happened. Yet there has been no lack of outside observers who have set forth explanations of why he began – and ended – the movement. A widely held view at the time is that it was a grand plot by a Machiavellian Mao Zedong to smoke out dissidents, to encourage intellectuals to freely express their opinions and then punish them for holding heterodox ideas. No doubt many of the victims of the Anti-Rightist campaign experienced their ordeals in this fashion. And the "smoking out" theory became the official explanation of a Communist Party attempting to rationalize a movement that was not under its organizational control. Liu Shaoqi, the most orthodox Leninist among CCP leaders, put it this way: "We allow the anti-socialist poisonous weeds to grow and confront the people with contrasts, so that . . . [the people] roused to indignation, rally together to uproot them."[23] But it is unlikely that Mao shared this need to maintain an image of Leninist infallibility. His attitude toward the Leninist party was ambivalent in many respects, and he set forth the Hundred Flowers policy as a personal initiative at the end of 1955, when he was engaged in struggle with most higher Party leaders over agrarian policy.

Some observers have suggested that the anti-Stalinist revolts in Eastern Europe crucially influenced the Hundred Flowers policy, most notably the Polish upheaval of October 1956 (which Mao supported on the basis of the principle of national independence from Moscow) and the Hungarian revolution of November (which Mao denounced as counter-revolutionary). While Mao mentions the anti-Soviet revolt in Hungary in the officially published version of *On the Correct Handling of Contradictions among the People*, citing the Hungarian events as one of the reasons for ending the Hundred Flowers campaign, the upheavals in Eastern Europe in 1956 obviously had little to do with the origins of the policy in late 1955.

A more plausible explanation for the rise and fall of the Hundred Flowers campaign might be sought in the enormous emphasis Mao placed on the value of struggle and the universality of contradictions. Correct ideas, Mao believed, emerge only in the struggle with incorrect ones, and in this dialectical process all ideas generate their opposites in an endless conflict that propels historical progress. It was with a faith in the value of ideological struggle that Mao encouraged intellectuals to criticize the Communist Party, for without being challenged Marxism and the revolutionary spirit would stagnate.

Yet at the same time as Mao extolled the value of struggle, he also believed that the great majority of intellectuals were part of a patriotic united front of "the people" whose contradictions among themselves, and with the Party, were basically "non-antagonistic." Such non-antagonistic contradictions could be resolved through peaceful ideological struggle and transformation – to the benefit of both the Party and the intelligentsia. Such was the optimistic premise on which the Hundred Flowers policy was based. But the candid and sometimes searing criticisms of the Communist system that were vehemently expressed in the spring of 1957 clashed with Mao's vision of a basically united people pursuing common socialist goals. For he interpreted critiques of the deficiencies of socialism in China as anti-socialist ideological assaults that went beyond the amorphous boundaries of "contradictions among the people." And when the era of "blooming and contending" seemed to bring threats of social disorder and ideological disunity, he did not hesitate to employ the repressive agencies of Party and state to end the movement and place himself at the head of the ensuing "Anti-Rightist" witch-hunt.

The suppression of the Hundred Flowers movement ensured that the Maoist pursuit of socialism would proceed without the right of the free expression of ideas and without popular democracy. These were among the fatal flaws in what observers would soon call "the Maoist vision."

6

Utopianism

At the beginning of 1958 Mao Zedong had every reason to feel triumphant. He had regained full control of the CCP the previous fall, in the course of the massive Anti-Rightist purge. The collectivization of agriculture, a movement launched on Mao's personal initiative, had been rapidly accomplished without plunging the country into either the violence or the economic chaos that had marked its Soviet counterpart of 1929–34. It had been characterized by the spontaneous peasant radicalism that Mao had prized so greatly since the mid-1920s. Moreover, Mao could claim (as most Party leaders also now did) that China had now completed "the transition to socialism" in the countryside as well as in the cities in a scant five years.

But for Mao, now 63 and increasingly impatient with the lethargic movement of history, the achievement of socialism (which was defined simply as the abolition of private ownership of productive property) was no time to pause to stabilize the new social system, a prescription for stagnation, he believed. As Mao warned in one of his many unpublished critiques of Stalin and Soviet theory: "We cannot go on consolidating [a new social system] for all time, or else we will make inflexible the ideology reflecting this system and make people incapable of adjusting their thoughts to new changes."[1] Rather it was necessary "to strike while the iron is hot" and ensure that "revolutions come one after another." "Our revolutions are like battles," Mao proclaimed. "After a victory, we must at once put forward a new task."[2] The new revolution Mao now contemplated would propel China through "the transition from socialism to communism." Only half a decade had passed since Mao had announced the beginning of the transition to socialism. Now, in 1958, he proclaimed the imminence of a communist utopia.

"Communism" is not defined in great detail in original Marxist theory, partly because of Marx's reluctance to draw utopian blueprints of the future. Nonetheless, there are several attributes of the envisioned communist society that have been generally assumed by Marxists over the generations, including Mao Zedong. One was the expectation that communism would be the time when people would be remunerated "according to need" rather than according to work, as with socialism. Communist society would be further distinguished by the realization of such ultimate Marxist goals as the abolition of the distinctions between mental and manual labor, between town and countryside, and between worker and peasant. And most radically, communism would bring about the abolition of the division of labor, which Marx regarded as the principal evil in history, as well as "the withering away of the state."

Such were some of the Marxian utopian social goals which Mao linked with a drive for increased production that he had launched under the slogan "the Great Leap Forward." The Great Leap had begun in late 1957 as a drive for greater productivity in both industry and agriculture, to produce "more, faster, better, and cheaper," as Mao exhorted. At the same time, Mao had become increasingly critical of the social and political consequences of Soviet-style industrialization. The First Five-Year Plan, which was drawing to an economically successful close, had more than doubled China's modern industrial capacity. But it also greatly expanded the hierarchical ranks of an increasingly privileged bureaucracy. It had spawned professional and technological elites who were separated from the masses of workers and peasants. It was creating an ever wider gap between the modernizing cities and the backward countryside, with the rural areas exploited for the benefit of the growing urban centers. Soviet-modeled industrialization further had sapped the revolutionary spirit of the Chinese Communist Party, Mao charged, turning self-sacrificing cadres into self-seeking careerists. The means that were being employed to build the material foundations for socialism were moving China away from, rather than toward, the socialist goals they were intended to serve. Mao conceived the Great Leap as a way of reconciling the means and ends of socialism as well as a way of thrusting China into the forefront of the world's industrialized nations.

The new economic strategy Mao proposed was at first little more than a set of vague economic prescriptions. The principal one was the notion of "simultaneous development," whereby the Soviet-borrowed emphasis on heavy industry would be accompanied by equal attention to the development of agriculture and light industries – with each of the three sectors stimulating the growth of the other two. Agriculture and light industry, requiring little capital investment, would generate capital for the even more rapid development of heavy industry. It was thus that Mao had declared: "If you have a strong desire to develop heavy industry, then you will pay attention to the development of light industry and agriculture."[3] This, the best of all possible economic worlds, Mao argued, could be gained by the intensive mobilization of the labor power of the people, China's greatest economic resource.

Mao Zedong's new developmental strategy demanded radical economic decentralization, with many decision-making powers passing from the central ministries in Beijing to local production units. The Maoist argument was that the full mobilization of labor power was dependent on releasing the initiative and creativity of the masses, which in turn was dependent on popular participation in local economic planning. The emphasis on local development was not intended to mean the abandonment of central economic planning, or a lessening of capital investment in the modern industrial sector. Indeed, Mao proposed even more ambitious goals for heavy industry. The new Maoist industrial policy of "walking on two legs" envisioned the rapid development of both large-scale urban industries and small-scale industries in the interior utilizing indigenous technologies and local resources. Since the latter were labor-intensive undertakings, Mao assumed that the rate of investment in heavy industry would remain steady or even increase.

As economic decentralization was being implemented in late 1957 and early 1958, Mao Zedong was undertaking a wide-ranging critique of Stalinist economic textbooks and Soviet developmental policies. The various writings and reading notes in which the critique appears were never officially published, but their contents were made available to high-level Party members. The Russians, he charged, greatly exaggerated the importance of heavy industry to the neglect of agriculture and light industry. Stalin, Mao wrote, was interested only in technology and technical cadre. "Stalin speaks only of production relations [economics]. . . . The role of people, the role of the laborer – these are not mentioned."[4] For Mao, by contrast, technology was not to remain a monopoly of an elite of scientific experts. The utopian hope that "the masses must make themselves masters of culture and science" was soon to become one of the popular slogans of the Great Leap Forward.

As Mao Zedong was attempting to formulate a new strategy of development, he repeatedly deplored that he and the Party had so uncritically borrowed Soviet models and methods in the early post-revolutionary years. "All we could do in our ignorance was to import foreign methods," Mao acknowledged. "Our statistical work was practically a copy of Soviet work. . . . We lacked understanding of the whole economic situation and understood still less the differences between the Soviet Union and China. So all we could do was follow blindly."[5]

"Poor and blank"

In January 1958, as tens of millions of laborers in the cities and the countryside were being mobilized for the ill-fated "backyard" iron and steel campaign, Mao predicted that China would achieve the economic levels of the advanced industrialized countries in 15 years. At the same time, Mao was seized by visions of a more or less imminent communist utopia. The notion of a social "great leap" was joined to the economic "great leap." The ultimate goals prophesied in classical Marxism soon were proclaimed to be in the process of being realized in the here and now. An enormous emphasis was placed on eliminating what Mao called "the three great differences" – the distinctions between mental and manual labor, between town and countryside, and between workers and peasants.

The expectation that communist goals could be successfully pursued well before their Marxian-defined material prerequisites were present was the logical culmination of a deeply rooted strain in Mao Zedong's thought. Ever since his youthful days during the New Culture and May Fourth movements, Mao had placed an enormous emphasis on the decisive role of human will and consciousness in history. It was a belief that sustained him during the long revolutionary years – and a belief that was fortified by the revolutionary victory against seemingly overwhelming material odds. Now, a decade after that victory, it was a belief that found renewed expression in Mao's inversion of the Marxian belief that the economic "base" fundamentally conditions the social, political, and ideological "superstructure." For Mao, communist goals could be pursued in the here and now, even in conditions of great material scarcity, in order to stimulate economic development. A communist "superstructure" was more the precondition than the product of modern economic development. The "leap" to a communist utopia, therefore, was not to be delayed. The Chinese people were to strike while the iron was hot.

In early 1958, as tens of millions of peasants were being mobilized for massive irrigation and construction projects, Mao Zedong was searching for an appropriate organizational form to combine the economic great leap (or what he usually called "the technological revolution") with a communist social revolution. This led to the establishment of "people's communes," an amalgamation of collective farms into much larger units intended to follow communist principles of work organization and remuneration. During the spring and summer Mao predicted (in increasingly fervent tones) the imminent realization of Marxist utopian goals and called for the reorganization of "industry, agriculture, commerce, education, and soldiers into big communes, thereby to form the basic units of society."[6]

The term "commune" occupies a hallowed place in the Marxist tradition, originating in Karl Marx's description of the Paris Commune of 1871 as the historical model for the "dictatorship of the proletariat." That this eminently urban revolutionary model, celebrating the heroism of the Parisian working class, should have been adopted to guide a movement of peasants in the post-revolutionary Chinese countryside, is one of the many incongruities in the history of Marxism in China.

During the Great Leap Forward campaign, Mao Zedong appeared in the guise of a prophet, predicting the imminent advent of a communist utopia. Three years of hard work, it was promised, would be followed by a thousand years of communist happiness. But while a deified Mao Zedong, and a Mao freed from the Leninist strictures of the Party, were essential to launching the adventure, the Great Leap was not Mao's doing alone. Utopian prophecies are of little historical significance if no one is listening. The Great Leap is incomprehensible without taking into account how Mao's visions of a communist utopia struck responsive chords among peasants who longed for economic prosperity and harbored anarchist dreams of a world without officials and bureaucrats.

Utopian expectations, both in Beijing and throughout much of the countryside, reached their zenith in the summer and fall of 1958. The ultimate communist goals prophesied in original Marxist theory, hitherto indefinitely postponed, now became ends to be striven for in the present. Economic abundance, along with the abolition of "the three great differences" and even "the withering away of the state," were no longer ritualized goals that resided in a distant future utopia but ones that were in the process of being realized in the here and now. The agency that would achieve these radical communist goals was the rural "people's commune." Some 24,000 communes, encompassing virtually the entire rural population of over 500,000,000 people, were organized during a period of less than six months by the hasty amalgamation of 750,000 collective farms.

In the radical Maoist literature of the time, the commune was pictured not only as the embryo from which the future communist utopia would grow, but also the product and producer of a new communist personality. The communes were to mold (and be molded by) people who conformed to Mao Zedong's ideal "red and expert," people who combined a communist consciousness with economic or scientific expertise. Such "red and experts" would perform a great variety of social and economic functions. At the same time, they would embody that vital "communist consciousness" upon which the new society inevitably would rest. Very soon, Maoist theoreticians proclaimed, "everyone will be a mental laborer and at the same time a physical laborer; everyone can be a philosopher, scientist, writer, and artist."

The visionary goals of the Great Leap were drawn from classical Marxist texts but the means employed to achieve them were not. At no time do Mao Zedong's departures from the premises of Marxism reveal themselves as starkly as they do in the theory and practice of the Great Leap. Many of the populist and "utopian socialist" features of Mao's thought that went into the making of Chinese Communist revolutionary strategy in the decades before 1949 reappeared during the Great Leap, often in exaggerated form. Prominent among these was the belief that the truly creative forces of revolutionary change reside in the countryside rather than in the cities. Just as Mao's strategy during the revolutionary years took the unorthodox form of mobilizing the radical forces of the countryside to "surround and overwhelm" the conservative cities, so the post-revolutionary ideology of the Great Leap assigned to the rural communes the task of carrying out the transition to a communist society. The cities, Guomindang strongholds during the civil war, were again viewed with suspicion as centers of moral corruption and bureaucratic conservatism – albeit now the conservatism of a Communist bureaucracy.

The powerful anti-urban biases, so prominent in Mao's thought during the revolutionary years, were tempered but did not vanish with the Communist victory over the Guomindang. In 1949, as the cities were falling to the peasant soldiers of the PLA, Mao Zedong proclaimed the beginning of a new communist era where "the city will lead the village." But at the same time he warned that living in the cities could corrupt the revolutionary spirit of the victorious Communists, lead to ideological decay among Party cadres, and undermine the rural revolutionary values of "plain living and hard struggle" in favor of the "love of pleasure" that urban life encouraged.[7] Mao's suspicion of the city, hardened by a quarter of a century of fighting in the rural hinterlands, remained even as he settled into Zhongnanhai in the heart of Beijing. His anti-urban biases re-emerged in the mid-1950s when, during the agricultural collectivization campaign, he again looked to the countryside and to the spontaneity of peasant radicalism for the sources of revolutionary social change.

Mao's anti-urbanism became more explicit, both in theory and practice, during the Great Leap. The communization of the countryside was accompanied by an ideological glorification of the virtues of rural life and an assault on the decadence of the cities. Party cadres were enjoined to practice the rural revolutionary tradition of leading "a hard and plain life" and to denounce officials who, corrupted by the cities, indulged in extravagance and adopted bureaucratic airs. The Maoist remedy was to dispatch such wayward city dwellers to the countryside, where they might acquire the proper revolutionary values. The distance between Mao Zedong and Karl Marx can be measured by Mao's belief that urban workers, intellectuals, and bureaucrats would be taught "proletarian" virtues by living and working among peasants in the countryside.

Mao Zedong's inversion of the Marxian analysis of the relationship between town and countryside reflected his abandonment of the proletariat as the agent of the historically redemptive communist future in favor of the peasantry. While this rural orientation was incongruous with the premises of Marxism, it was by no means an illogical outcome of the history of Marxism in a largely agrarian and pre-capitalist land. Indeed, it was perhaps an essential intellectual precondition for a successful revolutionary strategy in a land where a social revolution was desperately needed. Yet Mao did more than substitute peasants for workers as the principal revolutionary class. He also separated "class consciousness" from any social class moorings. "Proletarian consciousness" loomed large in Mao's vision and strategy of revolution. But it was neither an attribute of the actual proletariat nor of the peasants, however ardently he praised the peasants' revolutionary zeal and their "fine old culture."

Where then did "proletarian consciousness" reside? Mao is often portrayed as a super-Leninist who saw the Communist Party as the institutional incarnation of revolutionary truth. But Mao had witnessed the fallibilities of the Party many times since the 1920s. And in the late 1950s he had grown increasingly critical of the conservatism of the Party in power. In the end, it is difficult to escape the impression that by the time of the Great Leap Mao had come to believe that "proletarian consciousness" resided primarily in his own person and thought.

The separation of "proletarian consciousness" from the actual proletariat (or any other social class) reflected Mao Zedong's belief in the decisive importance of ideas and spiritual factors in history. In a land that lacked the Marxian-defined material and social prerequisites for socialism (much less communism), a reliance on "the objective forces of history" relegated the revolutionary to a passive observer standing on the historical sidelines. This would have been intolerable to Mao, whose activist temperament had always demanded political action in the here and now. That temperament had drawn him to anarchist ideas in the early May Fourth period. His subsequent conversion to Marxism came about less because of a burning intellectual attraction to the doctrine than because of the association of Marxism with the politically activist impulses released by the Russian Revolution. It is hardly surprising, then, that Mao Zedong never acquired any real Marxist confidence that socialism was imminent in the progressive movement of an objective historical process, a confidence which the modern Chinese historical situation did little to encourage. Rather, Mao retained a highly voluntaristic belief that the outcome of history depended on "subjective factors" – the consciousness, the moral values, and the actions of dedicated people.

Mao Zedong's extreme emphasis on the role of human consciousness and will in the making of history, apparent in his early pre-Marxian writings, reached its culmination during the Great Leap Forward campaign. To achieve the utopian social and economic goals of the movement, Mao counseled, it was only necessary to rely on "the creativity of the masses," recognize that a spiritually revitalized people would more readily respond to moral appeals than to monetary incentives, appreciate that "man is the decisive factor," and have faith in the emergence of "new men" of "all-round ability" who would mold social and economic reality in accordance with the dictates of their consciousness. Those who suggested that China lacked the necessary economic conditions for "the transition to communism" were accused of supporting the heretical "productive force theory," the eminently Marxist (but certainly non-Maoist) view that a communist society presupposed a high level of material development.

"Men do not build themselves a new world out of the fruits of the earth, as vulgar superstition believes, but out of the historical accomplishments of their declining civilization," Karl Marx counseled, as if he were forewarning Mao Zedong. "They must, in the course of their development, begin by themselves producing the material conditions of a new society, and no effort of mind or will can free them from this destiny."[8] In the Great Leap, it was precisely great efforts of "mind and will" that Mao relied upon.

By the time of the Great Leap Mao Zedong had abandoned such concessions as he had made to Marxist-Leninist orthodoxy on the historical progressiveness of capitalism. He had also abandoned the theory of New Democracy (the political form corresponding to the "bourgeois-democratic" phase of the revolution) in favor of "the dictatorship of the proletariat." The Marxist term, in its Maoist reincarnation, had little to do with the actual proletariat. It referred, rather, to the virtues and tasks that original Marxist theory had assigned to the proletariat – but which in the Maoist ideology of the Great Leap were attributed to the rural communes and their peasant inhabitants, who were presumably guided by "Mao Zedong Thought."

The utopian ideology of the Great Leap marked Mao Zedong's definitive rejection of the Marxist premise that socialism presupposes capitalism and the historical activity of the social classes directly involved in modern capitalist modes of production. It confirmed Mao's long-standing tendency to find the sources of socialism and communism in the social classes least influenced by capitalism, especially the tradition-bound peasantry. He was soon to reverse Marx even more explicitly, arguing that socialism and communism were easier to achieve in China than in the Western countries precisely because China was less burdened by capitalist economic relationships and bourgeois ideology.

Mao Zedong's rejection of the Marxist demand that socialism and communism were to be constructed on the social and material foundations of capitalism reflected his long-held belief in "the advantages of backwardness." It was a belief that involved more than the familiar notion that backward countries enjoyed the advantage of speeding up their development by borrowing the technologies of their advanced predecessors, while avoiding their social mistakes. Mao also believed in the intrinsic moral, social, and political virtues of backwardness itself, a prominent theme in the thought of the modern Chinese intelligentsia since the beginning of the 20th century, derived from late 19th-century anarchist and Russian Populist ideologies. It found its principal expression in the belief that China could modernize without suffering the social agonies of capitalism.

The idea of the advantages of backwardness appears in Mao Zedong's writings as early as 1919, prior to his conversion to Marxism, when he argued that China's backwardness in modern times augured well for its political and social future, since what "has been accumulating for a long time . . . will surely burst forth quickly."[9] The notion recurs sporadically in his Marxian writings over the decades, although usually disguised by the political need to repeat standard Marxist-Leninist orthodoxies. It was only on the eve of the Great Leap, when Mao had immunized himself from ideological pressures from Moscow as well as from more orthodox Marxists in the CCP, that Mao's belief in the revolutionary virtues of backwardness fully re-emerged. It found its most radical expression in the "poor and blank" thesis, set forth in April 1958:

> Apart from their other characteristics, China's 600 million people have two remarkable peculiarities; they are, first of all, poor, and secondly blank. That may seem like a bad thing, but it is really a good thing. Poor people want change, want to do things, want revolution. A clean sheet of paper has no blotches, and so the newest and most beautiful words can be written on it, the newest and most beautiful pictures can be painted on it.[10]

Mao Zedong's celebration of the virtues of being "poor and blank" reflected his faith in the peasantry as the agent of radical social change. For the peasants, if not necessarily "blank," were certainly poor and therefore the most eager for revolutionary change toward what now had been proclaimed China's pioneering "transition to communism." The "poor and blank" thesis also heralded the revival of that special faith in youth that Mao had inherited as a member of the May Fourth generation of intellectuals. If the peasants were revolutionary because they were poor, young people were potentially revolutionary because they were "blank." Youth, relatively uncorrupted by the influences of the old society, were amenable to the appropriate moral and ideological transformation; they were clean sheets of paper on which the newest revolutionary words could be written. "From ancient times the people who have created new schools of thought have always been young people without great learning," Mao declared in a speech delivered in March 1958. "When young people grasp a truth they are invincible and old people cannot compete with them."[11]

Mao Zedong's praise for the creativity of youth was accompanied by a growing hostility to intellectuals, to professionalism, and to formal higher education. "When the intellectuals had power," he observed in the early 1960s, "things were in a bad state and the country was in disorder." Thus he concluded "it is evident that to read too many books is harmful." To support this proposition, which of course he himself ignored, Mao offered historical examples from both China and the West. He noted that "Liu Hsiu [who suppressed a peasant rebellion and established the Later Han dynasty in AD 27] was an academician whereas Liu Pang [the famous peasant rebel who founded the original Han dynasty in 206 BC] was a country bumpkin." And to support his contention that "it is not absolutely necessary to attend school," Mao pointed to such creative geniuses as Benjamin Franklin and Maxim Gorky, neither of whom had much formal education. As for intellectuals, he proposed a drastic remedy to still their pernicious influences: "We must drive actors, poets, dramatists and writers out of the cities, and pack them off to the countryside."[12] No one could have imagined at the time that these seemingly offhand remarks were prophetic pointers to the future.

Mao Zedong's "poor and blank" thesis echoed one of the major themes of 19th-century Russian Populism. The Populists had argued that Russia's economic backwardness was a social blessing. Since its countryside was not yet suffering from capitalist encroachments, Russia had a unique opportunity to "skip over" the capitalist stage of development and achieve socialism on the basis of a pre-capitalist peasantry, whose social institutions and morality were not yet corrupted by Western bourgeois influences. Just as Alexander Herzen, the ideological founder of Russian Populism, proclaimed "we possess nothing" in declaring his faith in Russia's socialist future, so Mao Zedong proclaimed China to be "a clean sheet of paper" and saw in that alleged condition the promise of its imminent revolutionary leap to a communist utopia.

While Mao Zedong's celebration of the "advantages of backwardness" bears affinities with Russian Populism, it has nothing in common with either Marxism or Leninism. Both Marx and Lenin looked to the political and intellectual activities of the most modern social classes (the proletariat and the intelligentsia) to bring about the socialist future; they argued that a genuine socialist society could be constructed only on the material and social foundations of capitalism; and they took it for granted that the new society would inherit all the cultural accomplishments of the past. Mao Zedong, by contrast, placed his revolutionary faith in the moral virtues he found in backwardness, looked to those social groups uncorrupted by capitalist relationships and bourgeois ideology, celebrated the virtues of being "poor and blank," and saw peasants and youth as the bearers of socialism and communism. It is difficult to imagine a more profound departure from the premises of Marxist theory than Mao Zedong's "poor and blank" thesis.

Two years after setting forth the virtues of being "poor and blank," Mao was candid in stating its political and social implications – and sufficiently confident in his own ideological authority to revise Lenin in doing so. In notes he made while reading a Soviet text on political economy, he wrote: "Lenin said: 'The more backward the country, the more difficult its transition from capitalism to socialism.' Now it seems that this way of speaking is incorrect. As a matter of fact, the more backward the economy, the easier, not the more difficult, the transition from capitalism to socialism."[13]

Clash at Lushan

By late fall 1958 the hastily organized communes were running into difficulties. Food shortages, partly caused by the mobilization of peasants to work on irrigation and construction projects – and the consequent neglect of agriculture – were beginning to plague the land. Hunger was compounded by the exhaustion of the working population, as both urban workers and peasants were forced to labor long hours to meet unrealistic production goals. Organizational chaos in many of the more socially radical communes, and a precipitate decline in peasant morale, followed. At the end of November, Party leaders gathered in the industrial center of Wuhan to deal with the looming crisis. At a tense two-week meeting, the Central Committee was implicitly critical of Mao's Great Leap policies. The official resolution retained much of the utopian rhetoric with which the Great Leap began, but the aim was to bring the movement to an end, or at least moderate its radical thrust. The resolution, passed with Mao's reluctant assent, warned against "impetuous" actions and "utopian dreams" of bypassing the necessary stages of social development. Communism, the Central Committee counseled, must be built on the foundation of advanced productive forces, and this could be achieved only after "the lapse of considerable time." The resolution insisted on the socialist character of the communes and called for reversing the more radical communist social experiments that some communes had undertaken. The central authority of Party and state bureaucracies over the countryside was reasserted, circumscribing the autonomy of the communes.

Although Mao Zedong later complained that after the Wuhan meeting he was treated as a "dead ancestor" by most Party leaders, he had in fact recognized many of the excesses of the Great Leap and often took the lead in efforts to correct them, at least sporadically from December 1958 to the summer of 1959. He was critical of the radical egalitarian "communist wind" on many communes, the communes' arbitrary appropriations of peasant labor power, excessive exactions of grain, the general waste of labor, and unreasonable demands that were exhausting the working population. And he acknowledged that at the outset of the Great Leap he had failed to temper revolutionary zeal with "the practical spirit." Yet Mao's speeches and directives abounded with inconsistencies and ambiguities. While critical of many policies and practices of the time, he insisted on the long-term viability of the communes and the wisdom of the Great Leap in general. And while he felt free to admonish himself on occasion, he bristled under any criticisms from others that seemed to call his own judgments into question.

In the early months of 1959, as economic conditions further deteriorated, Mao's equivocal attitudes toward the Great Leap, and the reluctance of timorous Party leaders to propose anything that might run counter to the Chairman's rather ambiguous wishes, paralyzed such efforts as might have been made to shield the population from the looming debacle. The fate of the Great Leap and Mao's future as supreme leader of the CCP were issues that were fatefully joined in the dramatic confrontation between Mao and Peng Dehuai, China's Minister of Defense, when Party leaders gathered at the Jiangxi mountain resort of Lushan in July 1959.

Peng Dehuai was one of the great military heroes of the Communist Revolution. Five years younger than Mao, he was born into a poor peasant family in the same county in Hunan province where Mao had spent his relatively comfortable childhood. Unlike Mao, Peng had little formal education. At the age of nine he was indentured to work in a coal mine. He eventually joined the army of a Hunanese warlord, rose in the ranks and became a brigade commander in the Nationalist Army during the great revolutionary upsurge of 1925–7. Radicalized by the experience, he joined the Communists shortly after Chiang Kai-shek's counter-revolution of April 1927, and in 1928 led a force of several hundred soldiers to join Mao's guerrilla base in the Jinggang Mountains. Next to Mao and Zhu De, Peng was the most prominent figure in the Red Army during the revolutionary war. He commanded Chinese forces in the Korean War and shortly after was appointed Minister of Defense.

In the spring of 1959 Peng led a Chinese military delegation to the Soviet Union and Eastern Europe. During the six-week mission, he discussed his reservations about the Great Leap with Khrushchev and other foreign Communist leaders. Determined to bring his concerns directly to Mao, he wrote a long personal letter in mid-July while attending a conference of Communist leaders at Lushan that preceded the formal Central Committee plenum, detailing his criticism of the Great Leap and the communes. He cited the collapse of national planning, the oppressive economic conditions which had befallen the peasants, and the growing alienation of China's leaders from the people. Peng attributed these and other failings of the Great Leap to "petty bourgeois fanaticism" (extreme and misguided radicalism in the Marxist-Leninist lexicon), a familiar Leninist charge which the Comintern had hurled at Mao three decades before.

Although Peng's "Letter of Opinion" was a private communication, Mao had copies distributed to the 150 senior Party officials who had gathered in Lushan. He then responded to Peng's critique in a rambling – but remarkably revealing – talk to the assembled delegates on July 23. Mao's speech, apparently largely extemporaneous, curiously combined acknowledgments of his own responsibility for the failures of the Great Leap and a reaffirmation of the continuing validity of the basic policies of the past year. Mao conceded many of the criticisms made by Peng. He acknowledged that the system of national planning had collapsed. He accepted personal responsibility for the wasteful backyard steel campaign, as a result of which, he admitted, "we rushed into a great catastrophe." And the communes, he acknowledged, were organized "too quickly." In all, Mao conceded that the Great Leap had been "a partial failure" for which "we have paid a high price." "The chaos caused was on a grand scale and I take responsibility."[14]

While seemingly candid in admitting his errors, Mao Zedong implicitly absolved himself of blame by observing that even Confucius and Lenin had made mistakes. Indeed, Marx too was not infallible: "If you want to talk about haste, Marx also made many mistakes. Every day he hoped that a European revolution would arrive . . . [but] it had still not arrived when he died. . . . Wasn't this a case of impatience? Wasn't this petit-bourgeois fanaticism?"[15] Peng Dehuai's charge that the extremes of the Great Leap resulted from "petty bourgeois fanaticism" must have stung, for Mao repeatedly returned to the phrase during the course of his lengthy speech – and in similarly sarcastic tones.

Despite acknowledging failures and mistakes, Mao defended the policies of the Great Leap. To be sure, the transition to communism might take longer than originally envisaged, perhaps as long as "twenty five-year plans" (or a century), he now suggested. But while the future communist utopia was postponed, the drive to attain it was not. The rural communes, Mao insisted, remained the proper organizational forms for the transition to communism, however long and arduous the journey. He approved of communal mess halls because they conserved labor and material, even though he was aware that peasants were abandoning them *en masse*. And he still found great popular enthusiasm for communism.

Like most politicians in power, Mao Zedong seemed less concerned about the errors made in the Great Leap than about revealing those errors to the people: "If the paper you publish prints bad news every day, people will have no heart for their work. It wouldn't take as long as a year; we would perish within a week." Then, raising the spectre of the Communist regime collapsing, Mao issued a dramatic threat to those who were "wavering" in their support of the Great Leap: "I will go to the country-side to lead the peasants to overthrow the government. If those of you in the Liberation Army won't follow me, then I will go and find a Red Army, and organize another Liberation Army. But I think the Liberation Army would follow me."[16] The threat may have been mostly melodrama, but it conveyed the stark choice Mao offered Party leaders and especially PLA generals. Not only were they to choose between him and Peng Dehuai, but they were to declare whether they supported his policies on the Great Leap and his ultimate authority over the army as well. Although many Communist leaders now had the gravest doubts about the Great Leap, none of the delegates to the Central Committee plenum proved willing to follow Peng into a battle with potentially cataclysmic consequences.

The speech at the Lushan conference was revealing about how much Mao Zedong had been transformed over the decade he had been in power. Despite the fact that he acknowledged authorship of policies which had resulted in "chaos" and "catastrophe," he never once commented on how such conditions might be affecting the peasants whose interests he had so long championed and who had brought him to power in the first place. It is not that he could have been ignorant of the widespread reports of hunger in both the cities and the countryside. He was aware of many of the difficulties that were plaguing the movement since at least December 1958, when at the Wuhan conference he accepted (however reluctantly) the need to reverse, or at least mitigate, many of the more radical Great Leap policies. In the spring before the Lushan meeting, he had com-mented on the grossly exaggerated grain production figures, the food shortages, the failure of the backyard steel campaign, and the exhaustion of the working population. He had even warned that if the Party did not moderate its demands on the peasants, the Communist regime might suffer the fate of the Qin dynasty which unified China in 221 BC but whose oppressive rule was overthrown by a peasant rebellion within two decades.

Mao Zedong was too experienced a student of rural life not to have known what the failures he enumerated meant for the livelihood – and the lives – of the rural population. Yet he remained silent about the suffer-ing of the peasants. It was not so much out of ignorance that he failed to speak about the plight of the peasants than perhaps because of a degree of callousness over the loss of human life that had stamped itself on his personality and mentality. A certain indifference to death and human suffering was perhaps an inescapable consequence of the long and merciless revolutionary war which had consumed most of Mao Zedong's comrades and family – and often left him puzzled as why he alone had survived. But if a measure of indifference to death is a necessary attribute for a revolutionary, it is a fatal defect for the revolutionary who becomes a ruler – if not literally fatal for the ruler, then certainly for the ruler's subjects.

The protective shell that Mao Zedong had built to insulate himself from the costs of revolution was hardened by a self-imposed ignorance of real social conditions in the post-revolutionary years. In his youth and through much of his revolutionary career he had a passion for carrying out first-hand empirical investigations of the economic and social life of peasants (and before that of urban workers), which he related in meticulous detail in notes and reports. The principle of "seeking truth from facts" and the injunction that "practice is the sole criterion of truth," the slogans that were to be used so effectively against Mao by his successors, were precepts originally set forth by Mao himself. Much of his success as a revolutionary can be attributed to his application of those principles to actual social and political conditions.

In the post-revolutionary years Mao attempted to revive that tradition of local investigation by making "inspection tours" to various parts of the country and the countryside. But now he did so by traveling in a private and lavishly outfitted train. Surrounded by bodyguards, he spoke with peasants and workers who had been well rehearsed beforehand by local officials. It was a banal and universal pattern of political behavior, practiced by ancient Chinese emperors and modern American presidents alike. But for Mao the ruler it seemed sufficient. He still invoked an image of himself as the embodiment of the people. But "the masses," "the people," and even "the peasants" were becoming abstractions in the Maoist vocabulary.

Mao Zedong's growing estrangement from real social and economic life was epitomized by his visit to his native village of Shaoshan in July 1959, on his way to the Lushan conference. It was his first visit to Shaoshan since 1927 and he saw the promise of a bountiful harvest – "waving rows of rice and beans," as he wrote in a poem composed for the occasion. It took the blunt-spoken Peng Dehuai (who had seen hungry peasants and abandoned houses a few weeks earlier in nearby villages) to remind Mao that Shaoshan had been the recipient of generous and quite exceptional state aid. It is unlikely that Mao appreciated the reminder. He was certainly aware that his native village had been accorded special treatment.

He was too astute an observer of rural life not to know the difference between a real village and a Potemkin village. If he was deceived, it was only because he wished to be.

As Mao Zedong grew increasingly isolated from both the people and his revolutionary colleagues, he became more and more intolerant of any criticism of his policies, which he now took to be counter-revolutionary threats. Yet, as in earlier times, he urged everyone present to speak their minds, although perhaps now out of habit. At the Lushan conference he seemingly invited criticism: "If you don't agree with me then argue back. I don't agree with the idea that the Chairman cannot be contradicted."[17] However, this maxim was to be selectively applied, it soon became clear, and it was the Chairman who was to make the selections. It did not apply to Peng Dehuai, for one. When the Party's Politburo (and then the full Central Committee) formally convened at Lushan, Mao demanded Peng's political disgrace, hinting that Peng was conspiring with the Soviet Union to interfere in China's internal affairs.

There is no credible evidence that Peng, as Mao charged, had gone "behind the back of our fatherland to collude with a foreign country."[18] It was Peng's misfortune that his mission to the Soviet bloc coincided with the open outbreak of the Sino-Soviet conflict, which was to intensify over the remainder of the Mao era. It was just as Peng left Moscow that Khrushchev unilaterally abrogated the agreement of 1957 to provide China with modern military technology. And it was in mid-July 1958, when Peng wrote his "letter of opinion" to Mao, that Khrushchev publicly denounced the communes and the Great Leap. These developments, although largely coincidental, lent a surface plausibility to Mao's charges of "collusion" with foreigners and ensured that few would come to Peng's defense. Accordingly, the Central Committee unanimously condemned what was called "the anti-Party clique headed by Peng Dehuai." Peng was dismissed as Minister of Defense and his close associates in the PLA were purged. He was, however, permitted to retain his Party membership and even his seat in the Politburo, but he never again dared to question Mao's policies.

Peng Dehuai's political disgrace was not simply a matter of Mao's pique over having the wisdom of his leadership questioned. Also very much involved was the issue of control of the PLA. For Mao, who since 1927 had so keen an appreciation of the crucial importance of military power in Chinese politics, the question of who commanded China's military forces could not have been far from his thoughts. Peng was replaced as Minister of Defense – and as *de facto* head of the army – by Lin Biao, also one of the great military heroes of the Revolution but one whose personal and political loyalty to the Chairman was beyond question at the time. Over the next decade, the PLA was to assume an increasingly prominent role in domestic politics.

When the Standing Committee of the Politburo convened at Lushan on July 31, Mao Zedong not only demanded that Peng Dehuai be punished, but also (as if to justify the political deed) that the Great Leap policies Peng had criticized be reaffirmed. The full Central Committee duly complied, its members fearful of being branded "right opportunists" and followers of Peng's "anti-Party clique." The official resolution which issued from the plenum in late August was candid in acknowledging the failures of the Great Leap, at least the failures that Mao had already conceded, but nonetheless incongruously proclaimed the communes to be sound and called for a revival of the Great Leap campaign. It was a disastrously irresponsible decision, now motivated more by political fears than utopian visions. Hungry peasants and demoralized local cadres had no desire for further social experiments. The desperate attempt to revive the movement only served to delay confronting the deepening economic crisis. The Great Leap now gave way to an elemental struggle for survival.

Mao and the famine

Before the year 1959 was out, Mao Zedong had come to recognize the gravity of the crisis, somberly advising rural officials to pay attention "only to real possibilities." During 1960, as the communes atrophied into hollow administrative shells and the Great Leap descended into disaster, Mao began to withdraw from day-to-day political affairs, although without yielding ultimate authority over Party and state policies. Nonetheless regular state and Party bureaucracies began to reassert their power, many of their members looking more to Liu Shaoqi than to Mao for leadership – and for economic salvation. Mao's dominance at the Lushan meetings had proved a Pyrrhic victory. What remained of it was his control of the army, now under the command of his protégé Lin Biao.

In 1960 the economic crisis resulting from the Great Leap was exacerbated by a second consecutive year of natural disasters. Typhoons, drought, and floods ravaged 60 percent of the cultivated land. The desperate economic situation further deteriorated in the summer of 1960 when Khrushchev abruptly recalled the 1,400 Soviet scientists and engineers working in Chinese industries and laboratories, and on construction projects. They were ordered home, along with their blueprints. It was a heavy blow to the development of Chinese industry, which at the mid-point of the Second

Five-Year Plan had been growing at an annual rate of nearly 20 percent. But Mao Zedong, in 1960, seemed more preoccupied with the ideological quarrel with the Soviet Union than with the economic and human catastrophe left in the wake of the Great Leap.

In official statements and publications, Mao and other Chinese leaders attributed "the bitter years" of 1959–62 to a combination of natural disasters and Soviet treachery. While these external forces certainly aggravated the crisis, it was apparent that the organizational chaos of the Great Leap and the grossly exaggerated grain production figures were primarily responsible for the hardships suffered by the Chinese people in the early 1960s. And the term "the bitter years" was a euphemism for one of the worst famines in Chinese history.

It was not until the release of detailed mortality statistics in the 1980s that it became generally known that between 20 and 30 million people had perished, primarily in the years 1959–61. Before the 1980s most foreign observers had accepted official Chinese claims that one of the great accomplishments of the Communist Revolution was the elimination of mass starvation in a land where famine had been chronic over several millennia. Although it was known that the Chinese people had suffered widespread hunger and malnutrition, especially in 1960 and 1961, it was widely assumed that famine had been avoided through large grain purchases from Canada and Australia and an efficient system of rationing. Such was the impression that Mao Zedong (and other high officials) conveyed to foreign visitors in the years immediately after the Great Leap.[19]

Yet it is clear that Mao Zedong was aware by the summer of 1960, and likely well before, that wide areas of the countryside were afflicted with famine-like conditions, even though the magnitude of the disaster could not have been known at the time. As early as February 1959 he metaphorically hinted that Great Leap policies were in danger of repeating the bloody cataclysm and terrible famine that resulted from Stalin's collectivization campaign of 1929–33. "With the peasants," Mao warned, "he [Stalin] drained the pond to catch the fish. Right now, we have the same illness."[20] It was as if he were cautioning himself against ignoring the welfare of the peasantry. He thus continued the cautious retreat from the more radical policies of the Great Leap. Relative moderation prevailed until the fateful Lushan meetings in the summer of 1959, when, in a monumental act of self-deception, Mao Zedong convinced himself that hungry peasants were filled with great enthusiasm for building a communist utopia. The revival of the Great Leap in the fall of 1959 greatly aggravated the food shortages, further weakened the working population, delayed remedial measures, and ensured that the famine which had begun toward the end of 1959 would reach catastrophic proportions in 1960.

Mao Zedong, quite clearly, must bear the largest share of the moral and historical responsibility for the great famine. He was the principal author of the Great Leap and its main producer. And in the fall of 1959 he personally insisted on resurrecting the failed movement when every rational calculation of what would serve the welfare – and indeed the survival – of the people counseled that the adventure be abandoned. There is no need to invoke "the Maoist vision" to explain this final folly; it was prompted by the most mundane and petty of egotistic political motives.

However severe the historical judgment on Mao's role in the Great Leap must be, it does not follow that he stands condemned as a mass murderer no different from Hitler and Stalin, as some glibly portray him. Mao did not launch the Great Leap Forward with the aim of killing off a portion of the peasantry, as Stalin ordered his henchmen to "liquidate the kulaks as a class" or Hitler devised and implemented "the final solution." There is a critical moral distinction between the unintended consequences of political actions and wilful genocide. The blurring of that distinction does little to clarify the real moral and historical ambiguities that surround the revolutionary career of Mao Zedong.

China's hermetic political system also contributed to the famine that brought the Great Leap to its tragic conclusion. From the beginning of the movement, Party cadres were under enormous pressure from higher Party organs to meet unrealistic production goals. They often did so by inflating production figures, which often were further exaggerated as they passed up the bureaucratic ladder. Mao and other Party leaders, seized by messianic visions of a communist land of plenty, were only too eager to believe the spectacular results that were reported to them. Thus Mao initially announced that the harvest of 1958 had more than doubled the previous year's yield. This led to the fantastic belief that the countryside was flooded with an enormous surplus of food grains. Accordingly, the quotas of grain that peasants were required to sell to the government at low fixed prices were sharply raised – just as agricultural output was precipitously falling in 1959. Hunger and then famine resulted. The crisis was exacerbated when fearful and opportunistic local cadres concealed food shortages, thereby delaying or forestalling the arrival of relief supplies.

Mao Zedong later acknowledged that some Great Leap policies were mistaken, but he did so without any admission of personal responsibility.

In a speech delivered to a closed door meeting of the Central Committee in September 1962, he commented:

> In 1959 and 1960 a number of things were done wrongly, mainly because most people had no experience. . . . The most serious fault was that our requisitioning was excessive. When we did not have very much grain, we insisted on saying that we had. Blind commands were issued in both industry and agriculture.[21]

The deficiencies of China's political system does not relieve Mao Zedong of the major share of the responsibility for the human disaster that resulted from the Great Leap. It was Mao, after all, who took the lead in constructing China's Stalinist-modeled political apparatus, and then presided over it. The officials and cadres of the post-1949 bureaucratic apparatus were his one-time revolutionary comrades and followers who, like Mao himself, had undergone the transformation from revolutionaries to rulers. However much Mao had become disillusioned with the venality of some of his cadres, he could hardly denounce them without renouncing the revolution he had led. Mao's hostility to bureaucracy was real, but it was mostly directed to bending the bureaucracy to his own will, which he assumed to be the distillation of the popular will. At no time did Mao make a serious effort to bring the bureaucracy under popular democratic supervision. Political despotism remained deeply ingrained in Maoism – and it was the association of political despotism with the utopianism of the Great Leap that was largely responsible for the great human tragedy which finally brought the adventure to an end.

7

The Cultural Revolution and the Exhaustion of Maoism

It was not until October 1960, the deadliest year of the famine, that Mao Zedong fully recognized the need to abandon the policies of the Great Leap. He reluctantly postponed his vision of making the commune the communist "organizer of living and working." Agricultural production again was organized by the village-based production team, as it had been in the mid-1950s, private family plots were restored, and rural markets were reopened. The communes remained, but mostly as administrative structures overseeing rudimentary healthcare programs and small rural industries.

The retreat from the Great Leap was accompanied by Mao's withdrawal from the center of the political stage. He retired to what he called "the second front" of Party leaders, leaving his heir-apparent, the dour Leninist Liu Shaoqi, in charge of day-to-day Party affairs. He also left to Liu, the second-highest-ranking CCP leader and the President of the People's Republic, the responsibility for reviving the depressed economy.

In the early 1960s, Mao's thoughts – if not necessarily the canonized body of "Mao Zedong Thought" – took on uncharacteristically pessimistic overtones, dominated more by fears of the past than by utopian visions of the future. At the beginning of the Great Leap Mao had envisioned an imminent era of economic abundance. He now somberly concluded that it would take at least a century for China to attain the economic levels of Western capitalist countries.

Just as economic abundance was indefinitely postponed, so the achievement of a communist society seemed far more difficult – and even uncertain. Mao now was obsessed by fears that China would suffer a "bourgeois restoration," a foreboding that was sharpened by the increasingly bitter ideological quarrel with the Soviet Union. The controversy culminated in the spring of 1964 with the publication of the Maoist treatise *On Khrushchev's Phoney Communism and its Historical Lessons for the World*. The Soviet Union, enthusiastically emulated a decade earlier, was now portrayed as a wholly negative post-revolutionary example. Khrushchev's "revisionism,"

Mao charged, had resulted in a restoration of capitalism – and China, he warned, faced a similar danger.[1] Whereas at the outset of the Great Leap Mao confidently proclaimed that China was pioneering the transition from socialism to communism, he now acknowledged that the struggle between socialism and capitalism in China had yet to be decided.

Mao Zedong's anxieties about a "capitalist restoration" were less about actual capitalist economic activities than undesirable ideological tendencies and growing doubts that the Communist Party remained reliably revolutionary. He observed his once self-sacrificing cadres of the heroic revolutionary days turn into petty post-revolutionary bureaucrats. Not only were they tending to become politically conservative, but also corrupt. "At present," he contemptuously remarked, "you can buy a Party branch secretary for a few packs of cigarettes, not to mention marrying a daughter to him."[2]

Of far greater political consequence was Mao's growing suspicion of higher-level Party leaders, his comrades in arms during the desperate revolutionary years. In 1962, when Mao returned to Party affairs after more than a year of relative seclusion, he set forth the thesis – in far stronger terms than ever before – that classes and class struggle persist in a socialist society. A favorable outcome of that struggle was by no means guaranteed. "A country like ours can still move toward its opposite," Mao warned. It could even turn fascist.[3]

The social classes engaged in this struggle were never clearly identified. Presumably it was a struggle between "the bourgeoisie" and "the proletariat," a struggle between socialism and capitalism. But what remained of the Chinese bourgeoisie had been expropriated in the early 1950s, and now existed only as a dwindling number of aging pensioners collecting modest dividends on state bonds. And the proletariat, while it had grown significantly, still made up only a small percentage of the Chinese population, and in the early 1960s remained a politically inactive class. But by the terms "bourgeoisie" and "proletariat," Mao had in mind not actual social classes but rather the ideologies Marxist theory attributed to those classes. The struggle against "the bourgeoisie" was a struggle against "bourgeois ideology," whose social carrier was not necessarily the actual bourgeoisie.

Mao Zedong, of course, long had tended to think of class in terms of political consciousness and behavior rather than Marxian-defined social and economic criteria. What was startlingly new in the Maoism of the 1960s was the conclusion that "bourgeois ideology" resided primarily in the Chinese Communist Party. Whereas in the revolutionary years the

Party had been the Leninist incarnation of "proletarian consciousness," albeit with a notable absence of actual proletarians, in the 1960s the Party had become the principal carrier of bourgeois ideology. In a socialist society, Mao had warned, "new bourgeois elements" were still produced – and members of this new bourgeoisie, he ominously disclosed, operated in "the guise of Communist Party members." And from these propositions he came to the extraordinary conclusion that the main enemies of socialism in China were "those people in positions of authority within the Party who take the capitalist road."[4]

If there was confusion over the meaning of the term "bourgeoisie," the matter was further muddled by Mao's proclivity to use interchangeably the terms "bourgeoisie" and "bureaucracy." In 1965, for example, he charged:

> The bureaucratic class is a class in sharp opposition to the working class and the poor and lower-middle peasants. How can those people who have become or are in the process of becoming bourgeois elements sucking the blood of the workers be properly recognized? These people are the objectives of the struggle, the objectives of the revolution.[5]

The ambiguity surrounding the term "bourgeoisie" was to become a major source of confusion – and violence – during the Cultural Revolution.[6]

Mao versus the Party

In the early 1960s, as Mao was haunted by fears of "revisionism," by which he meant the death of the revolution, he became increasingly estranged from other Party leaders. Save for a small number of officials who managed to retain his confidence – the prime minister Zhou Enlai, the defense minister Lin Biao, the sinister Party secret police chief Kang Sheng, and the radical ideologist Chen Boda – Mao became increasingly suspicious of the loyalty and revolutionary credentials of most of his old comrades in arms. Liu Shaoqi, the highest-ranking Party member after Mao himself, and the Party's General Secretary, Deng Xiaoping, were particularly distrusted. When Mao launched the Cultural Revolution in 1966, Liu was to be branded "the number one person in authority taking the capitalist road," with Deng the number two capitalist-roader. It was less a matter of personal animus than the fact that Liu and Deng had come to control the Party apparatus – and Mao had come to regard the Leninist party as a conservative obstacle to revolutionary change. While Liu and Deng were the most prominent suspects, few of the 26 "old revolutionaries" who were members of the Party's ruling Politburo escaped the Chairman's critical scrutiny, although most were to physically survive the Cultural Revolution and politically thrive in the post-Mao era.

Mao Zedong was quite conscious of his estrangement from other Party leaders, most of whom had been his supporters and comrades since the darkest days of the revolution. "I am alone with the masses. Waiting," he told André Malraux, then De Gaulle's Minister of Cultural Affairs, shortly before the Cultural Revolution.[7] But if Mao was "with the masses," it was now primarily in alien form – through the medium of his personality cult.

In the early 1960s the cult of Mao Zedong became a deliberately manufactured phenomenon. To be sure, Mao's acolytes and the Party propaganda machine had played major roles in the business of cult building in earlier decades. But from the more or less spontaneous origins of the Mao cult among the peasants of north China in the early Yan'an era through its reincarnation during the Great Leap, the cult had grown largely in proportion to Mao's increasing political power and his enormous personal popularity. After the Great Leap, however, faced with a disillusioned and politically apathetic population, cult building was very much a contrived project, calculated to serve immediate political ends. The absence of popular spontaneity was glaringly revealed in the decision to assign the task of refashioning the cult to the People's Liberation Army, now under the command of Lin Biao.

The Political Department of the PLA published the first edition of *Quotations from Chairman Mao* in May 1964, and over the next three years issued no less than a billion copies of that soon to be fetishized "little red book." It was the Defense Minister Lin Biao who orchestrated mass campaigns to study Mao's writings, who turned the army into "a great school for the study of Mao Zedong Thought," and who made the most extravagant claims for Mao's ideas – "a spiritual atomic bomb of infinite power," Lin wrote shortly after China's first nuclear test in October 1964.

By the winter of 1964–5 the Mao cult was ubiquitous. Edgar Snow, who had observed the early manifestations of the cult when he interviewed Mao in his cave dwelling in Shaanxi in 1936, was shocked by the "immoderate glorification" of the Chairman when he visited China in January 1965:

> Giant portraits of him now hung in the streets, busts were in every chamber, his books and photographs were everywhere on display to the exclusion of others. In the four-hour revolutionary pageant of dance and song, The East is Red, Mao was the only hero. As a climax of that perfor-

mance . . . I saw a portrait copied from a photograph taken by myself in 1936, blown up to about thirty feet high. . . . [It gave me an] uneasy recollection of similar extravaganzas of worship of Joseph Stalin seen during the wartime years in Russia. . . . The one-man cult was not yet universal, but the trend was unmistakable.[8]

Mao Zedong did not object to the cult that was being built around him; indeed he took an active part in constructing it. He had already justified personality cults in general by distinguishing between correct and incorrect forms in ambiguously commenting on Khrushchev's speech denouncing Stalin, by implication justifying his own cult: "The question at issue is not whether or not there should be a cult of the individual, but rather whether or not the individual concerned represents the truth. If he does, then he should be revered."[9]

The cult of Mao Zedong served to permit Mao, the Chairman of the Communist Party, to stand above the Party as an institution, and to impose his personal political supremacy in the name of "the people." The political potency of the cult had been demonstrated in the collectivization campaign of 1955 and during the Great Leap. In the mid-1960s the cult was being refashioned and elaborated as Mao prepared his assault on a huge and increasingly bureaucratized Party apparatus that he could no longer easily bend to his will.

But Mao did not rely solely on his cult and his personal prestige. He also counted on the support of the PLA, the institution that was mainly responsible for fabricating the cult in its most recent incarnation. That Mao looked to a hierarchically organized army to promote an egalitarian social movement is of course rather incongruous. Yet it was an army which Mao himself had largely built since the late 1920s – and he regarded the PLA, perhaps more than the Communist Party, as the true institutional bearer of the values and conscience of the revolution.

Nonetheless, it was a celebrated Maoist maxim that "the Party commands the gun," and the primacy of the civilian authority of the Party had hitherto been strictly enforced by Mao. Now, in the years immediately preceding the Cultural Revolution, the guns of the PLA were no longer firmly in the hands of the Party. Beginning in 1963, the army, operating under the personal authority of Mao, began to intervene in civilian life. It mainly took the form of propaganda campaigns celebrating model soldiers who exemplified the Maoist virtues of heroic self-sacrifice on behalf of the people and the assignment of model military personnel to work in schools, economic enterprises, and government offices. While military intervention was very limited, it was sufficient to demonstrate that the

PLA was not under the control of the Party, and indeed was a potential alternative to it.

Mao Zedong's fears over the fate of the Revolution also found expression in a 1964 campaign to train "revolutionary successors." The campaign was directed to the youth of China, who were seen as relatively uncorrupted by the traditions of the past or by the "revisionist" influences of the present. This was very much in the spirit of the celebration of the "new youth" during the May Fourth era, the formative years of the young Mao's intellectual evolution. But the campaign also reflected how deeply the aging Mao had come to distrust the Chinese Communist Party. The Party, it was now clearly suggested, could not be relied on to continue the work of the revolution on its own.

The cultivation of "revolutionary" youth, the growing public prominence of a politicized army, and the further elaboration of the Mao cult, were all, in retrospect, prophetic pointers to the Cultural Revolution, which was to take the extraordinary form of an assault on the Leninist party and many of its veteran leaders.

In launching what was to be baptized the "Great Proletarian Cultural Revolution" in the late spring of 1966, Mao Zedong did not rely on the revolutionary spontaneity of the masses alone. He had made careful political preparations well beforehand. First and foremost, he made sure that he had the support of the PLA, which in the early 1960s underwent what Lin Biao called "living ideological indoctrination" in "The Thought of Mao." He also sought to neutralize his potential opponents in the Communist Party – and he did so in methodical fashion over the course of a year.

The slowly unfolding purge struck, one by one, the Party's veteran revolutionaries, most of them long-standing members of the Maoist faction who had joined the Party during the darkest days of the Revolution. Their downfall had been foreshadowed in January 1965, when Mao ominously warned that the struggle for socialism in China had to be fought against "those people in positions of authority within the Party who take the capitalist road."[10] There followed a lengthy period of increasingly Byzantine political intrigues and obtuse ideological polemics that were aimed at Liu Shaoqi and senior Party officials in the cultural and propaganda departments. Mao orchestrated the purge from behind the scenes, and indeed from outside Beijing. He had left the capital in November 1965, spending most of the next eight months in Hangzhou, demonstrating that even from afar, and at age 72, he had lost few of the skills in intra-party infighting that he had honed over nearly half a century. His erratic but deft political maneuvers and Delphic ideological pronouncements left his timid political opponents bewildered. No one was willing to openly challenge the Chairman of the Party, the leader of the Revolution, and the founder of the nation-state. Nor could Party leaders refuse to perform the public rituals surrounding Mao's cult, to the construction of which all had contributed.

Among the first to fall was the "Group of Five" (headed by Peng Zhen, a disciple of Liu Shaoqi and the fifth-highest-ranking Party leader) who had been appointed in January 1965 to carry out Mao's demand for a "cultural revolution." They were replaced by a new "Cultural Revolution Group" composed of radical Maoists, including Mao's wife Jiang Qing. As was the case with his surviving children and other relatives, Mao had kept Jiang Qing out of politics and away from the public limelight – until 1963, when she was given the task of "revolutionizing" the Peking opera.

The idea of "cultural revolution"

What Mao meant by "cultural revolution" was by no means entirely clear either to his opponents or his supporters. It seemed a rather innocuous notion at first, perhaps yet another campaign to ideologically remold writers and artists, many thought. Had they further pondered the intellectual origins of "Mao Zedong Thought," and their own history, they might have looked back to the New Culture movement and the May Fourth era (1915–21), the formative period in Mao's intellectual evolution. From the intellectual and political ferment of those years, when Mao's first published articles appeared in *New Youth* and other periodicals, he had been drawn to the idea of a "cultural revolution" advocated by the iconoclastic May Fourth intelligentsia. It was a notion that conveyed several fundamental beliefs that were to endure in Mao's worldview for half a century. First, very much in the May Fourth spirit, Mao rejected much of the traditional Chinese cultural heritage, which was seen not only as useless for China's modern regeneration but also morally evil and corrupt. To that dustbin of history, he added Western bourgeois culture as well. Secondly, like his New Culture mentors, he was convinced that human consciousness was the decisive factor in history. Cultural and intellectual transformation was not a substitute for effective political action, but it was the essential prerequisite for it. Finally, from the cult of youth erected by the May Fourth intellectuals, Mao derived a romantic faith in young people as the bearers of a new culture and a new society, for the youth were seen as relatively uncorrupted by the traditions of the past. The young students that Mao called forth to fight the first battles of the Cultural Revolution were the "new youth" so much celebrated during his own youth. Such were some of the beliefs that China's first cultural revolution of the May Fourth era imparted to Mao on the eve of his conversion to Communism, and which survived to mold his peculiar version of Marxism. They reappeared with a vengeance in the making of the "Great Proletarian Cultural Revolution" in the 1960s.

The term "cultural revolution" also appears in the Marxist-Leninist tradition. But it is noteworthy that Mao did not draw upon it. Lenin (among other Russian Marxists) was an advocate of a "cultural revolution" in the difficult years following the Bolshevik Revolution of 1917. For Lenin a cultural revolution meant bringing the customs and work habits of modern bourgeois culture to the people of a land still mired in feudal backwardness. The agents of such a cultural transformation were to be intellectuals and the advanced elements of the urban working class. The success of the cultural revolution was ultimately dependent on modern industrialization, for, as Lenin stressed again and again, "to be cultured we must achieve a certain development of the material means of production."[11] Moreover, Lenin assumed, as had Marx, that the new society would inherit all the cultural accomplishments of the past; it was essential, he emphasized, to "grasp all the culture which capitalism has left and build socialism from it."[12]

For Mao Zedong, by contrast, the notion of importing Western bourgeois culture to overcome the backwardness of China and its people was anathema – on both nationalist and revolutionary grounds. No less distasteful was Lenin's assumption that intellectuals were the bearers of modern culture. For Mao, especially at the time of the Cultural Revolution, intellectuals were to learn from the masses, not teach them. Nor did Mao accept the Leninist belief that a successful cultural revolution would proceed gradually, ultimately dependent on modern industrialization. For Mao, a cultural revolution would rather quickly bring about a revolutionary transformation of consciousness, which was in turn the essential precondition for modern economic development – at least if the latter was going to have a socialist outcome. Mao believed that "the subjective could create the objective" and that therefore the important question was the spiritual "remolding of people." And rather than foreseeing a socialist society inheriting the cultural legacies of the past, as Lenin assumed would be the case, Mao celebrated the socialist advantages of being "poor and blank." Had he been familiar with Lenin's concept of cultural revolution, Mao would have found little to embrace. Indeed, looking at the

Maoist version of "cultural revolution" in the light of its Leninist precedent only serves to suggest how far Mao Zedong had departed from the basic premises of Marxist theory.

Mao Zedong also departed from the Leninist conception of the "vanguard party." Mao had never fully accepted the Leninist view that the Marxist "consciousness" of an intellectual elite had to be imposed on the "spontaneous" movement of the masses to build a disciplined party organization capable of effective revolutionary action. Mao, by contrast, variously attributed true revolutionary consciousness to the Party, to the peasant masses, and to himself – as changing circumstances and his own political interests dictated. On the eve of the Cultural Revolution, he clearly had lost what faith he may have once had in the revolutionary credentials of the Party. The Cultural Revolution thus began with an extraordinary – and decidedly non-Leninist – call for the masses to rebel against the Chinese Communist Party and its organizations.

Rebellion: the Red Guard movement

The popular rebellion against the authority of the Party began on the campus of Beijing University in late May 1966. Younger radical professors, and then students, launched a campaign – unprecedented since the brief "storm in the universities" during the Hundred Flowers period – criticizing Party-appointed university administrators for having suppressed discussion of the political and cultural issues raised by Mao. The uprising was not entirely spontaneous. Mao Zedong had been preparing the political and ideological conditions for an assault against the existing Party apparatus since January 1965. And barely a week before the Beijing University rebellion took place, Mao had drafted a directive, issued in the name of the Party's Central Committee, appointing a new Cultural Revolution Group to replace the Group of Five. Lest there be any doubt that the political aim of the Cultural Revolution was to cleanse the Party, the "May 16" directive claimed that "representatives of the bourgeoisie" had infiltrated the Party at all levels, including the Central Committee, warned that "persons like Khrushchev are still nestling besides us," and charged that such revisionists were preparing to establish "a dictatorship of the bourgeoisie."

While the new Maoist-reorganized Cultural Revolution Group encouraged the uprising at Beijing University, what was really important was Mao's personal blessing. At the end of May, from his retreat in Hangzhou, Mao endorsed the first of the "big character posters" that appeared on a

Beijing University wall, which exhorted "all revolutionary intellectuals" to "go into battle." It was, Mao declared – in an allusion to the Paris Commune of 1871 – "the manifesto of the Beijing Commune of the 1960s" and it heralded "a wholly new form of state structure." His words were broadcast on Beijing radio and printed in the *People's Daily*, both organs now firmly in Maoist hands. Under the aegis of Mao's personal approval the mostly student movement spread with extraordinary rapidity – to other campuses in Beijing, to other cities, and from universities to middle schools.

By late June millions of students at universities and high schools in cities throughout China had joined the revolt, attacking verbally (and sometimes physically) school administrators and teachers, and protesting both heavy-handed Party control of the schools and archaic methods of teaching. The youth movement was factious from the outset, largely because of confusing but real social differences among the students. For as the Cultural Revolution became a mass movement, especially among young people, it revealed one of the great ironies of the Chinese Communist Revolution. And that was that the offspring of classes who had gained from the Revolution and were favored under the new order – workers and peasants – tended to be conservative supporters of the existing Communist regime. The sons and daughters of the social classes that had been deposed by the Revolution and who were discriminated against in the new society (and especially in the educational system) – landlords, the bourgeoisie, and intellectuals – were the most radical and ardent supporters of Mao Zedong and the attack against the established Party bureaucracy.

It was a paradoxical but eminently rational social division, the existence of which was only dimly perceived by the participants in the movement. The social divisions were further obscured by the pervasiveness of the Mao cult. All political factions, whether within the Party or among the more amorphous student movement, marched under Maoist banners, all copiously quoted Mao's writings and slogans, and all no doubt believed that they were acting in accordance with the Chairman's wishes and instructions.

The social differences, whether consciously recognized or not, were of course inherent in the student movement from the beginning. In early June, however, they were cemented into bitter factional divisions when Liu Shaoqi, in charge of the central Party apparatus, dispatched work teams to the campuses in order to bring the mushrooming student movement under the organizational control of the Party. It was a standard Leninist organizational device, and Mao, in his more Leninist moments, had also freely employed work teams. Liu and other leaders assumed that the Chairman of the Party naturally would have approved restoring order on the campuses, as he had during the Hundred Flowers campaign. Few could have imagined that a popular assault against the Party and its authority was precisely what Mao Zedong had in mind.

From the growing turmoil in the schools there emerged secret student societies who sought to counter the efforts of the work teams to bring the student movement under the organizational control of the Party. The new groups called themselves "Red Guards," the term derived from the local peasant militias who supported Mao's Red Army during the revolutionary years. The appearance of the Red Guards, a largely spontaneous movement, must have seemed to Mao to mark the timely political arrival of the young and uncorrupted "revolutionary successors" he had been cultivating for several years. He hastily left Hangzhou to finally return to Beijing after an absence of eight months, determined to shield the radical students from the onslaught of the Party apparatus. *En route*, he stopped at Wuhan, where he took a much-publicized swim in the Yangzi, allegedly covering a distance of 9 miles. The physical effort was intended to demonstrate his political vigor, distantly echoing his youthful essay published in the *New Youth* magazine half a century before, in which the physical fitness of the individual was a metaphor for the strength of the nation.

When Mao returned to Beijing in late July, he condemned the "fifty days of white terror" and ordered the Party work teams to disband in favor of "Cultural Revolution Small Groups," composed of pro-Maoist students and teachers. He also convened a meeting of the Party Central Committee at the beginning of August, the first in four years. Hitherto, Mao had conducted the Cultural Revolution on his own authority, sometimes in the name of the Central Committee, often simply in his own. He now felt the need for some formal Party sanction for the increasingly massive and radical movement he had called into being. But the sanction that issued from the raucous 12-day meeting of the 11th Plenum of the Central Committee was of dubious validity in terms of the Party's established Leninist procedures, for the sessions had been packed with Mao's supporters selected both from the membership of the Party and from the leadership of the student movement.

The first business of the Central Committee was to launch a purge of the upper levels of the Party organization, which included demoting several senior officials to ensure a Maoist majority on the Politburo. More strikingly, Lin Biao was elevated to the position of Vice-Chairman of the Party, making him Mao's heir-apparent in place of Liu Shaoqi. It was the beginning of a fall that was to culminate in Liu's imprisonment and death.

The Central Committee then set forth the goals of the Cultural Revolution, as Mao dictated them to the assembled delegates. The resulting document, known as the "16 Points," became enshrined as the charter of the Great Proletarian Cultural Revolution. From it, one can measure the successes and failures of the movement – at least from a Maoist viewpoint. The "16 Points" identified the enemies of socialism as "those within the Party who are in authority and taking the capitalist road." They were, it was charged, plotting a "bourgeois restoration," which it was the task of cultural revolutionaries to forestall. Thus the fantastic thesis that Mao had set forth in January 1965 now became the official policy of the CCP, albeit by means of a somewhat irregular meeting of the Central Committee.

On the question of who constituted "the bourgeoisie" and how they were to be identified, the Maoist document was less than entirely clear. It variously suggested that the bourgeoisie were the "capitalist roaders" who were to be found among the highest leaders of the Communist Party; members of the former bourgeoisie who had been expropriated by the Revolution and who were attempting "to stage a comeback;" or those who were carriers of "the four olds" – "old ideas, culture, customs, and habits" that "the exploiting classes [used] to corrupt the masses." The loose use of the term "bourgeoisie" was to create enormous confusion among the millions who responded to Mao's call to rebel against the existing Communist order. And it was to facilitate indiscriminate attacks on many groups and individuals who could vaguely be labeled "bourgeois" on a variety of grounds.

The most intriguing feature of the "16 Points" was the quasi-democratic means by which Mao proposed to carry out the Cultural Revolution. Since it now was made clear that the danger of a "bourgeois restoration" resided in the Party itself, especially in its highest organs, the Party could not be expected to rectify itself in conventional Leninist fashion. Rather, the purification of the Party was to come by popular pressure from outside its ranks. The means of carrying out the Cultural Revolution was to "boldly arouse the masses" and permit "the free mobilization of the masses," in contrast to the customary practice of mass mobilization under the leadership of the Party. The people were free to seek their liberation in their own fashion, it was now suggested.

On the place of the Party in China's future political structure, Mao was ambiguous, perhaps deliberately so. On the one hand, he emphasized the reorganization of political power in accordance with the democratic principles of Marx's description of the Paris Commune of 1871. It was a model that called for the democratic election of officials, who were to be subject to immediate popular recall, and who were to perform their public duties at ordinary workers' wages and without special privileges. The various "cultural revolutionary groups" that had recently sprung up at schools, factories, and elsewhere were to operate in accordance with these democratic principles and they were to become "permanent, standing mass organizations." On the other hand, the new popular cultural revolutionary organizations were not to replace the Communist Party but to stand alongside it. About the Party, Mao now said, 95 percent of its cadres were good, or at least amenable to ideological rectification. He thus left open the question of the future place of the Party in China's political structure.

The aims of the Cultural Revolution were described with chiliastic fervor. Distantly echoing the New Culture Movement of his youth, Mao Zedong proclaimed that the goal of the Great Proletarian Cultural Revolution was to bring about a fundamental transformation of the consciousness of the whole nation. It would be a revolution that would "touch men's very souls." And it would decide the "life and death struggle" between socialism and capitalism. Yet despite the bombastic revolutionary rhetoric that introduced and accompanied the movement, Mao's aims were more reformist than revolutionary. This is nowhere more apparent than in his considerations of the social class forces operating in China on the eve of the Cultural Revolution.

In the two years immediately preceding the Cultural Revolution, Mao had entertained the idea that the Chinese Communist Party had yielded a new "bureaucratic class" of rulers who exploited the people on the basis of their control of nationalized and collectivized property. Chinese socialism, he had come to believe, had produced a new bureaucratic ruling class that was "in sharp opposition to the working class and the poor and lower-middle peasants;" it was a class of new "bourgeois elements [who were] sucking the blood of the workers."[13]

Mao's notion of a new functional (but property-less) bourgeoisie rooted in the upper levels of the Chinese Communist Party conflated the terms "bureaucratic class" and "bourgeoisie." The concept of a "bureaucratic class" appeared in Mao's unofficial writings, which were widely distributed by Red Guards who ransacked Party archives during the Cultural Revolution. It was a portrayal of China's post-revolutionary class structure that appealed to the more radical anti-Party activists in the Cultural

Revolution, for it conformed to their own experiences and perceptions of the Communist bureaucracy. They argued, with considerable justification, that it was what Mao really meant by the term "bourgeoisie." But as the Cultural Revolution approached, Mao Zedong, realizing the political implications of the notion, drew back from publicly characterizing China's bureaucrats as a new ruling class. To do so would have demanded a political revolution and not simply a cultural one. It would have meant overthrowing the state he had founded and perhaps plunging into civil war the nation he had unified. And it would have forced him to condemn, as members of an exploiting bureaucratic class, virtually all of his old comrades and cadres from the heroic days of the Revolution. He preferred to believe that 95 percent of Party cadres were good or at least capable of redemption. Mao thus settled for a purge of the upper levels of the Party hierarchy and a "cultural revolution" that would spiritually revolutionize the people, especially the youth, and revitalize the socialist goals of the Revolution. It was an essentially reformist endeavor that Mao had in mind, albeit one that would employ the radical means of class struggle – or at least simulated class struggles. But no fundamental changes in post-revolutionary state and society were contemplated.

The Cultural Revolution, therefore, was intended to be an intense but non-violent political and ideological experience. The use of force was prohibited. Economic production was not to be disrupted. The rural areas were immunized from the movement as were scientists, technicians, and most urban industries. Mao Zedong's rhetoric was radical and pseudo-revolutionary, but he knew well the difference between a cultural revolution and a socio-political one.

The Red Guards, however, took Mao's revolutionary words quite literally – and soon acted on the Chairman's injunction that "to rebel is justified." Referred to in the "16 Points" as "courageous and daring pathbreakers," the Red Guards at first appeared to Mao as ideal "revolutionary successors." They were anointed the vanguard of the Cultural Revolution on August 18, when a million youths, many in paramilitary dress and most of them waving copies of *Quotations from Chairman Mao*, the "little red book," gathered in the square beneath the Gate of Heavenly Peace, a sacred site for modern revolutionaries since the May Fourth incident of 1919. In a ceremony filled with a strange combination of traditional symbolism and modern revolutionary fervor, Mao Zedong appeared atop the old imperial gate at the break of dawn, donned a red armband, and thus became the "Supreme Commander of the Red Guards." Over the next three months, some 13 million Red Guards flocked to Beijing from across the land – their travels facilitated by free trains and PLA assistance – to participate in seven more such mammoth rallies at Tienanmen to pledge their loyalty to the Chairman.

Yet the activities of the Red Guards were more socially chaotic than Mao expected, and less politically effective than he had hoped. Recognizing no authority save for the Chairman and his "Thought," which many of the youthful zealots interpreted in anarchistic and sometimes mystical fashion, the Red Guards embarked on a frenzied crusade against the "four olds," an indiscriminate attack against both traditional Chinese "feudal" culture and Western "bourgeois" culture. Museums and libraries were ransacked, homes were invaded, individuals were assaulted. In searching out "the bourgeoisie," the brunt of the cultural revolutionary attack fell on individual intellectuals, who were the most seemingly "bourgeois" in a land where the actual bourgeoisie had long ceased to exist. They also were the most vulnerable, which perversely encouraged attacks from all quarters. Subjected to ideological "struggle sessions," many were physically abused and some driven to suicide.

Mao Zedong's hostility to intellectuals, which assumed extreme proportions during the suppression of the Hundred Flowers campaign in 1957, created the atmosphere for the witch-hunt that the Cultural Revolution spawned. But the first attacks on intellectuals were instigated by high officials in the established Party apparatus who aimed to deflect the Maoist attack away from themselves. Indeed, many Red Guard groups had been organized – or were supported – by the Party apparatus precisely for that purpose, exacerbating the factionalism in the student movement. The Red Guards had become pawns in a bitter struggle among higher Party leaders.

The activities of the Red Guards in the late summer and early fall of 1966 were both humanly destructive and politically superficial. Although the charter of the Cultural Revolution (the "16 Points") had stipulated that "contradictions among the people" were to be resolved by "reasoning, not by coercion or force" and that the Cultural Revolution aimed to increase economic production, not hinder it, the teenage Red Guards paid scant attention to such restraints on their zeal. By late October Mao Zedong was becoming exasperated with his "revolutionary successors," acknowledging at a Party work conference that "the Great Cultural Revolution [has] wreaked havoc. . . . I myself had not foreseen that [the] whole country would be thrown into turmoil. . . . Since it was I who caused the havoc, it is understandable if you have some bitter words for me."[14]

Perhaps more distressing to Mao than the turmoil the Red Guards were creating was their preoccupation with what Mao regarded as superficial aspects of the "revisionist" threat – such as ideologically suspect teachers, school administrators, intellectuals, and hapless citizens wearing Western-style clothing. His real target was the Party bureaucracy, which most Red Guard organizations were reluctant to confront and which remained largely intact, even though semi-paralyzed, through most of the country.

In November and December 1966, efforts were made by Mao and the Cultural Revolution Group in Beijing to bring the sprawling Red Guard movement under control and to direct its very considerable political energies against the upper levels of the Party hierarchy. Although Mao had proclaimed the cultural revolutionary principle that "the masses must liberate themselves," he did not hesitate to employ such bureaucratic agencies as were under his personal control, not excluding secret police units, to manipulate the mass movement and to advance his political aims. Now such agencies were enlisted to identify government and Party officials that Red Guards were to attack – and facilitate their downfall. Many other departures from the original principles of the Cultural Revolution were to follow.

Mao Zedong's efforts to bring a degree of order and common purpose to the Red Guard movement were only temporarily successful. By 1967 rival Red Guard organizations became embroiled in endless cycles of violence and revenge. Eventually, Mao was to call on Lin Biao's army to remove the factious Red Guards from the political arena – and the PLA was to do so in sometimes bloody fashion, especially in the summer of 1968. But well before then, the Red Guards had been politically eclipsed when China's actual proletariat joined the Great Proletarian Cultural Revolution.

The urban working class

Rapid industrialization during the Mao era had greatly increased the numbers and importance of China's urban working class. After 1952, when industrial production had been restored to its highest pre-war levels (1936–7), modern industry grew at an average annual rate of 11 percent over the rest of the Mao era. By the time of the Cultural Revolution, the number of urban workers in modern industries had increased almost five-fold, from 3,000,000 in 1952 to about 15,000,000. Although the urban working class was still a small minority of the total working population, the net material value of urban industry now surpassed that of agriculture. Industrial workers, moreover, were strategically concentrated in a small number of large cities.

Mao Zedong, despite his rustic self-image, ardently promoted modern industrialization. Yet save for his brief career as a labor organizer in the early 1920s, he had demonstrated little interest in the political potential of urban workers either before or after 1949. While the Cultural Revolution was conceived and proceeded largely as an urban movement, Mao did not originally allow a role for the industrial proletariat, whose productive endeavors were not to be interrupted. The term "proletarian" in the Great Proletarian Cultural Revolution referred to a Maoist political consciousness that existed quite apart from the actual proletariat.

In the last months of 1966, however, Mao Zedong was forced to turn to the urban working class when the Cultural Revolution was stymied by the stubborn resistance of the Party bureaucracy. Many of the restraints on the organization of workers were relaxed and Red Guards were permitted to propagate the rebellious message of the Cultural Revolution in the factories. The most dramatic events, crucial for the nation-wide outcome of the Cultural Revolution, took place in Shanghai, China's most populous and most highly industrialized city. Mao Zedong's response to the revolutionary workers' movement in Shanghai revealed the social and political limits he had placed on the mass movement he had called into being.

In early November 1966 Shanghai workers joined rebellious Red Guards in verbal and sometimes physical attacks against municipal Party authorities and government officials. It was the harbinger of an extraordinary groundswell of self-organization among the proletariat in cities all across China. But in Shanghai insurgent workers were far more numerous than elsewhere, more militant in their demands and actions, and more explicitly hostile to the established Party apparatus. But they did not join the Cultural Revolution as a united body. In Shanghai, as elsewhere, the working class was socially and economically divided into relatively privileged permanent state workers, who enjoyed job security and social welfare benefits, and increasing numbers of exploited temporary and contract workers, who labored for meager compensation. With the unaccustomed freedom to organize brought by the Cultural Revolution, the socio-economic differences among the working population found immediate expression in the formation of competing political organizations. Yet, after a period of strikes, demonstrations, and sometimes violent factional fighting, the workers of Shanghai managed to achieve a sufficient degree of unity to overthrow the powerful Shanghai Party apparatus in the first week of 1967. The "January Revolution" was hailed in Beijing, and throughout the land, as a great popular victory over "revisionism." It marked, after all, the appearance of China's actual proletariat in the Great Proletarian Cultural Revolution, the first political victory of the urban working class since the great revolutionary upsurge of 1925–7.

To replace the discredited Shanghai Communist Party organization, radical Maoist intellectuals from the central Cultural Revolution Group who had placed themselves at the head of the workers' movement proclaimed a new Shanghai People's Commune, based, it was claimed, on the principles of the Paris Commune of 1871. It was to be a democratic "self-government of the producers" with elected officials who were to be subject to immediate popular recall. The standing army and police were to be abolished.

There was no lack of incongruity between these principles and the methods used by radical Maoists to establish the Shanghai People's Commune, not least of all their employment of the PLA and the secret police. But the democratic principles of Marx's model of the Paris Commune were loudly proclaimed and struck responsive chords among the citizens of Shanghai, no doubt partly a reflection of their antipathy to the dictatorial rule of the old Party municipal regime. It was anticipated that the newly announced form of government would win Mao Zedong's enthusiastic approval. Mao, after all, often had invoked Marx's image of the Paris Commune to support his policies, especially during the Great Leap and at the beginning of the Cultural Revolution. His acolytes in Shanghai had every reason to expect that the Chairman would laud their efforts.

The Shanghai People's Commune was formally proclaimed on February 5, 1967, its inauguration celebrated by 1,000,000 citizens who gathered in the central square of the huge metropolis. But Mao Zedong was silent. Eventually in mid-February he summoned two of the radical leaders of the Shanghai movement to an audience in Beijing. In the course of three conversations, Mao condemned the more egalitarian proposals of Shanghai's cultural revolutionaries as "extreme anarchism." He complained that the commune form of organization was politically feeble: "Communes are too weak when it comes to suppressing counter-revolution. People have come and complained to me that when the Bureau of Public Security arrest people, they go in the front door and out the back."[15] And most tellingly, Mao wondered whether the Paris Commune model left any place for the Communist Party, suggesting that the country would require the Party and its experienced cadres for many years to come. He thus recommended that the Shanghai Commune transform itself into a "Revolutionary Committee" based on the "triple alliance" of Army, Party, and the mass organizations formed during the Cultural Revolution – the political outcome of the struggles of the Cultural Revolution that Mao now demanded be universally implemented in provinces and municipalities across the land. The Shanghai leaders quickly complied, and after an uneventful 19-day history the Shanghai People's Commune became the Revolutionary Committee of the Municipality of Shanghai. Neither the birth nor the death of the Shanghai Commune was recorded in official Maoist histories of the Cultural Revolution.

The demise of the Shanghai Commune revealed that the personal power of Mao had become so great that merely a few words from the Chairman could decide not only the fate of individuals but also the outcome of great social movements. If Mao had suspended his Leninist convictions to launch a popular attack on the Party at the beginning of the Cultural Revolution, his response to the Shanghai Commune confirmed that his Leninist and authoritarian inclinations had once again come to the fore. A Leninist party, uneasily combined with a personal autocracy, were to dominate Chinese political life until the end of the Mao era in 1976.

The events in Shanghai also underlined how little Mao Zedong's conception of socialism had been influenced by the Marxian notion of the democratic "self-government of the producers," despite his emotional attachment to Marx's description of the Paris Commune. It is striking how rarely Mao found political democracy a desirable goal in itself, either in his long revolutionary career or in his voluminous writings. In the May Fourth era, to be sure, Mao was influenced by the powerful democratic currents of the time, expressing his admiration for Chen Duxiu's ideals of Western democracy and science, and praising democracy as "the great rebel."[16] After his conversion to Marxism in late 1920, however, the term "democracy" became more restricted in meaning. When it was not simply used as shorthand for the Marxist-Leninist concept of a "bourgeois-democratic" revolution, "democracy" referred to popular participation in – not popular control of – political life. For the most part, Mao regarded democracy (as participation or "mobilization") as a means to centralized ends, especially the ends of a Communist party operating in accordance with the Leninist principle of "democratic centralism."

It was only on the eve of the Cultural Revolution that Mao considered a democratic alternative to the Leninist party. That short-lived quest had found its principal expression in the "16 Points" of August 1966, where it was solemnly proclaimed that "the only method is for the masses to liberate themselves, and any method of doing things in their stead must not be used." A democratic strain also appears in Mao's increasingly frequent, if brief, references to the Paris Commune and the extensive literature produced by Maoist ideologists on the Marxian model.

Mao Zedong's rejection of the Shanghai Commune in February 1967, however, marked the end of his brief flirtation with the possibility of some sort of democratic alternative to the Leninist party. The remaining two years of the Cultural Revolution (according to the chronology of the great upheaval set forth at its official conclusion in April 1969) largely revolved around Mao's efforts to control the social and political forces he had unleashed and to restore order to the state and society that had emerged from the revolution. He now embarked on an agonizing retreat from the aims and principles of the Cultural Revolution that he had set forth in the summer of 1966, albeit disguising the retreat under an abundance of revolutionary rhetoric which became ever more extreme as it became further removed from social reality.

The role of the PLA

In the tortuous history of Mao's attempt to end the upheaval he had initiated – which was officially presented as a "deepening" of the revolution – the People's Liberation Army played a major role. A few weeks before he brought about the demise of the Shanghai Commune, Mao had ordered the PLA to enter the battles of the Cultural Revolution, instructing Lin Biao both to restore order and to assist the nebulous "revolutionary left." Mao's decision in favor of military intervention, although a limited intervention at first, was doubly incongruous. Since the revolutionary days it had been a principal Maoist maxim that "the Party controls the gun," a rule scrupulously enforced both before and after 1949. But now, after nine months of Maoist-inspired assaults, the Party had ceased to function as a national organization, its Central Committee having been superseded by *ad hoc* meetings of the Cultural Revolution Group of Mao loyalists who spoke in the name of the Party center. With the Party inoperative save on the local level, it was inevitable that the army would become the dominant political institution in China, responsible only to the personal authority of Mao. The political supremacy of the PLA reflected itself in the organization of provincial "revolutionary committees," with the army emerging as the dominant partner in the "triple alliance."

Military intervention was glaringly incongruous with the aims loudly proclaimed at the beginning of the Cultural Revolution. Among those goals, and ones which struck deeply responsive chords in Chinese society, were Mao Zedong's promises to combat bureaucratic elitism and promote egalitarianism – and allow the people to "liberate themselves" and do nothing "in their stead." Yet the army was the most bureaucratic and hierarchical organ of the state apparatus, and its intervention was bitterly resented by radical activists who had taken Mao's promises seriously. Those resentments deepened in February and March 1967 when the PLA, more inclined to establish order than assist "the revolutionary left," employed lethal force to disband many of the more radical Red Guard and workers' organizations in several provinces. That, in turn, produced a radical backlash against the army throughout much of the country, culminating in the "hot summer" of 1967.

Popular resentments against military intervention were intensified by the efforts of Mao and Zhou Enlai to rehabilitate Party officials who had been "overthrown" earlier in the Cultural Revolution and bring about a "great alliance" between the contending factions. Those resentments burst forth in a frenzy of violence in cities across the nation in the late spring and summer. Arms were seized from military installations and the battles between "conservative" and "radical" organizations became ever more lethal; the Foreign Ministry in Beijing was occupied by radical intellectuals who proclaimed a new "revolutionary" foreign policy; conservative PLA units in the industrial center of Wuhan mutinied, defying orders from the central government in Beijing; and the army as a whole was physically and verbally attacked, accused of suffering from the same "revisionist" influences as the Party. Mao Zedong, alarmed by the escalating violence, had embarked on a two-month tour of the more chaotic areas of the country at the beginning of the summer, fruitlessly attempting to unite the warring factions. He returned to Beijing at the end of August, sobered by his realization that to continue the Cultural Revolution as a mass movement threatened civil war. On September 5 he ordered the army to restore order, effectively ending the Cultural Revolution in fact, if not yet in name. Red Guards were told to return to their schools. The violence of the summer was blamed on a nebulous "ultra-left" faction of the movement, whose leaders turned out to be leading members of Mao's own central Cultural Revolution group – and who, Mao later decided, were actually "ultra-rightists." Purges, carried out by the Minister of Public Security Kang Sheng, accelerated, and they were directed not only against those who had opposed the Cultural Revolution but those who opposed ending it, leaving Mao Zedong both more powerful and increasingly isolated in an ever more Byzantine political world.

Yet the mass movement had acquired a radical life of its own, and it was to take another year for Mao to bring it under central control. The task fell mainly to the PLA, and it was carried out against radical workers and students with the brutality characteristic of a military campaign. The repression fell hardest on radical Red Guards who had taken Mao's revolutionary promises and slogans too seriously. The organizations that refused to disband on their own were crushed by the army in bloody battles and mass executions in various parts of the country. Of the estimated half-million citizens whose deaths can be directly attributable to the Cultural Revolution, the largest toll of human lives was taken by the PLA in its brutal repression of Red Guards during spring and summer of 1968.

Mao Zedong, on one poignant occasion near the end of the Cultural Revolution, accepted responsibility for crushing the very Red Guard movement he had called into being. Mao had arranged a meeting with the leaders of Red Guard organizations who were fighting the last futile – and now purposeless – battles of the Cultural Revolution on university campuses in Beijing. The somber gathering was held to inform the Red Guards that they had not passed the political test as worthy "revolutionary successors." In the course of his extemporaneous remarks, Mao referred to accusations that a behind-the-scenes "black hand" was to blame for the brutal repression of the Red Guard movement. "Who is the black hand?," Mao asked. "You still haven't captured him. The black hand is nobody else but me."[17]

Without Mao's support the Red Guard organizations quickly disintegrated – and when they did not the remnants of the movement were crushed by the army. Some students were permitted to remain in their schools, but under the PLA's supervision in the form of "Workers' Mao Zedong Thought Propaganda Teams." A far greater number were sent to live in the countryside where they were to undergo what Mao called "reeducation by the poor and lower middle peasants." But the real purpose was to remove the politicized youth from the cities. Over the next few years some 4 million young people were dispatched to the rural areas, there to become members of "the lost generation." Such was the fate of those who had been the first and most ardent to heed Mao's injunction that it was "justified to rebel." The right to rebel (and to organize) – which had been granted by Mao – was withdrawn by him as a now politically quiescent people bowed down to worship plaster icons of the deified leader to whom they had subordinated themselves.

As the Red Guard movement was coming to an end the PLA was finally completing the organization of provincial revolutionary committees, presumably based on the "triple alliance." The last of the revolutionary committees was formally established in September 1968, and like all the others it had come into being under the auspices of the army. PLA commanders chaired all but two of the 28 provincial and regional committees. And insofar as there was an "alliance" it was between the PLA and what remained of provincial Party organizations. In the meantime, Mao, having concluded that neither he nor China could do without the Leninist party, and now wary about the dominant role that the military had assumed in political life, was quietly promoting the rebuilding of the Communist Party, restoring to power many of the cadres and officials who had been "overthrown" in the Cultural Revolution.

Mao Zedong, who had launched the Cultural Revolution as an attack against a Communist Party whose revolutionary virtue had been corrupted by "capitalist roaders" plotting a "bourgeois restoration," now went to elaborate lengths to refurbish the Leninist image of an infallible Party organization. Thus Liu Shaoqi, long Mao's heir-apparent, was expelled from the Party at a rump meeting of the Central Committee in late 1968 not only because of his political errors in the years immediately preceding the Cultural Revolution, but also, it was now belatedly discovered, because he had been a traitor and an agent of the Guomindang since the early 1920s. The purpose of such absurd accusations, much like those Stalin leveled at the "old Bolsheviks" in the Moscow trials in the 1930s, was to picture the Leninist party as impeccably correct and attribute its deviations to enemy agents who had infiltrated it from without. And when the Ninth CCP Congress convened in April 1969 to formally conclude the Cultural Revolution, Mao made the astonishing claim – through the medium of the report delivered by his new "designated successor" Lin Biao – that the Cultural Revolution really had been a movement for "Party consolidation" all along.

In his brief opening address to the Ninth CCP Congress Mao Zedong proclaimed that the Cultural Revolution had concluded with a "victory" and had brought about "unity." And the words "victory" and "unity" were duly celebrated by China's surviving political leaders during the congress and after.

Yet Mao Zedong would have been hard pressed to explain the nature of the victory – had anyone dared to ask. The Cultural Revolution opened with stirring promises of popular democracy, but the students and workers who so ardently embraced those promises immediately subordinated themselves to the thoughts and person of Mao Zedong and his cult. The Cultural Revolution won much of its popular support as a movement against bureaucratic privilege, but millions who joined the crusade soon fell under the sway of the army, the most hierarchical bureaucratic agency of the state apparatus. Mao Zedong had launched the upheaval with a call to "bombard the headquarters" of the Chinese Communist Party, where the threat of a "bourgeois restoration" presumably resided, but the Cultural Revolution officially ended with the Maoist claim that it really had been a "Party consolidation movement." In 1966 Mao had enjoined cultural revolutionaries to uproot "the four olds," especially the pernicious superstitions inherited from traditional China, but he did not object to replacing them with the superstitious worship of "The Thought of Mao Zedong" and the primitive rituals performed around his cult. The Cultural Revolution was to train the youth of China as "revolutionary successors," but the military repression of those who heeded Mao's call to "dare to rebel" bred disillusionment and political cynicism among an entire generation of young urban Chinese. The urban proletariat became politically activated during the Cultural Revolution for the first time since Chiang Kai-shek's armies brutally crushed the workers' movement in 1927, but the vital working-class organizations that emerged during the brief period of freedom of organization were soon suppressed, and workers were once again reduced to political passivity. The Cultural Revolution, Mao claimed, was undertaken to forestall a "bourgeois restoration" and revitalize the spirit of socialism in the post-revolutionary era, but the betrayal of proclaimed principles by Mao above and the senseless violence engendered below served only to discredit the very idea of socialism for many Chinese and to create what soon was to be called a "crisis of faith" in Marxism.

It is striking that the political structure that emerged from the chaos of the Cultural Revolution was essentially the same Party-dominated bureaucracy that existed before the great upheaval – and which Mao had identified as the site and source of "revisionism." Mao Zedong had predicted in 1966 that the Cultural Revolution would bring a "wholly new form of state power" and Maoist ideologists had suggested a "system of general elections" based on the Paris Commune model. But Mao, distrustful of political democracy and fearful of chaotic conditions that might spiral out of his personal control, settled for the restoration of the Communist Party, albeit presumably ideologically rectified and shorn of his more prominent opponents. Yet even the personnel of the Party was much the same. Zhou Enlai reported that 95 percent of Party cadres purged during the Cultural Revolution had been reinstated by 1970.[18] More were to follow, including Deng Xiaoping, the "second leading person in authority taking the capitalist road." For Mao the preservation of the Party that he had been largely responsible for building since the mid-1930s, and the nationalist imperative to preserve the state that he had founded, proved more compelling than the risky business of yielding further to the radical impulses that had prompted him to launch the Cultural Revolution in 1966.

To be sure, several significant policy changes issued from the Cultural Revolution. Most notable among these was a reinvigorated program for building small-scale rural industries, a dramatic increase in primary and secondary education in the countryside, and a significant expansion of the rural healthcare system. While these lent a measure of credence to Mao's much emphasized goal of narrowing the gap between the cities and the rural areas, they were modest reforms that just as well could have been undertaken without the social and human costs exacted by the Cultural Revolution. Although Mao had been critical of occupational specialization and the existing division of labor in the years preceding the Cultural Revolution, his concern with maintaining agricultural and industrial production prevailed over his desire to restructure the social relations of production – in practice if not necessarily in ideology. Thus, apart from cosmetic changes, productive relations remained much the same in both the cities and the countryside. Radical demands that workers and peasants assume democratic control over the conditions of their labor, demands which came from below and sometimes from Maoist ideologists in Beijing, were denounced as "ultra-leftist" well before the Cultural Revolution had run its painful course.

The "victory" of the Cultural Revolution that Mao Zedong proclaimed in April 1969 was a hollow one, especially when set against the goals that had been set forth in 1966. And the new era of "unity" proved short-lived. Hardly had the Ninth CCP Congress concluded its business than new political struggles erupted in a Politburo whose membership largely had been selected by Mao. The most spectacular of the internal conflicts was between Mao and Lin Biao, the Minister of Defense and, according to the new Party constitution, Mao Zedong's "close comrade in arms and successor."

The struggle between Mao and his designated successor unfolded over a period of two years, from shortly after the close of the Ninth Congress to Lin Biao's abortive coup and death in September 1971. At the heart of the matter was Mao's determination to fully reestablish the supremacy of the Chinese Communist Party – since the Cultural Revolution had yielded nothing to take its place – and restore to power most of the Party's experienced officials and cadres who had been purged as "revisionists" or worse. Thus, in the months following the Ninth CCP Congress, Mao, recalling nostalgically the Party's heroic struggles during the desperate revolutionary days, expressed a new-found faith in "the old comrades who have made mistakes in the past."[19] And Mao claimed that from the beginning of the Cultural Revolution he had opposed the mistreatment of Party cadres.[20]

Mao's drive to restore the Communist Party to its former Leninist preeminence required doing away with several political incongruities which had resulted from the Cultural Revolution. One was the central Cultural Revolution Group in Beijing which, under Mao's personal auspices, had often substituted itself for the Party Politburo. The Group was abolished at the end of 1969 and its head, Chen Boda, Maoist ideologist *par excellence*, was expelled from the Party as "China's Trotsky."

Another incongruity was the cult of Mao Zedong, which during the Cultural Revolution had grown in extravagance in direct proportion to the increasing paralysis of the Communist Party. In December 1970, in a discussion with Edgar Snow, Mao acknowledged that his "personality cult" had been deliberately fabricated as a weapon to stimulate the masses to dismantle a Party bureaucracy over which he had lost control. Now that he had regained dominance it was time for the cult to be "cooled down."[21] While Mao suffered from no lack of public worship and official praise during his last years, the more extreme manifestations of his personality cult were muted in the early 1970s as the Party was being rebuilt. With uncharacteristic modesty, or perhaps feigned modesty, he now described such titles as "Great Helmsman," which he long had gladly accepted, as a great nuisance, and said he merely wished to be remembered as the school teacher he once briefly had been.[22]

A more formidable obstacle to the Leninist reconstruction of the post-revolutionary order was the anachronistic result of the Cultural Revolution that left Lin Biao's army the dominant institution in the People's Republic. Lin Biao was not only Mao Zedong's designated successor but the head of the PLA – and the military now controlled the revolutionary committees which the Cultural Revolution had yielded as the loci of political power in provinces and localities. Lin Biao's efforts to maintain the army's preeminent position in Chinese politics raised Bonapartist fears. Mao began to accuse Lin, and the PLA generals who had gathered around him, of "arrogance" and, hardly more than a year after Lin was formally named the Chairman's successor, Mao was maneuvering to depose him.

In the bizarre struggle for power that ensued, Lin Biao, ironically, became an even more ardent champion of Mao's personality cult, which he had played no small part in constructing. Yet it was in Lin's political interests to do so, for promoting the cult perpetuated the situation in the Cultural Revolution whereby the Party as an institution was subordinate to its leader. It was a way for Lin to hinder the rebuilding of the Party, which threatened to remove the PLA from the dominant political role it had assumed. And it also was a way to preserve Mao's status as supreme leader, a position which Lin Biao stood to inherit. Thus Lin proposed in 1970 that Mao officially be proclaimed a "genius" in the new state constitution that was being drafted. Mao, well aware of the political implications and purposes of the proposal, refused the title and later responded in fundamentalist Leninist fashion: "genius does not depend on one person or a few people. It depends on a party, the party which is the vanguard of the proletariat."[23]

The prolonged political intrigues that were to bring about the fall of Lin Biao make for a depressing commentary on the effects of the Cultural Revolution on Chinese political life. Mao moved carefully and methodically against his designated successor, taking special pains to ensure the loyalty of troops stationed in or near the capital. Lin and the generals allied with him responded with plans for a military coup that revolved around a plot to assassinate Mao. The coup proved abortive and on September 13, 1971, Lin Biao hastily fled on a Trident jet, apparently bound for the Soviet Union. Short on fuel, the plane crashed in Mongolia, killing all on board. The demise of Lin Biao was quickly followed by a massive purge of his supporters in both the military and civilian bureaucracies. The purge struck 11 of the 21 members of the Politburo, most of them PLA generals, revealing how much the military's influence in the Party had grown during the Cultural Revolution.

Mao and Nixon

In the second week of July 1971, two months before the fall of Lin Biao, it was announced – to the surprise of most Chinese and to the astonishment of the world – that Henry Kissinger, National Security advisor to President Richard Nixon, had visited Beijing. Kissinger's talks with Premier Zhou Enlai prepared the way for Nixon's dramatic journey to

China in February 1972 and the American President's meeting with Mao Zedong in the Chairman's study in Zhongnanhai. The Sino-US rapprochement that followed greatly alleviated, even if it did not end, a quarter-century of bitter hostility that was precipitated by American support of the Chiang Kai-shek regime during the Chinese civil war in the late 1940s. And it was to result – although after both Mao and Nixon had passed from the political scene – in the full normalization of relations between the two countries.

The understanding between Richard Nixon, who had built his career on an anti-Communist platform, and Mao Zedong, the most eminent of Communist leaders, seemed an incongruity to many people on both sides of the Pacific. But it was not inconsistent with a Maoist foreign policy that, while clothed in revolutionary rhetoric, was conservatively cautious in substance, based on narrow calculations of China's national self-interest. In Mao's view, the Soviet Union posed a greater danger to China than did the US – despite the *de facto* American military protectorate over the rump Guomindang regime in Taiwan, US bases which half-surrounded China, and the continuing intensification of the American war in Vietnam. The split between Moscow and Beijing had escalated from an increasingly bitter ideological dispute to bloody military clashes in 1969. More than a million Soviet troops were stationed along the 5,000-mile Sino-Soviet border, Soviet nuclear-armed missiles were targeted on Chinese cities, and the Russians hinted at a "preemptive" attack against Chinese nuclear installations, which since 1967 included hydrogen bombs. The Russian threat seemed particularly ominous after the Soviet invasion of Czechoslovakia in 1968. This was followed by the "Brezhnev doctrine," according to which Moscow arrogated to itself the right to intervene militarily in countries that made up what Soviet rulers still called "the Communist camp."

It was largely in response to the Soviet threat that Mao Zedong, in one of several Chinese overtures to Washington, told Edgar Snow that he would be happy to talk with Richard Nixon either in his capacity as tourist or president.[24] As it happened, Mao's invitation coincided with a new turn in American foreign policy that dictated a tactical accommodation with China to counter Soviet influence. Although Zhou Enlai was to play the most prominent public role in the negotiations that followed, China's new "America policy" was taken on Mao's initiative. Indeed, it hardly could have been even seriously discussed without the Chairman's approval.

Lin Biao was the most important opponent of the rapprochement with the US, less because of any special attachment to the proclaimed Chinese principle of "proletarian internationalism" than because of considerations of political power. His treatise *Long Live the Victory of People's Revolutionary War*, written in 1965, projected the Maoist revolutionary experience into a global vision of world revolution whereby "the countryside" of the economically backward continents would overwhelm the rich "cities" of Europe and North America. During the Cultural Revolution, this messianic revolutionary fantasy was widely taken as the essence of the Maoist worldview – but it was never one that Mao himself took seriously as a guide to China's foreign policy. However, it was a vision that was closely identified with Lin Biao, and thus Mao's policy of reaching an accommodation with the United States became one of the issues in the struggle between the Chairman and his designated "successor," although far less of an issue than the rebuilding of the Communist Party. The demise of Lin Biao two months after Kissinger's first visit to Beijing removed the last obstacle to the implementation of Mao's new foreign policy. Realpolitik diplomacy was now triumphant in Beijing as well as Washington.

When President Nixon visited Mao Zedong in February 1972, he was accompanied by Henry Kissinger, who described the celebrated journey as a "geopolitical necessity." Kissinger, a student of power, and much enamored of his subject, stood in awe of the elemental political power that the aged Chairman embodied. Kissinger noted, like many before him, that Mao's study was cluttered with books and manuscripts, covering the walls, the tables, and even the floor. "It looked like more the retreat of a scholar than the audience room of the all-powerful leader of the world's most populous nation," he observed. But what really struck him was the power Mao projected:

> there was no ceremony, Mao just stood there. . . . I have met no one, with the possible exception of Charles de Gaulle, who so distilled raw concentrated will power. . . . He dominated the room – not by the pomp that in most states confers a degree of majesty on the leaders, but by exuding in almost tangible form the overwhelming drive to prevail.[25]

Last years

The last years of Mao's rule were dreary and depressing, both for the Chairman and the land he so totally dominated. The rapprochement with the United States and Nixon's pilgrimage to Mao's study in what was once called the Forbidden City were Mao Zedong's last triumph. In a sense, save for his Pyrrhic electoral victory in November 1972, they were Nixon's last triumph as well. In the remaining years of the Mao era, growing waves of pessimism and cynicism swept over Chinese society, partly resulting from the festering wounds of the Cultural Revolution, and, for some, Mao Zedong's betrayal of the promise of the Cultural Revolution. The Lin Biao affair deepened public cynicism about their leaders when it was revealed – a year after the event – that yet another of Mao's anointed successors had been cast into oblivion. Mao and Lin Biao had in fact been close comrades in arms since 1928. Even the most devoted of the Chairman's followers must have wondered why it took Mao more than 40 years to penetrate the "false front" behind which stood a traitor.

The sense of dismay and disillusionment was not relieved by the debilitating factional political struggles that followed the fall of Lin Biao, the increasingly arbitrary employment of state power, and the Byzantine palace intrigues and obscurantist ideological quarrels that surrounded the dying Chairman's desperate and futile search for a worthy successor. The political turmoil was compounded by the death of virtually all the remaining members of the May Fourth generation of Communist political leaders in the early and mid-1970s. By 1976, the year in which both Zhou Enlai and Mao died, the chaos had spread from the Politburo to society at large. China was plagued by economic stagnation, rising social discontent, an upsurge of crime, and a rash of workers' strikes.

What Mao Zedong did leave to hold China together was not a viable successor but rather a revitalized Communist Party, which had risen phoenix-like from the ashes of the Cultural Revolution. The fall of Lin Biao in 1971 had removed the last obstacle to the rebuilding of the Party. By August 1973, when the delegates convened in Beijing for the Party's Tenth National Congress, Mao had succeeded not only in reestablishing the CCP in its orthodox Leninist form but, more quietly, restoring most of its pre-Cultural Revolution leaders, not excluding Deng Xiaoping, recently known as "the second leading person in authority taking the capitalist road." Mao presided over the Congress, but did not address the assembled delegates. His main efforts at the Congress were devoted to balancing the two factions into which the Party was increasingly divided: the veteran cadres and officials who had been attacked during the Cultural Revolution and who now looked to Premier Zhou Enlai for leadership; and a younger group of "radicals" whom the Cultural Revolution had catapulted into the upper ranks of the Party hierarchy. The leaders of the latter were soon to be known as the "Gang of Four," a label coined by Mao in 1975 after admonishing his radical disciples for their conspiratorial methods. Mao Zedong hoped – in vain, as it turned out – to preserve both the

Leninist party and what he took to be the legacy of the Cultural Revolution.

The problem of providing a credible explanation for the fall of Lin Biao was the occasion for Mao Zedong's last ideological campaign. Lin originally had been accused – when his demise was belatedly revealed to the Chinese people in 1972 – of having been an "ultra-leftist." But Mao soon realized that the accusation could intensify doubts about the validity of the Cultural Revolution, with which Lin Biao had been so intimately identified. Thus, at the Tenth Congress, Mao insisted that Lin had really been an "ultra-rightist," and had him posthumously expelled from the Party as a "bourgeois careerist," a "renegade," and a "fascist." To seal the "anti-rightist" case against Lin, he was also accused of having been an admirer of Confucius. The campaign to expose Lin's political sins thus merged with an ongoing minor academic debate which had come to focus on the reactionary role of Confucius in China's transition from a "slave" to a "feudal" society in the first millennium BC.

The strange "Criticize Lin, Criticize Confucius" campaign that dominated the official press for more than a year was filled with obtuse historical allusions to the Cultural Revolution, intelligible only to those familiar with the political struggles then raging behind closed doors in the Party Politburo. Mao Zedong appeared in the campaign in the guise of the First Emperor of the Qin dynasty who had acted in accordance with the progressive forces of history by uniting the various warring states into a centralized empire in 221 BC. Lin Biao, in turn, was pictured as the modern heir of the reactionary Confucian scholars who opposed the First Emperor by clinging to ancient territorial divisions, propagating outmoded ideas, and fostering antiquated social relations.

Mao Zedong's health began to deteriorate noticeably in the wake of the Lin Biao affair. Perhaps it was partly the physically arduous tour of the provinces he undertook in late summer 1971 to ensure the loyalty of local PLA commanders. Perhaps it was the shock of Lin Biao's treachery. By the time Mao met Nixon in February 1972, it was noted that a nurse stood by to steady him. He became bloated, suffering from congestive heart failure, for which he refused treatment. Other serious ailments followed, including motor neuron disease, lung infections, and cataracts. His speech became labored and eventually unintelligible, forcing him to communicate by writing brief notes on scraps of paper. Nonetheless, he continued to preside over Politburo meetings. He made a final visit to his native province of Hunan in the fall of 1974, remaining in the provincial capital of Changsha for five months. From there he continued to conduct affairs of state and Party, or at least to have the final word on most important policy and personnel decisions. But, for the most part, he spent his last years in the seclusion of his study in Zhongnanhai, where his public appearances were confined to brief meetings with visiting foreign dignitaries. In June 1976 it was announced that the Chairman was too frail to receive foreign visitors. During the summer, as Mao lay dying, the struggle between the "radical" Gang of Four and the "moderate" veteran Party officials intensified and swirled around him. The Chairman trusted neither faction and had selected Hua Kuofeng, a little-known Hunanese provincial official as his successor. "With you in charge, I am at ease," he had scribbled on a scrap of paper at the end of April 1976. It was a dubious claim to political legitimacy, and Hua was to play only a transitory role in keeping the now huge Communist bureaucracy together in China's passage to the post-Mao era.

A massive heart attack eventually ended Mao Zedong's life in the early morning of September 9, 1976. His embalmed body was put on display in a glass sarcophagus in the newly built Chairman Mao Memorial Hall, located on the square opposite the ancient Gate of Heavenly Peace. Tens of millions of tourists and pilgrims thronged to view Mao's corpse draped in the red flag of the People's Republic. The macabre burial place followed not an old Chinese imperial ritual but a modern Communist precedent, established in 1924 when Stalin had Lenin's embalmed body placed in a mausoleum in Moscow's Red Square. It was Lenin's body but Stalin's idea. In a sense, it was perhaps appropriate that the dead Mao should find a similar resting place. For Mao Zedong was both the Lenin and the Stalin of the Chinese Revolution, both the revolutionary founder and the post-revolutionary tyrant.

Epilogue: Progress and Tyranny, Marxism and Maoism

In traditional Confucian historiography Qin Shihuangdi, the First Emperor who in the year 221 BC united the various warring feudal states of ancient China into a centralized empire under the Qin dynasty, is portrayed as the epitome of the evil and tyrannical ruler, not least because he had burned Confucian books and buried alive Confucian scholars. Critics of Mao Zedong often have compared the Chairman with the First Emperor. Mao gladly embraced the historical analogy. At the beginning of the Great Leap in 1958, and again in the early 1970s, Mao praised the First Emperor and his Legalist minister Li Si for promoting progress in their day, unburdened by the traditions of the past. He also defended the harshness of Qin rule – and implicitly his own rule – as models of the revolutionary vigilance necessary to suppress reactionaries and hasten the progressive movement of history.

The analogy is compelling, in its positive as well as its negative implications. Just as the centralized imperial system established during the brief reign of the First Emperor was the political foundation for the economic and cultural achievements of traditional Chinese civilization for more than two millennia, so the Maoist revolution unified China after a century of disintegration, establishing the political preconditions for the industrialization of China and its pursuit of "wealth and power" in the contemporary world. The dates 221 BC and AD 1949 mark not only the establishment of centralized political dictatorships but also the two great social revolutions in China's long history.

The association of socio-economic progress and political tyranny is by no means peculiar to Chinese history. The incongruity is also characteristic of the great bourgeois revolutions that propelled the development of modern capitalism in the West. In the English civil war Cromwell fought valiantly against royal absolutism only to establish his despotic personal rule as Lord Protector. Robespierre, a disciple of Rousseau and a champion of popular democracy, presided over the Reign of Terror at the radical height of the French Revolution. In the Russian October Revolution, a bourgeois revolution in large measure, Lenin's revolutionary achievements during his abbreviated lifetime underwent a cruel metamorphosis after his death in the lengthy despotism of Stalin.

Mao Zedong thus stands in a long line of revolutionary tyrants – revolutionary in that they contributed to great socio-economic progress, tyrannical in their political methods. Mao began his political career as a servant of China's impoverished peasants and made himself their master in the process. He liberated the Chinese nation from the shackles of a century-long foreign impingement, only to bind the people of the nation to the alien shackles of his own deified image. At the end of the Mao era, the people (and particularly the peasants) who had given Mao Zedong his power in the first place bowed before plaster statues of the man who was at once their liberator and their master.

Yet if Mao Zedong's revolutionary career is viewed in broad historical terms, it seems clear that there is no necessary link between social revolution and personal tyranny. Mao appears on a larger historical canvas than his revolutionary predecessors – and for a far longer period of time. For the better part of two decades he was the dominant figure in the most massive – and perhaps the most heroic – revolution in world history. And for 27 years he was the unchallenged leader of the state that he founded in 1949. Over that long revolutionary era, and in the early post-revolutionary period, Mao was a sometimes ruthless leader of a Communist party organized in accordance with authoritarian Leninist precepts – but probably no more personally dictatorial than any effective leader would have been in similarly harsh and unforgiving political and historical circumstances. It was not until his late years that Mao became a tyrant. The ill-fated Great Leap Forward campaign marked the transition from Mao as the dominant leader of an authoritarian Leninist party to a personal tyrant ruling above the Party.

It is noteworthy, indeed it is essential to note, that Mao's greatest achievements occurred before the last tyrannical chapter in his political life. The revolution he led to victory against seemingly overwhelming odds was probably the greatest social revolution in modern world history. In its scope, scale and thoroughgoing character, the Chinese Communist Revolution dwarfed its French and Russian predecessors. No Marxist, at least not before Mao, could have foreseen a modern revolution that took the form of the mobilization of peasants in the backward countryside to "surround and overwhelm" the conservative cities. And few observers predicted the early post-revolutionary successes of the Maoist regime: the unification of China and the establishment of an effective central govern-

ment; the achievement of full national independence after a century of
foreign invasions and colonial impingements; the land reform campaign
which alleviated some of the worst abuses of the old landlord system and
provided funds to spur the modernization of one of the world's most backward lands; the consequent inauguration of a successful program of rapid
industrialization; impressive gains in literacy, education, and healthcare;
and, most strikingly, the near doubling of life expectancy over the quarter-
century of Mao's rule, from an average of 35 years in pre-1949 China to 65
years at the close of the Mao period in the mid-1970s.

These accomplishments were essentially the work of the 1950s, the first
decade of Maoist rule. Many of the progressive programs introduced in
that creative era of the People's Republic, particularly industrialization,
continued to advance in the period that is sometimes called "late Maoism,"
1958–76. But those final years of the Mao era, which coincided with Mao's
personal tyranny and the height of the Mao cult, yielded few lasting initia-
tives. What material progress there was in the late Mao period hardly
compensates for, indeed pales into insignificance, when weighed against
the famine that issued from the Great Leap and the human and social
destructiveness of the Cultural Revolution. The positive work of the Mao
era took place, for the most part, under the prosaic but efficient workings
of a Leninist party regime. It was a regime thoroughly dominated by Mao
Zedong, to be sure, but by Mao before he became an advocate of the doctrine of "permanent revolution" and assumed the guise of a utopian
prophet.

The achievements of the early Mao period were quite extraordinary but
there was nothing particularly socialist about them, save for the ideological
rhetoric in which they were sometimes clothed. National unification and
independence, the creation of a national market, political centralization,
and state promotion of industry – such are the typical features of all the
great bourgeois revolutions which have yielded modern capitalist economies. Even the land reform campaign of 1950–2, the most socially radical
result of the Maoist revolution, was well within bourgeois limits. Land
reform destroyed what remained of the pre-capitalist landlord-gentry
class, the dominant ruling group in traditional rural society, and thus was
the culmination of a great social revolution. But that social revolution
was a capitalist revolution, not a socialist one. What resulted from land
reform was a petty bourgeois system of individual peasant family proprietorship with peasants free to buy, sell, and mortgage their holdings.

Political democracy might be added to this brief enumeration of the
features of a bourgeois revolution. Ideally, a bourgeois (or what Marxists

call a "bourgeois-democratic") revolution produces a more or less democratic political system. In historical reality the emergence of political democracy, even in the most economically advanced countries, has been a long, drawn-out, tortuous, and often bloody process. In France, for example, the homeland of the classic bourgeois revolution, it was not until the establishment of the Third Republic in 1871, nearly a century after the great Revolution of 1789, that a viable system of political democracy was constructed. Dictatorships, restorations, and failed revolutions filled the intervening years.

There were few signs of any movement toward political democracy during the Mao period, and not many more in the post-Mao era. But in most essential respects the Maoist revolution performed the major tasks of the bourgeois revolution which previous Chinese regimes failed to accomplish. This, in turn, provided the necessary social and political prerequisites for the industrialization of the Mao period and the extraordinary economic revolution of the post-Mao years which has made China, in the words of the economic commentator Martin Wolf, "the workshop of the world," a title originally claimed by 19th-century England.[1] The dynamic capitalist revolution that has transformed China over the past quarter-century would have been impossible without the achievements of the Mao period, especially national unification and land reform.

For many years, before and after 1949, Mao Zedong emphasized the bourgeois character of the Chinese Revolution and the need to advance in accordance with the necessary "stages" of historical development set forth in Marxist-Leninist theory, even though all the stages would be traversed under the political leadership of the Chinese Communist Party. There were powerful objective as well as ideological reasons for Mao's insistence on the "bourgeois" limits of the Chinese revolution. Mid-20th-century China was among the most backward countries on earth, both economically and socially. Karl Marx often had warned of the futility – and the likely regressive historical consequences – of attempting to build a socialist society prematurely, that is, before capitalism had performed its necessary historical work of establishing the essential material preconditions for the new society:

> If the proletariat destroys the political rule of the bourgeoisie, that will only be a temporary victory, only an element in the service of the bourgeois revolution itself . . . so long as in the course of history . . . the material conditions are not yet created which make necessary the abolition of the bourgeois mode of production. . . . Men do not build themselves a new world out of the fruits of the earth, as vulgar superstition believes,

but out of the historical accomplishments of their declining civilization. They must, in the course of their development, begin by themselves producing the material conditions of a new society, and no effort of mind or will can free them from this destiny.[2]

Marx, therefore, insisted that every society must go through "the successive phases of normal development" and that those phases could not be avoided by "bold leaps" or "legal enactments."[3] Such strictures on the exercise of the revolutionary will appear throughout Marxist-Leninist literature and were reflected in Mao Zedong's theory of New Democracy and his emphasis on the necessary "stages" of development in post-revolutionary China, with the various social stages presumably more or less in conformity with the level of the material forces of production.

Yet Mao's subjective desire for socialism proved far more powerful than the influence of Marxist teachings on the objective material prerequisites for the new society. Thus, by the late 1950s, Mao's Marxian insistence on proceeding through the necessary stages of socio-economic development gave way to the notion of a "permanent" or "continuous" revolution, one that bypassed the "bourgeois-democratic" phase altogether; he claimed to have completed "the transition to socialism" in a few short years, and then proclaimed the imminence of communism. It was not Mao Zedong's impatience with the pace of history alone that was responsible for this rush toward utopia in the late 1950s. Mao had come to embody the increasingly radical expectations of peasants, rural Party cadres, and a good many higher Party leaders. He was also inspired, as were many others, by the striking successes of the Chinese Communist Party in the late 1940s and early 1950s – the stunning victory over the Guomindang, the rapid consolidation of Communist power, the successes of land reform and early industrialization, and the revolutionary fervors generated by the agricultural collectivization campaign of 1955–6. By late 1957 Mao Zedong had thrown off all conventional Marxian restraints on the revolutionary will, permitting him to embark on the tragic adventure of the Great Leap Forward. Standing above all institutions, he now became a tyrant as well as a utopian prophet, nearly oblivious to the human and social costs of his "great leap" to communism – and to the costs of the Cultural Revolution, an upheaval which in large measure grew out of the political tensions generated by the failure of the Great Leap.

The ideology that both produced and reflected the traumatic events of the Great Leap and the Cultural Revolution, a body of theory and practice that is sometimes called "late Maoism," was largely based on the Maoism of the revolutionary years. Revolutionary Maoism implicitly rejected many of the basic premises of Marxist theory. It was an ideology that ignored the Marxist insistence that capitalism was a progressive stage of development in world history and the necessary precondition for socialism. It was an ideology that abandoned the urban proletariat as the modern revolutionary class in favor of the peasantry and a celebration of the virtues of rural life. It was a doctrine that celebrated the revolutionary and socialist "advantages of backwardness." And, above all, "late Maoism" extolled the powers of the human will and spirit as the decisive factors in history. All these beliefs, which Marxists conventionally have labeled "utopian," were revived in extreme form on the eve of the Great Leap.

These distinctively Maoist intellectual and ideological notions left little Marxian content in the doctrine canonized as "The Thought of Mao Zedong," even though the latter was hailed as a new and higher stage in the evolution of Marxist-Leninist theory. But what Mao called "the sinification of Marxism," however far it strayed from the basic premises of the original doctrine, was probably necessary for the success of revolution in a land where a revolution was desperately needed. It is most unlikely that revolutionaries who thought and acted in accordance with orthodox Marxist-Leninist views could have succeeded in the Chinese historical environment.

Yet a Maoist doctrine that played so vital a role during the revolutionary years, bringing about an historically necessary revolution in the social state of China, paradoxically had disastrous human and political consequences when it was revived in the post-revolutionary era. Mao Zedong's removal of Marxian restraints on the revolutionary will in the late 1950s opened the way for the catastrophic consequences of the Great Leap Forward and the Cultural Revolution. It was not Mao's so-called "hardline Marxism" that was responsible for the debacles, but, in a sense, his lack of Marxism, or more precisely, his "utopian" departures from Marxian teachings on the imperatives of history. The inevitable failures of the Great Leap and the Cultural Revolution ensured that China's historical development would not, for the foreseeable future, proceed beyond bourgeois limits. The massive process of capitalist development in the decades since Mao's death, perhaps the most dynamic process of capitalist development in world history, is thus both the product of Mao's revolution and its negation, a capitalism that is at once the logical outcome of the Revolution that Mao Zedong led in an economically backward land and a capitalism that mocks his socialist claims and aspirations.

Notes

Chapter 1 Youth, 1893–1921

1 In late 1936, in northern Shaanxi, Mao related an account of his early life to the American journalist Edgar Snow. See Edgar Snow, *Red Star over China* (New York: Random House, 1938), pp. 111–67, 113; hereafter referred to as "Autobiography."

2 "Autobiography," p. 116.

3 Ibid., pp. 119–20.

4 Ibid., p. 120.

5 Ibid., p. 118.

6 Ibid., p. 121.

7 Ibid., p. 125.

8 On the peculiar origins and nature of modern Chinese nationalism, the crucial works remain: Benjamin Schwartz, *In Search of Wealth and Power: Yen Fu and the West* (Cambridge, Mass.: Harvard University Press, 1964); Joseph R. Levenson, *Liang Ch'i-ch'ao and the Mind of Modern China* (Cambridge, Mass.: Harvard University Press, 1959); and Levenson, *Confucian China and its Modern Fate: A Trilogy* (Berkeley: University of California Press, 1968).

9 "Autobiography," p. 128.

10 Mao Zedong, "Classroom Notes," Oct–Dec, 1913, in *Mao's Road to Power: Revolutionary Writings, 1912–1949*, ed. Stuart R. Schram (Armonk, NY: M.E. Sharpe, 1992), vol. I, pp. 113–27; hereafter *RW*.

11 "Autobiography," p. 132.

12 Mao Zedong, "A Study of Physical Education," in *RW*, vol. I, pp. 113–27.

13 Mao Zedong, "Letter to Xiao Zisheng," Aug 1915, ibid., p. 72.

14 Mao Zedong, "Essay on How Shang Yang Established Confidence by the Moving of the Pole," June 1912, ibid., pp. 5–6.

15 Mao Zedong, "A study of Physical Education," ibid., p. 113.

16 Ibid., p. 114.

17 Ibid., p. 120.

18 Ibid., p. 121.

19 Ibid., p. 121.

20 Mao Zedong, "Foreword to Xiao Zisheng's *All in One* Self-Study Notes," Summer 1917, ibid., pp. 128–9.

21 Mao Zedong, "Letter to Li Jinxi," Aug 23, 1917, ibid., p. 132.

22 Ibid., p. 136.

23 Mao Zedong, "*Evening School Journal*, Vol. I," Nov 1917, ibid., p. 152.

24 Chen Duxiu, *Duxiu wencun* [Collected Works], vol. 1 (Shanghai: Yadong tushuguan, 1922), pp. 35–40.

25 For an English translation of Mao's marginal notes and the sections of Paulsen's text to which they refer, see Mao zedong, "Marginal Notes to: Friedrich Paulsen, *A System of Ethics*," 1917–1918, in *RW*, vol. I, pp. 175–313.

26 "Marginal Notes," ibid., p. 310.
27 Ibid., pp. 263–4.
28 Ibid., pp. 237–8.
29 Ibid., p. 208.
30 Ibid., p. 194.
31 Ibid., p. 281.
32 Ibid., pp. 200–1.
33 Ibid., p. 273.
34 "Autobiography," p. 134.
35 Ibid., pp. 134–5.
36 Li Dazhao, "Bolshevism di shengli" [The Victory of Bolshevism] *New Youth*, vol. V, no. 5, Nov 15, 1918.
37 "Autobiography," p. 140.
38 Ibid., p. 135.
39 On anarchist influences in the early Chinese Communist movement, see Arif Dirlik, *Anarchism in the Chinese Revolution* (Berkeley: University of California Press, 1991); and Dirlik, *The Origins of Chinese Communism* (New York: Oxford University Press, 1989). On populist influences on Chinese Marxism, see Maurice Meisner, *Li Ta-chao and the Origins of Chinese Marxism* (Cambridge, Mass.: Harvard University Press, 1967).
40 Mao Zedong, "Manifesto on the Founding of the *Xiang River Review*," July 14, 1919, in *RW*, vol. I, pp. 318–20.
41 Ibid., p. 319.
42 Ibid., p. 320.
43 Mao Zedong, "The Arrest and Rescue of Chen Duxiu," July 14, 1919, ibid., p. 329.
44 Mao Zedong, "The Great Union of the Popular Masses," July 21 and 28, Aug 4, 1919, ibid., pp. 378–89.
45 Ibid., p. 380.
46 Alexander Herzen, "The Russian People and Socialism," in Herzen, *From the Other Shore* (London: Weidenfeld and Nicolson, 1956), pp. 165–208.
47 Mao Zedong, "The Great Union of the Popular Masses," in *RW*, vol. I, p. 389.
48 Li Dazhao's response to the Russian October Revolution is discussed in Maurice Meisner, *Li Ta-chao and the Origins of Chinese Marxism* (Cambridge, Mass.: Harvard University Press, 1967), pp. 60–70.
49 Mao Zedong, "For the Germans, the Painful Signing of the Treaty," July 21, 1919, in *RW*, vol. I, p. 365.
50 Mao Zedong et al., "Proposal that the 'Human Revolutionary Government' Convene a 'Hunan People's Constitution Convention' to Enact a 'Hunan Constitution' in order to Build a 'New Hunan'," Oct 5–6, 1920, ibid., pp. 568–9.
51 Mao Zedong, "Commentary on the Suicide of Miss Zhao," Nov 16, 1919, in *RW*, vol. I, p. 422.
52 Mao Zedong, "The Evils of Society and Miss Zhao," Nov 21, 1919, ibid., pp. 427–30.
53 Mao Zedong, "Concerning the Incident of Miss Zhao's Suicide," Nov 21, 1919, ibid., pp. 431–3.
54 Mao Zedong, "The Question of Love – Young People and Old People," ibid., p. 440.
55 Lu Xun, "Diary of a Madman," *Selected Works of Lu Hsün* (Peking: Foreign Languages Press, 1956), pp. 8–21.
56 Mao Zedong, "Oppose Unification," Oct 10, 1920, in *RW*, vol. I, p. 579.
57 See Mao Zedong, "The Founding of the Cultural Book Society," July 31, 1920, ibid., pp. 534–5; and "First Business Report of the Cultural Book Society," Oct 23, 1920, ibid., pp. 579–82.

58 Mao Zedong, "Reply to Zeng Yi from the Association for Promoting Reform in Hunan," ibid., pp. 526–7.

Chapter 2 Communism and Marxism

1 "Autobiography," p. 139.
2 Mao Zedong, "Manifesto on the Founding of the *Xiang River Review*," July 14, 1919, in *RW*, vol. I, p. 318.
3 Mao Zedong, "The Great Union of the Popular Masses," July 21, 1919, ibid., p. 380.
4 Mao Zedong, "Letter to Zhou Shizhao," March 14, 1920, ibid., pp. 504–7.
5 On the "problems and isms" debate, see Chow Tse-tsung, *The May Fourth Movement* (Cambridge, Mass.: Harvard University Press, 1960), pp. 218–22; Maurice Meisner, *Li Ta-chao and the Origins of Chinese Marxism* (Cambridge, Mass.: Harvard University Press, 1967), pp. 105–11; and Jerome B. Grieder, *Hu Shih and the Chinese Renaissance* (Cambridge, Mass.: Harvard University Press, 1970), ch. 6 and *passim*.
6 Mao Zedong, "Statutes of the Problem Study Society," Sept 1, 1919, in *RW*, vol. I, pp. 407–13.
7 Mao Zedong, "Letter to Luo Aojie," Nov 25, 1920, ibid., pp. 599–600.
8 Mao Zedong, "Letter to Xiao Xudong, Cai Linbin (Cai Hesan), and Other Members in France," Dec 1, 1920, in *RW*, vol. II, pp. 6–7.
9 Ibid., pp. 8–9.
10 "Autobiography," pp. 140–1.
11 Chang Kuo-t'ao, *The Rise of the Chinese Communist Party, 1921–1927: Volume One of the Autobiography of Chang Kuo-t'ao* (Lawrence, Kansas: The University Press of Kansas, 1971), pp. 140–1.
12 Mao Zedong, "Appeal to the 300,000 Citizens of Changsha in Favor of Self-Rule for Hunan," in *RW*, vol. I, p. 572.
13 Mao Zedong, "Letter to Luo Xuezan," Nov 26, 1920, ibid., p. 607.
14 Li Dazhao, "Youth and the Villages," Feb 20–3, 1919, in *Li Dazhao xuanji* [Selected Works] (Beijing: People's Publishing House, 1959), pp. 146–50.
15 On Mao Zedong's activities as a labor organizer in the early 1920s, see Lynda Shaffer, *Mao and the Workers: The Hunan Labor Movement, 1920–23* (Armonk, NY: M.E. Sharpe, 1982); and Angus McDonald, *The Urban Origins of Rural Revolution* (Berkeley: University of California Press, 1978).
16 Mao Zedong, "Hunan under the Provisional Constitution," July 1, 1923, in *RW*, vol. II, p. 170.
17 Ibid., p. 171.
18 Mao Zedong, "The Beijing Coup d'Etat and the Merchants," July 11, 1923, ibid., p. 179.

Chapter 3 Peasant Revolution

1 The best, and the most passionate, account of the revolutionary movement of the mid-1920s remains Harold Isaacs, *The Tragedy of the Chinese Revolution* (Stanford, Ca.: Stanford University Press, 1951).
2 Mao Zedong, "An Analysis of the Various Classes among the Chinese Peasantry and their Attitudes toward the Revolution," Jan 1926, in *RW*, vol. II, p. 304.
3 Mao Zedong, "The National Revolution and the Peasant Movement," Sept 1, 1926, ibid., pp. 387, 389.
4 Karl Marx and Frederick Engels, *Selected Works* (Moscow: Foreign Languages Publishing House, 1950), vol. I, p. 37.
5 Mao Zedong, "Some Points for Attention in Commemorating the Paris Commune," March 18, 1926, in *RW*, vol. II, p. 367.

6 Chen Duxiu, *Zhungguo geming wendi lun wenchi* [A Collection of Articles on Problems of the Chinese Revolution] (Shanghai: Xinqingnian she, 1927), p. 39.

7 Well before Mao Zedong came to recognize the revolutionary potential of the peasantry, the young Communist intellectual Peng Pai had immersed himself in the peasant movement in Guangdong province, which produced China's first rural soviet in late 1927. For a brilliant study of the social origins of the modern peasant movement in Guangdong from a broad historical viewpoint, see Robert B. Marks, *Rural Revolution in South China: Peasants and the Making of History in Haifeng County, 1570–1930* (Madison: University of Wisconsin Press, 1984).

8 "Autobiography," pp. 143–4.

9 Mao Zedong, "The Bitter Sufferings of the Peasants in Jiangsu and Zhejiang, and their Movement of Resistance," in *RW*, vol. II, pp. 414–17.

10 Benjamin I. Schwartz, *Chinese Communism and the Rise of Mao* (Cambridge, Mass.: Harvard University Press, 1952), p. 76.

11 Mao Zedong, "Report on the Peasant Movement in Hunan," Feb 1927, in *RW*, vol. II, p. 430.

12 Ibid., p. 433.

13 Ibid., p. 430.

14 Engels, "The Peasant Question in France and Germany," in Marx and Engels, *Selected Works*, vol. II, p. 384.

15 Mao Zedong, "Report on the Peasant Movement in Hunan," Feb 1927, in *RW*, vol. II, pp. 462–3.

16 Ibid., p. 434.

17 Ibid., pp. 434–5.

18 Ibid., pp. 487, 505, 508.

19 "Autobiography," pp. 144–5.

20 Mao Zedong, "The Hunan Problem," July 4, 1927, in *RW*, vol. III, p. 11.

21 Mao Zedong, "Remarks on the Report of the Representative of the International at the August 7 Emergency Conference," Aug 7, 1927, ibid., p. 30.

22 Mao Zedong, "Report of the Jinggangshan Front Committee to the Central Committee," Nov 25, 1928, ibid., p. 94.

23 Ibid., pp. 114–15.

24 Ibid., p. 102.

25 Ibid., p. 96.

26 Ibid., p. 97.

27 Ibid., pp. 97–8.

28 Mao Zedong, "A Letter from the Front Committee to the Central Committee," April 5, 1929, in *RW*, vol. III, p. 159.

29 "Autobiography," pp. 157–8.

30 Mao Zedong, "A Letter," April 5, 1929, in *RW*, vol. III, p. 155.

31 Ibid., pp. 154–5.

32 Mao Zedong, "Eight Great Conditions for Victory," Dec 22, 1930, in *RW*, vol. III, pp. 718–20.

33 Cited in Jerome Chen, *Mao and the Chinese Revolution* (New York: Oxford University Press, 1965), p. 156.

34 Mao Zedong, "Report to the Central Committee," Sept 17, 1930, in *RW*, vol. III, p. 528.

35 Mao Zedong, "A Letter," April 5, 1929, in *RW*, vol. III, pp. 157–8.

36 As Steven Averill has pointed out in "The Origins of the Futian Incident," in Tony Saich and Hans Van de Ven (eds), *New Perspectives on the Chinese Communist Revolution* (Armonk, NY: M.E. Sharpe, 1995), p. 102; for an earlier account of the Futian incident (pp. 218–37) and an excellent study of Mao's changing political fortunes during the

Jiangxi years, see John E. Rue, *Mao Tse-tung in Opposition, 1927–1935* (Stanford, Ca.: Stanford University Press, 1966).

37 Mao Zedong, "Conclusion of the Joint Conference and Announcement of the Establishment of the Front Committee," Feb 16, 1930, in *RW*, vol. III, p. 269.

38 Averill in Saich and Van de Ven (eds), *New Perspectives*, pp. 88–91.

39 Ibid., p. 107.

40 As pointed out in Schwartz, *Chinese Communism*, pp. 172–88.

41 Mao Zedong, *Report from Xunwu*, trans. and with an introduction by Roger R. Thompson (Stanford, Ca.: Stanford University Press, 1990); the Thompson translation, with minor revisions, is reproduced under the title "Xunwu Investigation" in *RW*, vol. III, pp. 296–418.

42 Mao Zedong, "Oppose Bookism," May 1930, in *RW*, vol. III, pp. 419–26.

43 "Autobiography," p. 166.

Chapter 4 Nationalism and Social Revolution, 1935–49

1 "Autobiography," p. 167.

2 Edgar Snow, *Red Star over China* (New York: Random House, 1938), p. 177.

3 Edgar Snow, "Interview with Mao," *New Republic*, vol. 52, Feb 27, 1965, pp. 17–23.

4 Mao Zedong, "Problems of Strategy in China's Revolutionary War," in *RW*, vol. V, p. 481, n. 72.

5 Mao Zedong, "On Tactics against Japanese Imperialism," Dec 27, 1935, ibid., pp. 86–102.

6 Ibid., p. 100.

7 Mao Tse-tung, *On New Democracy* [1940] (Peking: Foreign Languages Press, 1954), p. 82.

8 Leon Trotsky, *The Third International after Lenin* (New York: Pioneer Publishers, 1936), p. 224.

9 Mao Zedong, "Interview with Edgar Snow on Internal Affairs," July 18–19, 1936, in *RW*, vol. V, p. 268.

10 Mao Zedong, "On Tactics against Japanese Imperialism," ibid., p. 86.

11 Mao Zedong, "Letter from the Red Army to All Officers and Men of the Northeast Army," Jan 25, 1936, ibid., p. 113.

12 Mao Zedong, "Interview with Edgar Snow on Special Questions," July 23, 1936, ibid., p. 285.

13 An essential study for understanding the reasons for the Communist successes during the wartime years – and the civil war that followed – is Chalmers Johnson, *Peasant Nationalism and Communist Power* (Stanford, Ca.: Stanford University Press, 1962). Although perhaps a bit romanticized, the best general book on Maoist policies and practices during the crucial revolutionary years remains Mark Selden, *The Yenan Way in Revolutionary China* (Cambridge, Mass.: Harvard University Press, 1971).

14 Among the most important studies on the nature of Maoism and its relationship to the Marxist and Leninist traditions are Benjamin I. Schwartz, *Chinese Communism and the Rise of Mao* (Cambridge, Mass.: Harvard University Press, 1951); Schwartz, *Communism and China: Ideology in Flux* (Cambridge, Mass.: Harvard University Press, 1968); Stuart R. Schram, *Mao Tse-tung* (New York: Simon and Schuster, 1967); Schram, *The Political Thought of Mao Tse-tung* (New York: Praeger, 1969); and Schram, *La 'Révolution permanente'* (Paris: Mouton, 1963).

15 Mao Zedong, "The Great Union of the Popular Masses," Aug 4, 1919, in *RW*, vol. I, p. 389.

16 Helen Foster Snow [Nym Wales], *Inside Red China* (New York: Da Capo Press, 1977), p. 265.

17 Mao Tse-tung, "On Contradiction," Aug 1937, in *Selected Works* (London: Lawrence and Wishart, 1954), vol. I, p. 332; hereafter *SW*, 1954.

18 "The Great Union of the Popular Masses," July 21, 1919, in *RW*, vol. I, pp. 378–80.

19 Mao Zedong, "The Question of Love – Young People and Old People," Nov 25, 1919, ibid., p. 440.

20 Mao Tse-tung, *The Chinese Revolution and the Chinese Communist Party* (Peking: Foreign Languages Press, 1954).

21 For an unusually perceptive account of the theory and practice of the notion, see Thomas Lutze, "New Democracy: Chinese Communist Relations with the Urban Middle Forces, 1931–1952," Ph.D. dissertation, University of Wisconsin-Madison, 1996 [publication in preparation].

22 Mao Tse-tung, "The Present Situation and Our Tasks," in *Selected Works of Mao Tse-tung* (Peking: Foreign Languages Press, 1961), vol. IV, p. 168; hereafter *SW*, 1961.

23 Mao Zedong, "Reading Notes on the Soviet Union's 'Political Economy,'" in *Mao Zedong sixiang wansui* [Long Live the Thought of Mao Zedong] (Taipei: n.p., 1967), pp. 333–4; hereafter "Reading Notes."

24 Snow, *Red Star*, p. 67.

25 Ibid., pp. 66–7.

26 Mao Tse-tung, "Reform Our Study," May 1941, in *Selected Works of Mao Tse-tung* (Peking hereafter *SW*, 1967; Foreign Languages Press, 1967), vol. III, pp. 17–25; "Rectify the Party's Style of Work," Feb 1, 1942, ibid., pp. 35–51; "Oppose Stereotyped Party Writing," Feb 8, 1942, ibid., pp. 53–68; and the two "Talks at the Yenan Forum on Literature and Art," May 2 and May 23, 1942, ibid., pp. 69–98.

27 Mao Tse-tung, "Talks at the Yenan Forum," May 2 and 23, 1942, ibid., pp. 69–98.

28 On Ding Ling's essay of March 8, 1942, and its political repercussions, see Merle Goldman, *Literary Dissent in Communist China* (Cambridge, Mass.: Harvard University Press, 1967), pp. 22–4, 93.

29 Wang Shiwei, "Wild Lilies" (Part Two), in Dai Qing, *Wang Shiwei and "Wild Lilies"* (Armonk, NY: M.E. Sharpe, 1994), p. 20.

30 Ibid., pp. 66–9.

31 The clash between political demands and intellectual integrity has been the subject of many studies. Among the most interesting are: Paul G. Pickowicz, *Marxist Literary Thought in China* (Berkeley: University of California Press, 1981); Kung Chi-keung, "Intellectuals and Masses: The Case of Qu Quibai," Ph.D. dissertation, University of Wisconsin-Madison, 1995; Merle Goldman, *Literary Dissent in Communist China* (Cambridge, Mass.: Harvard University Press, 1967), and T.A. Hsia, *The Gate of Darkness* (Seattle: University of Washington Press, 1968).

32 Liu Shaoqi, *Collected Works* (Hong Kong: Union Research Institute, 1968), pp. 14, 30–1, 179.

33 Snow, *Red Star*, p. 73.

34 James F. Byrnes, *Speaking Frankly* (New York: Harper, 1947), p. 228.

35 Vladimir Dedijer, *Tito Speaks* (London: Weidenfeld and Nicolson, 1953), p. 331; and Milovan Djilas, *Conversations with Stalin* (New York: Harcourt, Brace & World, 1962), p. 182.

36 Mao Tse-tung, "Talk with the American Correspondent Anna Louise Strong," Aug 1946, in *SW*, 1961, vol. IV, p. 101.

37 Ibid., p. 103.

38 Mao Tse-tung, "The Present Situation and Our Tasks," Dec 25, 1947, ibid., p. 161.

39 Mao Tse-tung, "The Concept for Operations for the Liaoshi-Shenyang Campaign," Sept and Oct 1948, ibid., p. 262.

40 Ibid., p. 261.

41 Maro Tse-tung, "Statement on the Present Situation by Mao Tse-tung, Chairman of the Central Committee of the Communist Party of China," Jan 14, 1949, ibid., p. 317.
42 Mao Tse-tung, "The Chinese People have Stood Up!", in *Selected Works of Mao Tse-tung* (Peking: Foreign Languages Press, 1977), vol. V, pp. 16–17; hereafter *SW*, 1977.

Chapter 5 Mao Zedong in Power: Nationalism and Modernization, 1949–57

1 Deng Xiaoping, Interview with Oriana Fallaci, *Washington Post*, Aug 31, 1980, p. D4.
2 Mao Tse-tung, "On the People's Democratic Dictatorship," June 30, 1949, in *SW*, 1961, vol. IV, pp. 411–24.
3 Ibid., p. 419.
4 Ibid., p. 418.
5 Mao Tse-tung, "Talks at the Chengtu Conference," March 1958, in *Mao Tse-tung Unrehearsed: Talks and Letters, 1956–71*, ed. Stuart R. Schram (Harmondsworth: Penguin Books, 1974), pp. 102–3; hereafter *TL*.
6 Ibid., p. 101.
7 Ibid., p. 99.
8 Fei Xiaotung, *China's Gentry* (Chicago: University of Chicago Press, 1953), p. 119.
9 Mao Tse-tung, "Be a True Revolutionary," June 23, 1950, in *SW*, 1977, vol. V, p. 38.
10 Mao Tse-tung, "Talk on Questions of Philosophy," Aug 18, 1964, *TL*, p. 216.
11 Barrington Moore, *Social Origins of Dictatorship and Democracy* (Boston: Beacon Press, 1966), p. 410.
12 Mao Tse-tung, "A Single Spark Can Start a Prairie Fire," Jan 1930, in *SW*, 1954, vol. I, p. 118.
13 Li Fuchun, "Report on the First Five Year Plan for Development in the National Economy of the People's Republic of China in 1953–1957," in Robert Bowie and John K. Fairbank (eds), *Communist China, 1955–59: Policy Documents with Analysis* (Cambridge, Mass.: Harvard University Press, 1962), p. 48.
14 Mao Tse-tung, "On the Cooperative Transformation of Agriculture," July 1931, 1955, in *SW*, 1977, vol. V, pp. 201–2.
15 Ibid., pp. 184–207.
16 Ibid., pp. 184–5.
17 Ibid., p. 195.
18 Mao Tse-tung, *On the Historical Experience of the Dictatorship of the Proletariat* (Peking: Foreign Languages Press, 1961), pp. 7–18.
19 Mao Tse-tung, *On the Correct Handling of Contradictions among the People* (Peking: Foreign Languages Press, 1957).
20 Ibid., p. 58.
21 Ibid., p. 50.
22 Ibid.
23 Liu Shaoqi, "The Present Situation, the Party's General Line for Socialist Construction and its Future Tasks," May 5, 1958, in Bowie and Fairbank (eds), *Communist China*, p. 434.

Chapter 6 Utopianism

1 Mao Zedong, "Reading Notes," p. 272.
2 Mao Tse-tung, "Sixty Points on Working Methods," in Jerome Chen (ed.), *Mao Papers: Anthology and Bibliography* (London: Oxford University Press, 1970), pp. 62–3.
3 Mao Tse-tung, "On the Ten Great Relationships," April 25, 1956, in *TL*, p. 63.

4 Mao Tse-tung, "Economic Problems of Socialism in the USSR," in *A Critique of Soviet Economics*, trans. Moss Roberts (New York: Monthly Review Press, 1977), pp. 130–1.

5 Mao Tse-tung, "Talks at the Chengtu Conference," in *TL*, pp. 96–9.

6 Quoted by Chen Boda, "Under the Banner of Comrade Mao Zedong," *Hongqi* [Red Flag], July 16, 1958.

7 Mao Tse-tung, "Report to Second Plenary Session of the Seventh Central Committee of the Communist Party of China," March 5, 1949, in *SW*, 1961, vol. IV, pp. 363–4, 374.

8 Karl Marx, "Die moralisierende Kritik und die kritisierende Moral," in Marx, *Selected Writings in Sociology and Social Philosophy*, ed. T.B. Bottomore and Maximilien Rubel (London: Watts, 1956), p. 240.

9 Mao Zedong, "The Great Union of the Popular Masses," July 21 and 28, Aug 4, 1919, in *RW*, vol. I, p. 389.

10 *Hongqi* [Red Flag], June 1, 1958, pp. 3–4.

11 Mao Tse-tung, "Talks at Chengtu," in *TL*, pp. 118–19.

12 Mao Tse-tung, "Remarks at the Spring Festival," Feb 13, 1964, ibid., pp. 204–7, and "Talks at Chengtu," ibid., pp. 119–20.

13 Mao Zedong, "Reading Notes," pp. 333–4; the notion of "the advantages of backwardness" in early 20th-century Chinese intellectual history is insightfully analyzed by Wang Yann-iee in "The Chinese Idea: A Study in Chinese Thought, Politics, and the Intel-lectual History of Capitalism," Ph.D. dissertation, University of Wisconsin-Madison, 1997.

14 Mao Tse-tung, "Speech at the Lushan Conference," July 23, 1959, in *TL*, pp. 142–6.

15 Ibid., p. 146.

16 Ibid., p. 139.

17 Ibid., p. 144.

18 Mao Tse-tung, "Speech at the Enlarged Session of the Military Affairs Committee and the External Affairs Conference," Sept 11, 1959, in *TL*, p. 151.

19 See, for example, Edgar Snow, *The Other Side of the River* (New York: Random House, 1961), p. 620.

20 Mao Zedong, "Speech at the Chengchow Conference," Feb–March 1959, *Chinese Law and Government*, winter 1976–7, p. 18.

21 Mao Tse-tung, "Speech at the Tenth Plenum," Sept 24, 1962, in *TL*, p. 190.

Chapter 7 The Cultural Revolution and the Exhaustion of Maoism

1 Editorial Departments of Renmin Ribao and Hongqi, *On Khrushchev's Phoney Communism and its Historical Lessons for the World* (Peking: Foreign Languages Press, 1964), p. 65 and *passim*.

2 Mao Tse-tung, "Talks on Questions of Philosophy," Aug 18, 1964, in *TL*, p. 217.

3 Mao Tse-tung, "Speech at the Tenth Plenum," Sept 24, 1962, ibid., p. 189.

4 Mao Zedong, "Some Problems Currently arising in the Course of the Rural Socialist Education Movement" ("The Twenty-three Articles"), in Richard Baum and Frederick Teiwes, *Ssu Ch'ing* [The Four Cleans] (Berkeley: University of California Press, 1968), Appendix F, pp. 118–26.

5 *Selections from Chairman Mao*, Washington, D.C.: Joint Publications Research Service, no. 49826, p. 23.

6 On the issue of social class and its ambiguities during the Cultural Revolution, see the superb study by Richard Curt Kraus, *Class Conflict in Chinese Socialism* (New York: Columbia University Press, 1981). How the confusion over social class was experienced by radical Red Guards is analyzed by Lin Weiran, "An Abortive Chinese Enlightenment

– the Cultural Revolution and Class Theory," Ph.D. dissertation, University of Wisconsin-Madison, 1996.

7 André Malraux, *Anti-Memoirs* (New York: Holt, Reinhart, & Winston, 1968), p. 375.

8 Edgar Snow, *The Long Revolution* (New York: Random House), pp. 68–9.

9 Mao Tse-tung, Talk at the Chengtu Conference," March 10, 1958, in *TL*, p. 100.

10 "The Twenty-three Articles," in Baum and Teiwes, *Ssu-Ch'ing*, p. 120.

11 V. I. Lenin, "On Cooperation," Jan 6, 1923, in *Selected Works* (Moscow: Foreign Languages Publishing House, 1952), vol. II, part 2, p. 723.

12 Cited in Richard Stites, "Iconoclastic Currents in the Russian Revolution," in Abbott Gleason, et al. (eds), *Bolshevik Culture* (Bloomington: Indiana University Press, 1985), p. 17.

13 *Selections from Chairman Mao*, Washington, D.C.: Joint Publications Research Service, no. 49826, p. 23.

14 Mao Tse-tung, "Talk at Central Work Conference," Oct 25, 1966, in *TL*, p. 271.

15 Mao Tse-tung, "Talks at Three Meetings with Comrades Chang Ch'un-ch'iao and Yao Wen-yuan," Feb 1967, ibid., pp. 277–8.

16 Mao Zedong, "The Great Union of the Popular Masses," Aug 4, 1919, in *RW*, vol. I, p. 385.

17 *Miscellany of Mao Tse-tung Thought (1949–1968)*, Washington, D.C.: Joint Publications Research Service, no. 61269-1-2, vol. II, p. 470.

18 Snow, *Long Revolution*, p. 13.

19 Mao Tse-tung, "Talk at the First Plenum of the Ninth Central Committee of the Chinese Communist Party," April 28, 1969, in *TL*, p. 287.

20 Snow, *Long Revolution*, p. 174.

21 Ibid., pp. 18–19, 169.

22 Ibid., p. 169.

23 "Summary of Chairman Mao's Talks with Responsible Comrades at Various Places during his Provincial Tour," Aug–Sept 1971, in *TL*, p. 293.

24 Snow, *Long Revolution*, p. 172.

25 Henry A. Kissinger, *The White House Years* (Boston: Little Brown & Co., 1979), p. 1058.

Epilogue

1 Martin Wolf, "The New Workshop of the World," *Financial Times*, Nov 25, 2003; available at FT.com (Nov 26, 2003).

2 Karl Marx, "Die moralisierende Kritik und die kritisierende Moral," in his *Selected Writings*, p. 240.

3 Karl Marx, "Preface to the First [German] Edition of Kapital," *Capital*, trans. Samuel Moore and Edward Aveling (Chicago: Charles H. Kerr and Co., 1906), pp. 14–15.

Writings of Mao Zedong

Mao Tse-tung, *The Chinese Revolution and the Chinese Communist Party* (Peking: Foreign Languages Press, 1954)

Mao Tse-tung, *On New Democracy* [1940] (Peking: Foreign Languages Press, 1954)

Selected Works of Mao Tse-tung, 4 vols (London: Lawrence and Wishart, 1954) [*SW*, 1954]

Mao Tse-tung, *On the Correct Handling of Contradictions among the People* (Peking: Foreign Language Press, 1957)

Mao Tse-tung, *On the Historical Experience of the Dictatorship of the Proletariat* (Peking: Foreign Languages Press, 1961)

Selected Works of Mao Tse-tung, 4 vols (Peking: Foreign Languages Press, 1961) [*SW*, 1961]

Quotations from Chairman Mao Tse-tung (Peking: Foreign Languages Press, 1966)

Selected Works of Mao Tse-tung, 4 vols (Peking: Foreign Languages Press, 1967) [*SW*, 1967]

Mao Zedong sixiang wansui! [Long Live the Thought of Mao Zedong] (Taipei: n.p., 1967) ["Reading Notes"]

Mao Zedong sixiang wansui! [Long Live the Thought of Mao Zedong] (Taipei: n.p., 1969)

Mao Tse-tung Unrehearsed: Talks and Letters, 1956–71, ed. Stuart R. Schram (Harmondsworth: Penguin Books, 1974) [*TL*]

Miscellany of Mao Tse-tung Thought (1949–1968), 2 vols (Washington, D.C.: Joint Publication Research Service 61269-1-2, 1974)

Mao Tse-tung, *A Critique of Soviet Economics*, trans. Moss Roberts (New York: Monthly Review Press, 1977)

Selected Works of Mao Tse-tung, 5 vols (Peking: Foreign Languages Press, 1977) [*SW*, 1977]

The Writings of Mao Zedong, 1949–1976, ed. Michael Y.M. Kau and John K. Leung, 2 vols (Armonk, NY: M.E. Sharpe, 1986–92)

Mao Zedong, *Report from Xunwu*, trans. and with an introduction by Roger R. Thompson (Stanford, Ca.: Stanford University Press, 1990)

Mao Zedong, *Mao's Road to Power: Revolutionary Writings, 1912–1949*, ed. Stuart R. Schram, 7 vols (Armonk, NY: M.E. Sharpe, 1992–) [*RW*]

Bibliography

Barme, Geremie R., *Shades of Mao: The Posthumous Cult of the Great Leader* (Armonk, NY: M.E. Sharpe, 1996)

Baum, Richard, and Frederick Teiwes, *Ssu Ch'ing* [The Four Cleans] (Berkeley: University of California Press, 1968)

Benton, Gregor (ed.), *Wild Lilies: Poisonous Weeds* (London: Pluto Press, 1982)

Bowie, Robert, and John K. Fairbank (eds), *Communist China, 1955–59: Policy Documents with Analysis* (Cambridge, Mass.: Harvard University Press, 1962)

Breslin, Shaun G., *Mao* (New York: Longman, 2000)

Byrnes, James F., *Speaking Frankly* (New York: Harper, 1947)

Chang Kuo-t'ao, *The Rise of the Chinese Communist Party, 1921–1927: Volume One of the Autobiography of Chang Kuo-t'ao* (Lawrence, Kansas: The University Press of Kansas, 1971)

Cheek, Timothy, *Mao Zedong and China's Revolution: A Brief History with Documents* (Boston: Bedford and St Martin, 2002)

Cheek, Timothy and Tony Saich (eds), *New Perspectives on State Socialism in China* (Armonk, NY: M.E. Sharpe, 1997)

Chen Duxiu, *Duxiu wencun* [Collected Works], 4 vols (Shanghai: Yadong tushuguan, 1922)

Chen Duxiu, *Zhungguo geming wendi lun wenchi* [A Collection of Articles on Problems of the Chinese Revolution] (Shanghai: Xinqingnian she, 1927)

Chen, Jerome, *Mao and the Chinese Revolution* (New York: Oxford University Press, 1965)

Chen, Jerome (ed.), *Mao Papers: Anthology and Bibliography* (London: Oxford University Press, 1970)

Chevrier, Yves, *Mao and the Chinese Revolution* (Northampton, Mass.: Interlink Books, 2004)

Chow Tse-tsung, *The May Fourth Movement* (Cambridge, Mass.: Harvard University Press, 1960)

Dai Qing, *Wang Shiwei and "Wild Lilies"* (Armonk, NY: M.E. Sharpe, 1994)

Davin, Delia, *Mao Zedong* (Stroud, Gloucestershire: Sutton Publishing, 1997)

Dedijer, Vladimir, *Tito Speaks* (London: Weidenfeld and Nicolson, 1953)

Deutscher, Isaac, *Stalin: A Political Biography* (New York: Oxford University Press, 1949)

Dirlik, Arif, *The Origins of Chinese Communism* (New York: Oxford University Press, 1989)

Dirlik, Arif, *Anarchism in the Chinese Revolution* (Berkeley: University of California Press, 1991)

Djilas, Milovan, *Conversations with Stalin* (New York: Harcourt, Brace & World, 1962)

Domes, Jurgen, *Peng Te-huai: The Man and the Image* (Stanford, Ca.: Stanford University Press, 1985)

Fei Xiaotung, *China's Gentry* (Chicago: University of Chicago Press, 1953)

Feigon, Lee, *Chen Duxiu: Founder of the Chinese Communist Party* (Princeton, NJ: Princeton University Press, 1983)

Feigon, Lee, *Mao: A Reinterpretation* (Chicago: Ivan R. Dee, 2002)

Gleason, Abbott, et al. (eds), *Bolshevik Culture* (Bloomington: Indiana University Press, 1985)

Goldman, Merle, *Literary Dissent in Communist China* (Cambridge, Mass.: Harvard University Press, 1967)

Grieder, Jerome B., *Hu Shih and the Chinese Renaissance* (Cambridge, Mass.: Harvard University Press, 1970)

Herzen, Alexander, *From the Other Shore* (London: Weidenfeld and Nicolson, 1956)

Hsia, T.A., *The Gate of Darkness* (Seattle: University of Washington Press, 1968)

Isaacs, Harold, *The Tragedy of the Chinese Revolution* (Stanford, Ca.: Stanford University Press, 1951)

Johnson, Chalmers, *Peasant Nationalism and Communist Power* (Stanford, Ca.: Stanford University Press, 1962)

Kissinger, Henry A., *The White House Years* (Boston: Little Brown & Co., 1979)

Kraus, Richard Curt, *Class Conflict in Chinese Socialism* (New York: Columbia University Press, 1981)

Kung Chi-keung, "Intellectuals and Masses: The Case of Qu Quibai," Ph.D. dissertation, University of Wisconsin-Madison, 1995

Lenin, V.I., *Selected Works* (Moscow: Foreign Languages Publishing House, 1952), 2 vols

Levenson, Joseph R., *Liang Ch'i-ch'ao and the Mind of Modern China* (Cambridge, Mass.: Harvard University Press, 1959)

Levenson, Joseph R., *Confucian China and its Modern Fate: A Trilogy* (Berkeley: University of California Press, 1968)

Li Dazhao, *Li Dazhao xuanji* [Selected Works] (Beijing: People's Publishing House, 1959)

Li Zhisui, *The Private Life of Chairman Mao* (New York: Random House, 1994)

Lifton, Robert Jay, *Revolutionary Immortality: Mao Tse-tung and the Chinese Cultural Revolution* (New York: Random House, 1968)

Lin Weiran, "An Abortive Chinese Enlightenment – the Cultural Revolution and Class Theory," Ph.D. dissertation, University of Wisconsin-Madison, 1996

Liu Shaoqi, *Collected Works* (Hong Kong: Union Research Institute, 1968)

Lutze, Thomas, "New Democracy: Chinese Communist Relations with the Urban Middle Forces, 1931–1952," Ph.D. dissertation, University of Wisconsin-Madison, 1996 [publication in preparation]

McDonald, Angus, *The Urban Origins of Rural Revolution* (Berkeley: University of California Press, 1978)

MacFarquhar, Roderick (ed.), *The Hundred Flowers Campaign and the Chinese Intellectuals* (New York: Praeger, 1960)

MacFarquhar, Roderick, *The Origins of the Cultural Revolution*, vol. I: *Contradictions among the People* (London: Oxford University Press, 1974)

MacFarquhar, Roderick, *The Origins of the Cultural Revolution*, vol. II: *The Great Leap Forward, 1958–1960* (New York: Columbia University Press, 1983)

MacFarquhar, Roderick, *The Origins of the Cultural Revolution*, vol. III: *The Coming of the Cataclysm, 1961–1966* (New York: Oxford University Press and Columbia University Press, 1997)

Malraux, André, *Anti-Memoirs* (New York: Holt, Rinehart & Winston, 1968)

Marks, Robert B., *Rural Revolution in South China: Peasants and the Making of History in Haifeng County, 1570–1930* (Madison: University of Wisconsin Press, 1984)

Marx, Karl, *Capital*, trans. Samuel Moore and Edward Aveling (Chicago: Charles H. Kerr and Co., 1906)

Marx, Karl, *Selected Writings in Sociology and Social Philosophy*, ed. T.B. Bottomore and Maximilien Rubel (London: Watts, 1956)

Marx, Karl, and Frederick Engels, *Selected Works*, 2 vols (Moscow: Foreign Languages Publishing House, 1950)

Meisner, Maurice, *Li Ta-chao and the Origins of Chinese Marxism* (Cambridge, Mass.: Harvard University Press, 1967)

Meisner, Maurice, *Marxism, Maoism, and Utopianism* (Madison: University of Wisconsin Press, 1982)

Meisner, Maurice, *Mao's China and After*, 3rd edn (New York: The Free Press, 1999)

Moore, Barrington, *Social Origins of Dictatorship and Democracy* (Boston: Beacon Press, 1966)

Pickowicz, Paul, *Marxist Literary Thought in China* (Berkeley: University of California Press, 1981)

Rue, John E., *Mao Tse-tung in Opposition, 1927–1935* (Stanford, Ca.: Stanford University Press, 1966)

Saich, Tony, *The Rise to Power of the Chinese Communist Party* (Armonk, NY: M.E. Sharpe, 1996)

Saich, Tony and Hans Van de Ven (eds), *New Perspectives on the Chinese Communist Revolution* (Armonk, NY: M.E. Sharpe, 1995)

Schram, Stuart R., *La "Révolution permanente"* (Paris: Mouton, 1963)

Schram, Stuart R., *Mao Tse-tung* (New York: Simon and Schuster, 1967)

Schram, Stuart R., *The Political Thought of Mao Tse-tung* (New York: Praeger, 1969)

Schram, Stuart R., *Mao Zedong: A Preliminary Reassessment* (New York: St Martin's Press, 1983)

Schwartz, Benjamin I., *Chinese Communism and the Rise of Mao* (Cambridge, Mass.: Harvard University Press, 1952)

Schwartz, Benjamin, *In Search of Wealth and Power: Yen Fu and the West* (Cambridge, Mass.: Harvard University Press, 1964)

Schwartz, Benjamin, *Communism and China: Ideology in Flux* (Cambridge, Mass.: Harvard University Press, 1968)

Selden, Mark, *The Yenan Way in Revolutionary China* (Cambridge, Mass.: Harvard University Press, 1971)

Shaffer, Lynda, *Mao and the Workers: The Hunan Labor Movement, 1920–23* (Armonk, NY: M.E. Sharpe, 1982)

Short, Philip, *Mao: A Life* (New York: Henry Holt, 2000)

Smedley, Agnes, *Battle Hymm of China* (New York: Knopf, 1943)

Smedley, Agnes, *The Great Road* (New York: Monthly Review Press, 1956)

Snow, Edgar, *Red Star over China* (New York: Random House, 1938) [including Mao's account of his early life, pp. 116–67: "Autobiography"]

Snow, Edgar, *The Other Side of the River* (New York: Random House, 1961)

Snow, Edgar, *The Long Revolution* (New York: Random House, 1971)

Snow, Helen Foster [Nym Wales], *Inside Red China* (New York: Da Capo Press, 1977)

Spence, Jonathan, *The Search for Modern China* (New York: Norton, 1990)

Spence, Jonathan, *Mao* (London: Weidenfeld and Nicolson, 1999)

Terrill, Ross, *Mao: A Biography* (New York: Harper & Row, 1980)

Trotsky, Leon, *The Third International after Lenin* (New York: Pioneer Publishers, 1936)

Union Research Institute (ed.), *The Case of P'eng Teh-huai, 1959–1968* (Hong Kong: Union Research Institute, 1968)

Wakeman, Frederick, *History and Will: Philosophic Perspectives on Mao Tse-tung's Thought* (Berkeley: University of California Press, 1973)

Wang Yann-iee, "The Chinese Idea: A Study in Chinese Thought, Politics, and the Intellectual History of Capitalism," Ph.D. dissertation, University of Wisconsin-Madison, 1997

Wylie, Raymond F., *The Emergence of Maoism: Mao Tse-tung, Ch'en Po-ta and the Search for Chinese Theory, 1915–1945* (Stanford, Ca.: Stanford University Press, 1980)

Index

Lightning Source UK Ltd.
Milton Keynes UK
UKOW031057010312

188151UK00002B/52/P